A WOMAN OF

Hillary Rodham Clinton is the ___ ___ ___ ___ ___ ___ ___ guing First Lady in recent me ___ ___ ___ ___ ___ ___ from the Monica Lewinsky sc ___ ___ ___ ___ ___ ___ more popular than ever, a wo ___ ___ ___ ___ grace under pressure has won respect and admiration around the world. This behind-the-scenes, up-to-date biography reveals the complex, often contradictory woman behind the headlines. It offers a candid and insightful look at our First Lady— who she is, where she's been, and what role she might play after she and Bill Clinton leave the White House.

A *New York Times* bestseller for eight weeks when it was first published in January 1993, *HILLARY CLINTON: THE INSIDE STORY* has been completely revised and updated. It offers:

- insights into Hillary's enduring love for Bill Clinton, their dynamic and difficult relationship, and why she stays committed to her marriage
- Hillary's struggles to find an acceptable role as First Lady
- the challenges Hillary has faced as a mother to Chelsea and an independent career woman
- how Hillary has handled the scandals and accusations that have dogged the Clintons for years—and have culminated in only the second impeachment of a president in U.S. history
- how Hillary's advocacy of women and children throughout the world is being transformed into a political agenda that might someday catapult her into public office

WITH 8 PAGES OF UPDATED PHOTOS

JUDITH WARNER has cowritten books on former *Vogue* editor Grace Mirabella and former House Speaker Newt Gingrich. Since 1995, she has lived in Paris, where she was until recently a special correspondent for *Newsweek* magazine. Her articles on French politics and society have also appeared in the *New York Times*, the *Boston Globe*, and the *Village Voice*.

HILLARY CLINTON
— THE —
INSIDE STORY

Judith Warner

A SIGNET BOOK

SIGNET
Published by New American Library, a division of
Penguin Putnam Inc., 375 Hudson Street,
New York, New York 10014, U.S.A.
Penguin Books Ltd, 27 Wrights Lane,
London W8 5TZ, England
Penguin Books Australia Ltd, Ringwood,
Victoria, Australia
Penguin Books Canada Ltd, 10 Alcorn Avenue,
Toronto, Ontario, Canada M4V 3B2
Penguin Books (N.Z.) Ltd, 182–190 Wairau Road,
Auckland 10, New Zealand

Penguin Books Ltd, Registered Offices:
Harmondsworth, Middlesex, England

First published by Signet, an imprint of New American Library,
a division of Penguin Putnam Inc.

First Printing, January 1993
First Printing (Revised and updated edition), August 1999
10 9 8 7 6 5 4 3 2 1

Ⓓ REGISTERED TRADEMARK—MARCA REGISTRADA

Printed in the United States of America

CONTENTS

ACKNOWLEDGMENTS

For the revised edition of this book, I owe a special debt of gratitude to the encouragement and foresight of Michelle Lapautre, my literary agent in Paris. I also owe special thanks to Melanne Verveer and her staff in the Office of the First Lady for their very gracious and extensive help.

I could not have written this book without Max Berley, who conducted many of the bedrock interviews and enriched the text with his critical judgment. Julia Flannery Berley lent critical support.

I am very grateful for the help of Kim Witherspoon and Josh Greenhut, and to Liza Featherstone for her important contribution to the 1993 edition.

I would like once more to extend a round of thanks to all the people who contributed their time and thoughts to this book, both in 1992, and in preparation for the current edition. I am particularly indebted to Charles Flynn Allen, who permitted me the free use of interview transcripts used in preparation for his book *The Comeback Kid*, cowritten with Jonathan Portis. Articles and background interviews by Garry Wills, Christophe Buchard, Eleanor Clift, and Gail Sheehy provided invaluable material. I would like to thank the *Arkansas Democrat-Gazette* for the use of its library and the American Library in Paris for providing an oasis of Americana in a foreign city.

Do all the good you can, in all the ways you can, in all the places you can, at all the times you can, to all the people you can, as long as you ever can.

—JOHN WESLEY

Chapter 1

Hillary Through
the Looking-Glass

In late January 1991, Hillary Rodham Clinton took her daughter, Chelsea, to San Francisco to spend a holiday weekend with three of her closest friends and their daughters.

The mother-daughter weekend had been planned long in advance. It meant arranging schedules, coordinating vacations, and, ultimately, braving the skies in the middle of the Gulf War, when American airports were on high terrorism alert. Nothing, however, would have kept Hillary away. She loved nothing better than the company of smart and funny female friends. For four glorious days the women and girls rowed boats in Sausalito, ate Chinese takeout food, visited the city's planetarium, talked and talked and laughed.

There was only one ripple in their bliss. One afternoon, while the friends sat drinking Irish coffee in a curbside San Francisco cafe, a passerby stopped and asked one of them if she might by any chance be the famous actress Mary Steenburgen.

Yes, Steenburgen said with a grimace, I am.

The passerby then rounded the table and asked Steenburgen's neighbor if she was the television reporter and talk show host Nancy Snyderman.

Yes, Snyderman said. Yes, indeed.

Once the passerby moved out of sight, Hillary Clinton, First Lady of Arkansas, turned to Connie Fails, Little Rock's one and only known dress designer, and smiled. "Isn't it great," she said, "to be in a place where nobody knows who we are?"

Hillary Rodham Clinton has always shunned the public eye. It has always tended to judge her sharply. It has had a way of confronting her with the aspects of her life she prefers to forget: namely, Bill Clinton's infidelity. And it has always forced her to assume false identities. In Arkansas, intensely negative public scrutiny of Hillary's appearance, her choice to keep her maiden name and to pursue an independent career almost put a premature end to her husband's political career. Public scrutiny of the failings of her marriage almost kept her husband from running for president. It pushed an already taxed marriage almost to the brink of disaster. And once Clinton did run, and then did win the presidency, the unrelenting glare of national scrutiny very nearly shattered Hillary's faith in the public-service calling she'd followed all her life.

For Bill Clinton's 1992 presidential campaign, Hillary had done all she could to comply with the dictates of national taste. She'd traded in her headband, her sharp tongue, her loftiest ambitions, and her pride in the powerful, strongly independent role she'd cultivated through years of advocacy work in Washington and Arkansas. As she had during the dark days of Bill Clinton's political misfortunes of the early 1980s, she submerged her own voice in the larger message of candidate Clinton. And once he was elected president, she'd thought she could reap the reward. She'd be able to get back to work and stop living her life as spectacle. She reclaimed her maiden name, her private life, and the active, public role of policy maker and political counsel that she'd always enjoyed in her marriage. She held press conferences and committee meetings and tried to reform the nation's system of health care. Her private self retreated behind a veil of mystery. And Hillary Rodham Clinton would have been very content if, for her entire time in the White House, it could have remained so hidden.

Unfortunately, fate had other plans. One day during the federal government shutdown in 1995, Monica Lewinsky, a twenty-one-year-old White House intern, showed the upper strap of her thong underwear to the President of the United States. She brought him some pizza. He took her into a windowless corridor just outside the Oval Office. And the rest became the story that will dominate the end of the American century.

Hillary Clinton, who not so long ago was called "the most powerful woman in the world," will now go down in history as the most famously betrayed. And yet this same woman who not long ago was seen as a dangerous schemer, a cross between Lady Macbeth and the Wicked Witch of the West, has become a heroine. She has become an icon of American womanhood, an ideal image of forbearance, dignity, grace under pressure, and forgiveness. Formerly vilified as a "radical feminist who has little use for religious values or even the traditional family unit," as a right-wing fund-raising letter once put it, she is now championed as an example of "family values." Once so hated that a group called the Committee for Decent Family Values used a live elephant to stomp on her effigy in an event staged outside the Republican National Convention, she is now the darling of progressives and traditionalists alike. She is being showered with offers to occupy her time after the White House: a possible Senate seat, lucrative book contracts, top billing on the national lecture circuit.

She is, by all counts, now the most popular woman in America. Her steely reaction to the Monica Lewinsky scandal has pushed her public approval rating to unprecedented highs. She is visibly more popular with congressional Democrats than is the President. In the run-up to the congressional elections of November 1998, she was the number one guest speaker on the campaign trail. Candidates shunned Bill Clinton, but they begged for help from Hillary. She was a universal crowd pleaser. With her stump speeches on child care, education, Social Security, and the environment, she captivated audiences grown weary with Monica Lewinsky. "The attraction of Mrs. Clinton is that she focuses on the issues rather than the distractions swirling around Washington, D.C.," explained one congressional candidate in Washington state. "The President is a distraction."

As she made the rounds in Oregon, New York, and California, she made Washington, D.C., look like a more and more distant swamp. As her husband fell ever deeper into an abyss of his own making, she exuded a sense of promise and hope. "There is something about your style, about your grace, about your strength, about your motherness, about your wifeness, about your maturity, about your patriotism, about your strength of reasoning," raved the Reverend Jesse Jackson, introducing Hillary to a mostly black audience at a Democratic rally on Chicago's South Side. "Hillary, you've walked through rain and you're not wet. You've walked through fire and there's not a singe on your clothing." Political scientist Ruth Mandel put it more succinctly: "Hillary sends a message that mothers tell their kids: 'You pick up and you go on.' "

Thanks to Hillary's efforts, challenger Charles Schumer defeated Senator Alfonse D'Amato, the once invincible-seeming conservative Republican from New York. By campaign's end, New York state Democrats were trying to tempt Hillary to run for Senate in the year 2000. It was hard to believe that this was the same woman who just a few years earlier had testified on Capitol Hill in shame. D'Amato, as head of the Senate Whitewater Committee, had hounded her mercilessly for years. He and his Republican colleagues had left no stone unturned in trying to prove that the First Lady, as a practicing lawyer in Little Rock, Arkansas, had intervened to keep state regulators off the scent of a corrupt local savings and loan institution run by her business partner in the failed real estate venture known as Whitewater. Although they, with the help of independent counsel Kenneth Starr, would fail to bring charges against Hillary, they would manage ultimately to convince the public that she had something to hide.

In 1996 polls had shown that a strong majority of Americans thought that the First Lady was a liar.

They thought she'd bent the rules to enrich herself and her friends. They thought she'd do anything to further the political career of her as husband and her own political dreams. They saw her as a craven yuppie who believed she was above the law. She was a hypocrite, a fraud. On January 26, 1996, the first First Lady ever to enter the White House with an independent career of her own had become the first one ever to be called to testify before a grand jury. As Hillary mounted the stairs to the courtroom, 51 percent of Americans said they disapproved of her. That was another "first:" she was now the most unpopular First Lady in history.

But Monica Lewinsky changed all that.

As the weight of lurid details accrued about the President's eighteen-month affair with the young White House intern, Hillary Rodham Clinton was reborn in public opinion. She was no longer an arrogant harridan. She was a woman *wronged*. As her face drooped in resignation and pain, the female voters who had always repudiated her—older women and non-working mothers—suddenly welcomed her with open arms. For the first time ever, non-college-educated women outnumbered educated women as her supporters. And as Hillary stood by her husband and proclaimed herself a loving and supportive spouse, the older men who had long despised her fell silent.

Americans admired what they saw as Hillary's quiet dignity. They identified with her refusal to be seen as a victim. They saw her allegiance to Clinton as a reasoned choice—a vindication of the often inexplicable choices they were forced to make in their own lives. "Hillary Clinton represents for so many Americans the problems and struggles in their own lives," a senator who watched Hillary raise money for the Democrats explained to the *New York Times*. "She's obviously a symbol for a generation of people with deep personal problems in complex times. And she has survived." For the first time in her life Hillary Clinton was Everywoman. "There but for the grace of God," mused a Democratic candidate for the House of Representatives, watching Hillary endure at a campaign stop in Milwaukee, Wisconsin. "She has dealt with it with so much dignity and grace, it has resonated with people." Gloria Borger, a contributing editor for *U.S. News & World Report*, summed it up. "We're all Hillary Clinton now."

Hillary Rodham Clinton spent early 1999 flirting with the idea of a Senate candidacy. She drew record crowds to her speeches and fund-raising events in New York, pointed barbs from her possible Senate seat contender Rudolph Giuliani, and heightened interest from the Monica-weary media. She watched it all with a rather jaundiced eye. After all, at this late date she has no illusions about the fealty of public opinion. She's been up, she's been down, she will no doubt go down again. "She often says: when people put you up on a pedestal, they can just as easily knock you down," said the first lady's chief of staff, Melanne Verveer. "She says she's just a Rorschach test for what's going on in the country."

The fact is, in the wake of the Monica Lewinsky scandal, Hillary Rodham Clinton has taken new form in the American imagination. After years of offering Americans a mirror in which they saw nothing more than their most crippling anxieties about women and families, she now makes people feel good. Whereas once she seemed to loom above as a kind of strict and punishing ideal—of women as they should be, according to the vision of a progressive, educated, and above all privileged part of the population—she is now someone people can relate to. Now that she's been humbled and demoralized, now that all the contradictions, compromises, and heartbreak in her life have been laid bare for the public to see, she represents American women as they feel they really are. And she is being hailed, for the first time in many quarters, as a First Lady for our time.

It's said that Hillary has "grown into" her role. It's said that she has changed. But in fact, cosmetic variations and election-year spinning aside, Hillary Rodham Clinton hasn't really altered. She is the same person in 1999 as she was when she first grabbed the nation's attention in 1992: an ambitious, upper-middle-class professional woman who'd attended the country's best schools, made a name for herself at a prestigious law firm, and developed a reputation for political acumen that rivaled her husband's. She is still a child of the 1960s who, at her Wellesley College graduation, challenged authority in calling for "more immediate, ecstatic, and penetrating modes of living." She is still a women's rights activist, a sometimes rigid-sounding moralist. She still has a sharp, sarcastic tongue and suffers fools poorly. She's never really developed an eye for home decoration, and her fashion sense still occasionally leaves something to be desired.

So why is she now so acceptable? Because Hillary

Clinton's long-held insistence that her true self was deformed by the public eye is true. The woman the country alternately loves and hates *isn't* Hillary Rodham Clinton at all. That woman is a creation of the media—and of the Clintons' own spin doctors. She is a projection of the country's hopes, fears, and desires. She is not a real person. "The tragedy of people like Hillary Clinton is that they ultimately become more useful and important to the society they live in as symbols for what people want them to represent than for who they really are as human beings," says Carl Sferrazza Anthony, who has written on the lives of many former first ladies and has collaborated on a number of historical projects with Hillary Clinton. "Everyone continues to categorize and label and use Hillary Clinton for their own purposes rather than see her as a complex human being. People don't like to see themselves in a complex way, much less a public figure."

Something in the larger culture has happened to make America embrace Hillary Rodham Clinton as a native daughter. What happened doesn't, in the end, say all that much about Hillary Clinton, but it does say a lot about America in the Clinton era.

In 1992 the country was wracked by growing pains. It had been evolving for decades, changing from a nation of stay-at-home moms and bread-winning dads to one where 60 percent of mothers worked, 50 percent of couples divorced, and a growing number of unmarried working mothers soldiered on alone. Economic forces had rendered the 1950s-era nuclear family obsolete. Women worked because they had to, because, in many parts of the country, all but the nation's wealthiest families had been priced out of access to desirable housing, affordable health care, and acceptable schools. But twelve years of Republican leadership had succeeded in keeping Americans from facing up to these changes. The Republicans, backed by the extreme right-wing social crusaders who provided much of the party's funding, succeeded in convincing many Americans that the purer, simpler world of the 1950s (1954, as Ronald Reagan once specified) could be resurrected. All that was needed was for women to stop working, for homosexuals to go back in the closet, and for the government to stop giving money to people who lacked the moral fiber to make good on their own. The weight of resentment that this political discourse generated, the weight of guilt borne by women and the anger directed at them, ultimately drove America to a near-perpetual state of rage. This rage expressed itself in the fury of the "culture wars" that conservatives like Patrick Buchanan and William Bennett waged in the 1980s and early 1990s. In 1992 it focused on Hillary Clinton.

When I first began reporting on Hillary Clinton, in November 1992, I was fascinated by that rage. I wanted to understand what it as about this relatively innocuous woman—this political wife and mother, lawyer, and children's advocate—that could inspire such passionate hatred. The "inside story," I wrote, in the book I first published in 1993, was that far from being a godless liberal and radical feminist, Hillary Clinton was a deeply religious, socially conservative, moderate pragmatist. My conclusion: that the woman so loathed, so vilified by Buchanan and his friends was a work of pure projection.

But I was guilty of some projection of my own. Like many young women, I was swept up in the moment of feminist fervor that ushered Bill Clinton into office. To so many of us the ascension of Clinton, and especially of his *wife*, to the White House just after the publication of Susan Faludi's *Backlash*, the Anita Hill hearings, and the William Kennedy Smith date rape case, felt like the start of a revolution. And so, in the 1993 version of *Hillary Clinton: The Inside Story*, I quoted Gloria Steinem, hailing the Clinton couple as an example of "the family as democracy." I quoted Naomi Wolf, calling the Clintons a model of the "equal partnership family," and Hillary "the embodiment of the feminist future."

The criticism from conservatives—from older conservative men in particular—was predictable. On a talk radio program in Florida I was accused of being a lesbian—"in love with Hillary Clinton." But more interesting, and more surprising, was the negative reaction of a large number of women. Not just Phyllis Schlafly-like women of the hard-line right, but middle-of-the-road, apolitical women, baby boomers, and older women alike (though not younger ones.) There was something about Hillary Rodham Clinton that just rankled these women. The word that came up, over and over again, was "phony."

It wasn't so much that Hillary embodied all the changes of modern American life; it was that she seemed so damn smug. What right had she to seem so happy and self-satisfied while millions of American women struggled with the choices they'd made in their lives? What right had she to this "co-candidacy," this "equal partnership marriage" when most women her age—of whatever political persuasion—were still screaming at their husbands to empty the dishwasher and pick up their socks? There was something about Hillary that struck people as coldly elitist. To many she seemed inhuman. She was free to utter all the pious reassurances that she could: "This is how I define my personhood—Bill and Chelsea," she'd tell *Glamour* magazine. Something about it all rang false.

And, of course, something was. The truth was, America hadn't changed as much as we all liked to think. The baby boomers had proved largely successful in changing society, but they couldn't change themselves. They'd created a world they were not socialized to inhabit. They said they wanted personal and political equality between men and women, but their psyches had been wired in the pre-feminist 1950s. And so even Americans of Hillary's age and Hillary's background raged at the seeming seamlessness of her life. There was something about her that just *stank*.

There was, for example, the story that Hillary and her husband sold the American people in 1992. That they had had "problems in their marriage." That he had "caused pain." That the pain had healed and they'd worked their problems out—and now had moved to a state of beatitude from which they could project a perfectly equitable image of respectful male-female relations. Then along came Monica—and real life claimed a victory. The idea that Hillary could have it all: a top career and a well-adjusted child *and* a doting husband had turned out to be a myth. Feminists gnashed their teeth while the rest of the nation's women chortled sympathetically. *Hillary,* they said, *welcome to the club.*

The fact was that a silent majority of Americans had never been able to relate to the vilified or idealized portraits of Hillary Rodham Clinton created by politicians and the media. They had also grown to recognize that the recent changes in American society were neither uniformly negative *nor* positive. And the have-it-all "co-presidency" boosterism that had ushered Hillary Rodham Clinton into the White House and billed her to the public as an unqualified heroine had offended them. They couldn't identify with this First Lady—even if they wanted to. She simply had to come down to earth and be cut down to size. The Starr report would do this, and then some.

But is the "new," "real," "human," and beloved Hillary Clinton of 1999 any less a projection? I think not. After conducting scores of interviews with Hillary Rodham Clinton's friends and colleagues, her teachers, political allies and critics, and after reading all that I could both by and about the First Lady, I have come to think that the wounded woman now celebrated by American men and women is no more real than the Hillary-as-harpy of 1992. The real Hillary Rodham Clinton resides elsewhere than in the figure of the long-suffering wife who has so calmly and with so much dignity stood by her husband in his time of travail. It can't be found in press releases from her office stating that her love for Bill Clinton is "compassionate and steadfast"—or in the breathy commentary of friends and pundits. The real Hillary Rodham Clinton resides in the policy-addled prose of *It Takes a Village.* It resides in her speeches, her lectures, her Sunday school teachings, her spiritual sessions with ministers and theologians. It has shown up in Bangladesh and Beijing, in Senegal and Belfast, having tea with women fighting to end sectarian violence and staging plays to teach villagers about the hazards of female genital mutilation.

The truth is that Hillary Rodham Clinton's selfhood is grounded in a certain idea of herself as a public servant. The truth is also that she is not a woman that most women—most people—can "relate to." She is not deeply wounded. She is not a victim. She is like many powerful men before her—motivated by ideals, faith, and the drug-like high of top achievement, devoted to but not defined by the relationships in her life. That self-containment, a rare thing in most women's lives, may serve to explain some of the elements that seem inexplicable about her marriage. "The very idea of marriage to her is difficult," says an old friend. "She's a very independent, self-motivated, self-directed woman. . . She doesn't need much intimacy. She needs the space to live her own life."

Understanding Hillary Clinton means breaking with traditional notions of what defines a woman's life. It also means a change in language. Hillary Clinton's life doesn't lend itself to analysis through the terms of psychological jargon so prevalent in America today. Hillary herself doesn't psychologize—not about herself or about other people. Her inner world isn't structured by the abuse-and-recovery cycles of popular psychology. It is instead held together by a core of spiritual beliefs that grow out of her strong religious faith, her Methodism, which places great emphasis on social responsibility and good works. It is tempting to want to dig deeper. To look for some kind of missing piece, for some dark secret, that will explain the seeming contradictions in Hillary Clinton's life through a master narrative of psychological complexity. But that story simply wouldn't be true—just as reports that she is borne through her life's crises in "denial" or even in a state of "disassociation" just don't ring true. Hillary Clinton is a person who has constituted her inner self through her public actions, in parallel with the demands of her faith. As a result, her private self and her public self are amazingly similar. And that is the real inside story: what you see is what you get.

Chapter 2

Coming of Age

Park Ridge, Illinois, was the kind of place where parents dreamed of moving and children loved to live in the early 1950s. Hugh and Dorothy Rodham were parents with dreams, and highest among their dreams was to make their children happy. A few years after the war, joining the mass movement of Americans who were then fleeing the crowded cities, they took the plunge into the suburbs. Hugh was a salesman who was then working hard at building up his own small textile business. Dorothy was a stay-at-home mother with great hopes for her family, especially for her smart little preschool girl, Hillary.

Park Ridge, then as now, was mostly a bedroom community made up of families whose fathers or mothers commuted to Chicago daily. Most had moved to the suburb, which had been incorporated as a city only a few decades earlier, in the 1940s and 1950s. They were drawn by the promise of excellent schools, densely tree-lined streets, gaslight-style street lamps shining over stone-engraved street signs, and family-sized houses ranging from modest to substantial. There were landmark buildings, too, in the central Uptown area. The Pickwick Theater, and, of course, the nearby lake.

There was only one slightly noisy inconvenience. "I grew up," Hillary once joked, "under flight patterns at O'Hare Airport."

Hillary and her two younger brothers, Hugh and Tony, lived with their parents in a large, Georgian-style yellow brick house, with tall trees out front and a well-tended yard. It was a comfortable house, surrounded by others just like it, on a quiet street with neighbors just like them. Families left their doors unlocked, and the children considered each others' backyards their own. All through the neighborhood, children ran from house to house, rode their bikes in circles down the middle of drowsy streets, or pedaled off for a ride down bigger boulevards, where the older trees grew together to form a canopy over their heads.

The Rodham family, well off but not rich, solid in their bonds, fit in well in the neighborhood. Methodists, of Welsh and English descent, they blended in easily in a community that was, above all, homogeneous. It was homogeneously white, homogeneously Christian. It was a homogeneously conservative community, home of later anti-abortion fighters Henry Hyde and Penny Pullen, filled with dyed-in-the-wool Republicans and a few John Birchers too. It was also, not coincidentally, a dry town, though liquor was sold just one township over, and road trips out and deliveries in were frequent enough that any white panel truck that crossed the city line and pulled into a private alleyway was immediately considered suspect.

The most important thing that the families of Park Ridge had in common was an unflagging belief in education. They were themselves a highly educated, upper-middle-class group, and they wanted their children to do even better. They were even willing to pay for it.

"I've often kidded my father, who has never been a fan of taxes or government, about moving to a place that had such high property taxes to pay for school," Hillary Clinton told Bill Clinton's Arkansas biographer, Charles F. Allen, co-author with Jonathan Portis of *The Comeback Kid.* "But even though it was a very conservative Republican community, there was just no griping during the fifties and sixties about paying for good education."

The Rodhams worked hard to instill in Hillary the sense that the biggest responsibility of her young life was to be sure she got the best education possible. "Learning for learning's sake," her mother said. "Learning for earning's sake," her father joked.

Dorothy Rodham herself had not gone to college. She had married Hugh, a Penn State University graduate, and devoted her life to him and their children. She seemed at peace with her life. But she promised herself that her daughter would have more options. Her daughter, she swore, would never be so unsure of her knowledge that she would drop out of conversations, or simply play a supportive audience to her husband's stronger voice. She would say and do whatever she wanted.

"I was determined that no daughter of mine was going to have to go through the agony of being afraid to say what she had on her mind," she said. "Just because she was a girl didn't mean she should be limited. . . . I don't know whether you could say that was unusual at the time," she told a reporter from the *Washington Post*. "I guess it was more of an accepted role to stay within your own scope."

Hillary's scope, Dorothy decided, would be as wide and dream-filled as possible. It would be as big as Hillary's belief in herself could make it. As Hillary recalled years later: "[My parents] told me that it was my obligation to go to school, that I had an obligation to use my mind. They told me that an education would enable me to have a lot more opportunities in life, that if I went to school and took it seriously and studied hard, not only would I learn things and become interested in the world around me, but I would open up all kinds of doors to myself so that when I was older I would have some control over my environment. It was education for education's sake," she told the *Arkansas Democrat*, "but also it was the idea that school was a real pathway to a better opportunity."

Fortunately, where doing well in school was concerned, Hillary didn't need much prodding. As a student in her local home district 64, she, along with every other school child in America, watched with an almost personal dismay as the Russians launched the first Sputnik rocket into space. In her first public service-minded move, she swore that she'd devote herself to science.

Home life taught Hillary that she could do anything and everything. "I felt very fortunate because as a girl growing up I never felt anything but support from my family," she later recalled to Charles Allen. "Whatever I thought I could do or be, they supported. There was no distinction between me and my brothers or any barriers thrown up to me that I couldn't think about doing something because I was a girl. It was just: if you work hard enough and you really apply yourself, then you should be able to do whatever you choose to do."

The outside world, however, wasn't quite as encouraging. While Hillary was still in junior high school, she decided she wanted to be an astronaut. It was the early 1960s, and the nation, under President Kennedy's leadership, was thinking moonward. Hillary Rodham wrote to NASA and asked them what she needed to do to start training. She included mention of her background and academic strengths. NASA wrote back telling her that girls need not apply. It was, she said, "infuriating." She told the *Washington Post*: "I later realized that I couldn't have been an astronaut anyway, because I have terrible eyesight. That somewhat placated me."

Even if Hillary had been the kind of girl whose ambitions could have been derailed by this sort of setback, her parents wouldn't have allowed it. Dorothy's investment in seeing Hillary have the life she'd never had was too great. And Hugh was a self-made man, a son of the Great Depression who had attended college on a football scholarship. He knew how close he had come to not receiving a college education at all. His hold on middle-class life felt fragile, and failure seemed an ever-present threat. His love for his daughter led him to project his own fears onto her. She had to succeed, had to outdo herself constantly. If she didn't, disaster lay just around the corner.

"My father would come home and say, 'You did

well, but could you do better? It's hard out there,' "
Hillary recalled. "I would come home from school
with a good grade, and my father would say, 'Must
have been an easy assignment.' " In later years Hillary took a charitable view of her father's constant
worrying. "His encouragement was always mixed
with realism." But it didn't make for the most pleas-
ant atmosphere growing up. Hugh Rodham's emotional parsimony could translate into downright
tight-fistedness. He balked at giving his children
pocket money and laughed at the thought of doing
as other parents did and rewarding them with a dol-
lar or two for mowing the lawn or washing the car.
"They eat and sleep for free!" he'd tell his wife.
"We're not going to pay them for it as well!"

From a very early age Hillary was encouraged to
earn her own money. She started baby-sitting when
she was herself little more than a child, helped out in
a day-care center, and, when she was slightly older,
worked as a salesgirl in a store. Vacations were spent
in similarly remunerative activity. Dorothy did not
tolerate sloth. She had big plans for her daughter,
and she figured a sense of responsibility couldn't
hurt.

A girl with a different psychological makeup might
have buckled under the weight of such great parental
expectations. She might have internalized Hugh's
chronic dissatisfaction. Or might have rebelled as a
teenager, breaking free for a while of the yoke of
perfect girlhood. But achievement gave Hillary Rodham a reason to be. She became the sum total of her
good grades and good acts. If there was a risk involved in so much self-betterment, it wasn't acknowl-

edged in the high-achieving world of Park Ridge. It probably never would have dawned on anyone there to raise the question of whether being such a perfect little girl could carry a cost to the soul.

Soon Hillary was working just as hard at polishing her soul as she was at perfecting her report card. In high school she met Don Jones, a Methodist minister fresh out of Drew University Theological School who had just been assigned to the Rodhams' church, First Methodist, to work with the parish's teenagers. Jones would become the first major outside influence on Hillary Rodham's life. He showed her that there were people and places far beyond the picket fences of her stable, middle-class world. He led her forward as the placid certainties of her world—the fortress mentality of mid-century America—crumbled in the gathering storm of the 1960s. "We were just getting out of the Eisenhower era, the Pat Boone era, the passive period, and moving into a revolutionary decade where many things would happen," Jones recalls. "Kennedy had just been elected, and the civil rights law would be passed within two yeas. That's when I first got in touch with Hillary."

Hillary's crowd of friends was too young then to drive cars and wasn't even allowed into downtown Chicago without their parents. Jones took the youth group on trips into the inner city. They visited a recreation center in one of the city's toughest neighborhoods and met with a black gang and Hispanic groups. Under his leadership Hillary and some of the other high school girls began to organize baby-sitting brigades for the children of migrant workers who were living in what were then farmlands not far to the west and south of Park Ridge.

"He just was relentless in telling us that to be a Christian did not just mean you were concerned about your own personal salvation," she recalled to *Newsweek*.

"I don't think those kids had seen poverty before. I don't think they had interacted with kids that weren't like themselves," Jones says. "Religion, going to church, tended to function there for most people to reinforce their rather traditional conservative values. And so when I came in and took that white youth group, that middle-class youth group, into the inner city of Chicago, that was something quite radical. That wasn't common practice for North Shore Chicago"

Jones had studied under the theologian Paul Tillich and had been exposed to creative new methods of relating theology to art and culture. He took these teachings with him to Park Ridge, where he exposed the high school kids to Picasso, e.e. cummings, and Stephen Crane. While some played the guitar, the group sang folk songs, Bob Dylan songs, then talked about the lyrics. Jones screened films like *Requiem for a Heavyweight* and *The 400 Blows*.

"I did things like I took a print of Picasso's *Guernica*, took it into the inner city, set it on the back of a chair, and asked both groups, the city group, the suburban group, to sit there and look at that painting, and not say anything, and then we talked about it in terms of their experience," Jones recalls. "I asked them if it reminded them of anything, even what kind of music they would set it to—just to even out the playing field, so as not to give a discursive advantage to the better-educated kids. I might ask them simple things like: what strikes you, grabs you? Some kids would say, the baby and the mother crying and wailing, or the broken arm, or the lightbulb in the middle. And then I would say things like: did this remind you of any experience you had? What was interesting was that the inner-city kids were able to relate to the tragedy, the tragic dimensions of that painting better than the suburban kids. I remember one girl from Chicago started crying and said, 'Why did my uncle have to die just because he parked in the wrong parking place?' And she started to tell us that just three days before her uncle parked in the wrong parking place and some guy pulled out a gun and said that's my parking place, and they got into an argument and the guy shot her uncle."

Sherry Heiden, who was also a member of the youth group from Park Ridge at that time, recalled those inner-city visits as part and parcel of the golden age of the early sixties, when hope was still on the rise and drugs had not yet come to infiltrate the schools. "It was a time when a lot of the idealism that was going to fuel the sixties and early seventies was becoming known about," she says. "We believed in the incredible social changes that can happen if you shift your mind and change your perspective."

A high point for Hillary came in 1962 when, through Jones, she met Dr. Martin Luther King Jr. He was addressing a Sunday Evening Club meeting, a weekly event which drew preachers from around the country to give talks in Orchestra Hall in downtown Chicago. After King's talk Jones took his youth group backstage. He stood next to King and introduced the teenagers to him one by one. Hillary Rodham's eyes were shining as she shook his hand.

Hillary started frequently dropping by Jones's office at the church in the afternoons after school. She liked to talk about ideas. Jones introduced Hillary, in small doses, to the difficult theological writings of Dietrich Bonhoeffer, Reinhold Niebuhr, and Paul Tillich. Then he decided to present her with a different kind of challenge.

He reached back from his desk and took a small paperback book off his bookshelf.

"Here," he said, "you ought to read this. And we'll talk about it later."

Hillary glanced at the book jacket. It was J. D. Salinger's *Catcher in the Rye*, a scandalous book in those days.

She took the book and went away. She never said anything about it to Jones. But a few years later she wrote him to thank him for having given it to her to read, saying that the character of Holden Caulfield had helped her to understand her brother Hugh. Hugh Rodham was a few years younger than Hillary, but already he was causing his family some trouble. Nothing serious. He just wasn't the perfect child that his sister was.

"Hughie was kind of a rascal," Jones says. "A roustabout. I think I played some role in taming him."

(Hugh Rodham went on to become a football player at Penn State University and then a highly respected public defender in Miami.)

Jones's eventual move to another church was an end of an era at the Youth Ministry. Though he and

Hillary kept in touch by letters, the new pastor was cut of quite a different cloth. "[He] thinks I'm a radical," Hillary wrote to Jones.

She too was entering into a new stage in her life, preparing for college. She was also living out the highs and lows of a high school social life. The rules of the game didn't at first come all that naturally to her.

"I saw a lot of my friends who had been really lively and smart and doing well in school beginning to worry that boys would think they were too smart, or beginning to cut back on how well they did or the courses they took, because that's not where their boyfriends were," Hillary told the *Washington Post*. "And I can recall thinking, 'Gosh, why are they doing that?' It didn't make sense to me."

It didn't interest her all that much either. She did as she liked, dressing for comfort, wearing glasses, prioritizing studying over worrying about her next date. As a child, Hillary told the magazine *Vanity Fair*, she had literally beaten her way to parity with the neighborhood boys. At her mother's urging, she had punched a neighborhood bully who had been making her life miserable. "I can play with the boys now!" Hillary ran home and bragged to her mother.

"Boys responded well to Hillary," her mother later recalled. "She just took charge, and they let her."

Hillary's crowd was full of all-American overachievers like herself. They went to football and basketball games, to school dances and afterward to restaurants. They didn't do drugs, didn't drink, and didn't get into much trouble with their parents. Their social life centered around hanging around talking and watching TV in the home of Hillary's friend Betsy Johnson.

Hillary organized circuses and amateur sports tournaments to raise money for migrant workers. She participated in a school talent show with later folk singer Steve Goodman and her friend and longtime admirer Rich Ricketts, and scolded them for not rehearsing enough. She had an incredible ability to rally high school boys to do her service-oriented bidding.

"She always had the energy and the drive and the ability to size people up and know who was going to be able to work hard and who was just doing it for reasons other than real dedication," her friend Sherry Heiden says, laughing.

She went ice skating and skiing and tobaggoning with the youth group. And she played softball. She loved team sorts. In those pre-Title VII school days, though, there were no girls' athletics teams. Girls who wanted to lead, to excel outside of the academic arena, were advised instead to get into the school clubs and student government. Which is just what she did.

Hillary became a senior leader—a sort of assistant teacher—in her last year of high school. She was vice president of her junior class, and a member of the national honor society. Recalls Kenneth Reese, who was Hillary's driver's-ed teacher and student council coordinator during her senior year, "She was a forceful person, confident, obviously motivated, and she was able to get things done. She was active and she was a leader. The kids just kind of automatically looked up to her because she spoke out for things that she believed in. She would take an unpopular stance on something, and she would be willing to be in the minority position, and be able to support that position."

She graduated at the top five percent of her class. She is said to have earned every Girl Scout badge. She was the girl voted most likely to succeed by her senior class. (The boy in her class voted most likely to succeed died of a drug overdose four years later.) At her graduation she won so many awards that, Dorothy Rodham later said, "It was embarrassing."

The importance of Dorothy Rodham's influence on Hillary Clinton's early education cannot be overestimated. She instilled in her daughter the sense of the unlimited possibilities of learning—and of her own limitless potential. And she believed in herself too. Sherry Heiden recalls that Mrs. Rodham was the only mother she knew who started taking community college courses "just for the thrill of it, just to do something with her mind" in her free time. "Dorothy was a big influence on Hillary. She has such an interest in the world and such an interest in people's minds," Heiden says. Her mother provided Hillary with a model for self-esteem—and an image of how to maintain it in a household dominated by a rather difficult man.

When it came time to apply to college, Hillary decided to go East—an "adventurous and cosmopolitan" thing to do in that place at that time, recalls Kenneth Reese. She had been inspired by two young teachers in her high school who had attended the women's colleges Smith and Wellesley, in Massachusetts. "They were both so bright and smart and terrific teachers, and they lobbied me so hard to apply to these schools which I had never thought of before," she recalled to Charles Allen. "And then when I was accepted, they lobbied me hard to go and be able to work out all of the financial and other issues associated with it." She eventually decided upon Wellesley. The campus had, she noted, looked very pretty in photographs. It seemed elegant—and intimidating too. But Hillary wouldn't stay intimidated for long.

The 1960s, Hilary Clinton once said, appeared to her as "years dominated by men with dreams, men in the civil rights movement and the Peace Corps, the space program." She went to college intent upon finding her place in that man's world of social progress. Wellesley was then the right place to do it.

"There was a sense of coming of age on campus then," a classmate recalls. "A sense of empowerment."

Hillary arrived at Wellesley a Park Ridge Republican with box-pleat skirts, Peter Pan blouses, and loafers with knee socks. In high school she had gone door-to-door canvassing for the right-wing candidate Barry Goldwater; now the former Goldwater Girl became president of the campus Young Republicans. She was an outspoken opponent of big government and high taxes, and, though her heart bled for the poor, she believed in self-reliance and in the responsibility of local governments to look after their own. All of that changed rather quickly.

When Hillary began college in the fall of 1965, the Goldwater-Johnson election, in which she had spoken out for the right with all the passion due to her seventeen years, was becoming ancient history. A great deal had happened in the world during the last six months of her senior high school year. Dr. Martin Luther King Jr. had led the march on Selma, Alabama, and white Northern Americans had for the first time seen fire hoses and police dogs set to rain hate on African Americans down South. Hillary Rodham, who only two years before had clasped and shook Dr. King's hand in Chicago's Orchestra Hall, saw white policemen in storm-trooper boots using cattle prods on peaceful black and white demonstrators, saw federal troops called in to keep the peace. The images could not have failed to make their mark on her. She came to college hungry to learn their meaning.

Hillary majored in political science and also studied psychology. Her mentor was a professor named Alan Schechter, part of a new breed of teachers in the humanities and social sciences who led classroom discussions with an eye to advocacy, and who was particularly excited by the civil rights movement. She studied with him through the assassination of Martin Luther King Jr. and Robert Kennedy, the fall of the Black Panthers, the Weathermen, the war and the protests. "We were in school when everything seemed to be falling apart at the seams," Kris Olson Rogers, a Wellesley friend who is now United States Attorney in Portland, Washington recalls. "And the campus often reflected the unrest in society at large."

Hillary certainly did. In the course of her first year she became radicalized—up to a point. She started to wear horn-rimmed glasses, granny skirts, and muslin dresses. Her academic career became a search for "relevance." She edged her way leftward through the moderate Rockefeller wing of the Republican party and by 1968 was campaigning for the Democrat Eugene McCarthy, thinking about women's issues, and talking about minority rights and the needs of the poor.

"There was a sea change in Hillary," recalls Jeff Shields, a Chicago attorney who began dating Hillary during her freshman year. "There was a great deal of change going on in the country, and she reflected it."

Shields recalls Hillary's transformation from a college freshman unsure in her views to a competent political thinker who loved nothing more than a good debate. Hillary, Shields recalls, always seemed to have a political mission—even before she had a vision to go with it. "She was someone who wanted to be involved and have an impact," he says. "She didn't have fixed ambitions in terms of knowing that she wanted to be elected to some office, and she certainly didn't give any indication that she was looking to attach herself to a politician—and I'm sure probably would have been offended by that concept if someone had raised it at that time."

Some friends say that the actual philosophical change that went on in Hillary Rodham's mind during college has been exaggerated. Her early Goldwater support in Park Ridge and her Young Republicanism, they say, was a last gasp of unconscious parent mimicking. Hillary, they stress, was never a hard-core conservative.

"Most of her thinking seemed to be based, as all of ours was based, on her parents' perspective," her friend and political comrade-in-arms (and later White

House collaborator) Eleanor "Eldee" Acheson recalls. Acheson, who came from a liberal, highly political family, was quickly drawn to her smart, intense classmate with the big light-up smile, who wore thick, heavy-rimmed glasses like Eldee's own, and whose long hair flopped negligently in a clip at the back of her neck. She welcomed her classmate's shift to the left. In the fall of 1968 Eldee drove Hillary around the state as the two young women campaigned for Senator Hubert Humphrey, doing literature drops and phone banks in Massachusetts and New Hampshire. "I never got into a conversation with her in which I thought that she held conservative views that would translate into being discriminatory about blacks or Catholics or Jews or anybody. I don't remember that kind of substantive conservatism," Acheson says.

At Wellesley, Acheson, Hillary, and a handful of friends settled in nearby rooms in the modern dormitory complex Stone-Davis which was known as the place where student leaders lived. They were a group of earthy, intense, committed, politically active young women. Almost all were from relatively conservative, middle-class backgrounds like Hillary's, and almost all were struggling through breaking with the political preferences of their parents.

It was a sylvan setting for study: tall trees, elegant New England landscape, old stone Gothic buildings, a windowed dining room overlooking the foliage. Hillary followed a rigorous schedule. She made frequent trips into the Roxbury section of Boston, where she worked teaching poor children to read. Boston then was embroiled in controversy over busing and voting access for African Americans. Hillary and her friends got involved in working on an alternative newspaper in the black community and participated in inter-campus activist groups with Harvard and MIT. In the evenings she often sat up late in the Stone-Davis dorm common area, holding a sort of social issues salon, dreaming of changing the world or, at least, bringing some hint of reform to Wellesley.

In some ways Wellesley in Hillary's time still had one foot in the 1950s. First-year students had to be in their dorm rooms by nine o'clock most nights, and the nights they were allowed out till one A.M. were few and far between. Freshman women were assigned a "big sister," who helped them out with orientation, gave advice, kept them out of trouble, and exchanged gifts with them at Christmas. First-year students weren't allowed to have cars, go away for the weekends without parental permission, or have boys in their rooms in the early years. When weekends came, they took the nearby Green Line train to Boston, where they knocked around the bookstores and cafés of Harvard Square. There were mixers and dances around Harvard and some coregistration with the men at MIT, but it wasn't a roaring social scene. "The biggest social life on campus was tea on Wednesday afternoon, you know, one lump or two," Kris Olson Rogers says.

But Wellesley, like the nation, was changing. In Hillary's freshman year the greatest number of black students ever admitted had entered the school. They formed the campus' first African-American women's association, and took on the university, charging that a secret quota policy was being used to keep their numbers down. There were talks of strikes and other political action. Hillary emerged as a mediator. "She did a sort of shuttle democracy among all the groups," Rogers says. "She had a talent for serving as a bridge between different groups of students. She tried to keep everybody talking and figured out a way to move the institution out of its inertia and also accommodate the concerns of black students."

Rogers suggests that it was precisely Hillary's not-long-distant conservatism which made her such a natural mediator between the students and the rather staid administration. "As she evolved personally into more Democratic politics, I think Hillary was able to not close off those channels of communication from her earlier roots. She definitely gained from them an empathy for various segments of the population who very often in those days weren't speaking to each other at all."

Hillary also fought the college administration to loosen restrictions and helped lead protests against Wellesley's rigid academic distribution requirements and for a pass-fail grading system. As president of the college government her senior year, she organized the first set of teach-ins on the Vietnam War on campus. The protest was mild, however, compared to the anti-war activities at other schools in the fall of 1968. Wellesley, as an all-women college, was not subject to the pains of the draft firsthand. There was no ROTC chapter and there were no CIA recruiters coming around to fish for likely new conscripts. Protest remained an academic, intellectual concern, not a matter of civil disobedience, and certainly nothing that would stand in the way of any liberal, pragmatic, ambitiously career-minded young woman's future.

"She was really very mainstream," Shields says. "She was not a counterculture person."

Hillary Rodham had met Jeff Shields when she went out on a date with his roommate. She dated him through the first half of her freshman year at Wellesley, along with a number of other men—"poli-sci, earnest idealist, policy activist, good government types, not wild-eyed radicals," Rogers recalls.

Shields, a Harvard College student two years ahead of her, remembers Hillary as a serious, active, and intellectual young woman, who knew how to have fun but primarily spent her time living, breathing, and talking politics.

She took him on long walks around the lake at Wellesley, talking all the while. He followed. "She listened to what people were thinking about and were interested in reading, and then she'd read that author's work and come back and be able to discuss it, which was a fairly impressive thing," he says. After a few turns around the lake, Hillary gave Shields a copy of Thoreau's *Walden*. They also discussed Locke and the early political philosophers.

"It was a relationship based on a lot of discourse," he says.

There were also football games and dances and private parties in the suites of Winthrop House, Shields' Harvard dorm. Hillary was outgoing and could chat with anyone. She loved to dance, loved the Beatles and the Supremes, and was considered attractive—in an athletic, un-fussed-over way. "She was not a woman who spent a lot of time thinking of how she looked or what she wore," a classmate recalls.

She saved her passions for politics. She poured her heart into her senior thesis: a comparative study of community-action programs for the poor, analyzing them to determine the conditions under which the participation of the poor in taking control of their lives could have a lasting positive impact. Her conclusion was that on a short-term basis participation of the poor in trying to improve their lives would help them, but the betterment would be temporary, and broader programs with more sustained help were needed to achieve longer-term impact.

She also reveled in the study of constitutional law. She looked forward to her weekly seminars with Professor Schechter and a small group of other seniors, many of whom had been involved in the anti-Vietnam movement, or in campaigning for Eugene McCarthy or Bobby Kennedy. The students shared an unhappiness with the course that their country was taking. They saw their brothers, cousins, and boyfriends going off to war. They felt the government was out of touch. They were involved, and committed, and believed that the fact of having been college students in the late 1960s was itself of historical importance. They were frustrated with the fact that, at their graduation, no one would be there to talk about their shared history.

"We need a class speaker, one of us," someone decided. Hillary and Eldee Acheson agreed. With Schechter's coaching and encouragement, they took the idea to Wellesley President Ruth Adams. Adams, not surprisingly, said no.

The constitutional law scholars made their case. They took the idea to the student body, and it was enthusiastically approved. Then they set to finding a speaker who would go over well with the administration. A good student, a class leader, a popular woman, who they could honestly say spoke for the class. They settled on Hillary Rodham. She was a natural choice—president of student government, a straight-A honors student, well-known and popular on campus. Having been a go-between for so long between so many groups, she was one of the only women whom everyone could claim as a fair representative of their interests.

The administration agreed. Miss Adams specified only that the speaker and her remarks were to reflect a consensus of the graduating class, and that her remarks be "appropriate" and not embarrass the college. In a "consensus" style typical of the day, Hillary opened the speechwriting process to suggestions from her classmates. They deluged her with ideas, poems, quotations. They wanted her to talk about what they had seen in the past four years, they said: the escalation of the Vietnam War, the assassinations of Martin Luther King and Bobby Kennedy, and the riots in the cities. A small committee of speechwriters, including Acheson, sifted through the ideas and came up with a tentative draft.

A few days before commencement, Miss Adams demanded the right to review the speech. Acheson and friends refused.

At Wellesley College at that time it was traditional

for the administration to invite an outside speaker to graduation. The year Hillary graduated, the invited speaker was Senator Edward Brooke, a liberal Republican from Massachusetts. The commencement scheduler, clearly not anticipating a war of words from the pulpit, scheduled Brooke to speak right before Hillary. It was a rather unfortunate mistake.

There were a lot of prominent guests in the audience that day. Eldee Acheson's grandfather, Dean Acheson, former secretary of state under Truman, was there with his wife. Paul Nitze, who had been deputy secretary of Defense during the Vietnam War, was there for his daughter Nina. There were other prominent people from business, the financial world, and government. There was more press coverage than usual.

Senator Brooke spoke for his allotted time without incident. Without substance, many of Hillary's classmates believed. After he finished speaking, Hillary Rodham approached the pulpit. She looked small and rather young in her oversized cap and gown. She faced her classmates, her parents, the board of trustees, and the reunited alumnae. Then she began.

Senator Brooke's remarks, she said, reflected just the kind of disconnected, irrelevant thinking that had led this country astray for four years. "I find myself in a familiar position, that of reacting, something that our generation has been doing for quite a while now. . . . I find myself reacting just briefly to some of the things that Senator Brooke said," she said. A few gasps were heard within the audience. The graduating students exchanged sideways glances and checked their smiles. For a few minutes Hillary spoke extemporaneously, rebuking Brooke. Then she segued into her prepared remarks.

The "challenge now is to practice politics as the art of making what appears to be impossible, possible. . . . We're not interested in social reconstruction; it's human reconstruction," she said. Her speech wound and wondered, its form and its abstraction striking as opposite a note to Brooke's traditional address as possible. "Words have a funny way of trapping our minds on the way to our tongues, but they are necessary means even in this multimedia age for attempting to come to grasps with some of the inarticulate, maybe even inarticulable things that we're feeling. We are, all of us, exploring a world that none of us understands and attempting to create within that uncertainty. But there are some things we feel, feelings that our prevailing, acquisitive, and competitive corporate life, including tragically the universities, is not the way of life for us. We're searching for more immediate, ecstatic, and penetrating modes of living."

It was a moving, if somewhat tortuously written speech. But few in the audience made the attempt to follow it. The long sentences were punctuated by the sounds of folding chairs creaking and screeching. A low murmur of whispered commentary buzzed under her words. "Hillary had just sort of launched off on her own," Acheson, one of the leaders of the speechwriting campaign, recalls. "Some people, largely mothers, thought it was just rude and never got off that point. Another group thought she was absolutely right. It distracted a lot of people." The students loved it.

An excerpt from Hillary's speech—and her picture—made *Life* magazine. Published alongside a few others, it seemed absolutely tame.

"Traditionally, commencement exercises are the occasion for fatuous comments on the future of the graduates present . . ." read the abridged text of revolt-minded Stephanie Mills, a senior from Mills College. "My depressing comment on that rosy future, that infinite future, is that it is a hoax. . . . Our days as a race on this planet are, at this moment, numbered, and the reason for our finite, unrosy future is that we are breeding ourselves out of existence. . . . I am terribly saddened by the fact that the most humane thing for me to do is to have no children at all."

"Realities exist but they're not real to me," was the catchphrase of another excerpt, this time from a speech by Brown University's student leader, Ira Magaziner (later to serve with Hillary on her disastrous health care reform effort).

By the time Hillary Rodham graduated from Wellesley College she had enjoyed triumphs and gained a notoriety far beyond even her most ambitious dreams. Her commencement speech had received national press notice. She would enter Yale University with a reputation to proceed her. She was well-liked and, even better, respected. "I thought she'd be the first Supreme court justice who was a graduate of Wellesley," Alan Schechter recalls.

But outside of the sheltered enclave of the progressive women's college, life wasn't always so triumphant. Hillary's conversion to the Democratic party put her in direct conflict with her conservative father.

When fights flared between them, the bottom line always was politics. Hillary's switch to the Democratic party was not, one might say, in a time of university takeovers, "tuning out and turning on," a major rebellion. But in her family it was, and the dissenting words at the dinner table sometimes cut deep.

"All of us talked about the difficulties of going back home again," Kris Olson Rogers recalled of that time. "Our personal evolutions mirrored so much what was going on in the times."

Outside the family, there were other problems as well. "People gave her a hard time because she wanted to be the best," Dorothy Rodham remembered to *Paris Match*. "I think that those years were those of her greatest challenge. She was a young woman and was the equal of men. At that time, that wasn't yet accepted."

"She was an unusual young woman," a classmate said. "She wasn't the same as other people in that everybody was usually more or less of something, and Hillary was really quite unique. She had a very strong personality. She wasn't everybody's cup of tea."

While Hillary's class was considered a swing year in terms of the changes affecting the school and the country, it did not by any means mark a radical break with past classes in terms of students' personal ambitions. Although Wellesley was known as a place full of extremely intelligent, highly motivated intellectual women, the majority of students still saw themselves as unlikely to do anything other than marry and raise families after college, and to use their superior Wellesley educations to be "serious adjuncts" to their husbands' professional careers. Although Hillary's class was the first to produce any number of graduates aimed for law school, virtually none of even the most ambitious of those women envisioned entering politics as a viable possibility for their future lives.

Given her political inclinations, law school was a natural choice for Hillary Rodham. She considered Harvard Law but leaned toward Yale, in part because of its emphasis on political philosophy, and partly due to an unpleasant experience she had with a professor at Harvard. This professor, a distinguished, elder scholar, looked her up and down with distaste when a friend of Hillary's introduced her and said she was considering attending Harvard Law School. "We don't need any more women," he said. Hillary went to Yale.

Shields himself by that time as at Yale Law, although after one last Harvard-Yale football game together, the pair's relationship had all but fizzled out. "The primary basis of our relationship was cerebral," he says. "It was one of those situations where both parties become less romantically interested in each other on a parallel track but remain friends."

Yale Law School marked the beginning of a new intellectual journey for Hillary Rodham. It also poised her for a romantic adventure. Just what would result in the end, when romance and intellect met, no one could then have expected.

Yale Law School in the early 1970s was, as it is today, the most public service–oriented of the top law schools. The generation of law students who filled Hillary Rodham's class of 1972 had as young teenagers formed their dreams through the words and speeches of John F. Kennedy, and had come of age in the turbulence of the late 1960s. They were a group who hoped for change and believed that the system could make it happen. They studied Charles Reich's *Greening of America* and discussed revolutionizing conventional notions of property. They demonstrated, they taught-in. In Hillary's second month on campus they went on strike.

Many of the professors at Yale inspired Hillary as models of the kind of professional career paths she might take toward public service. Several professors teaching there at that time had been members of John F. Kennedy's administration, including Burke Marshall, who had been director of the Civil Rights Division in the Justice Department during Kennedy's administration and was responsible for the drafting of a civil rights agenda for the federal government at that time in the South.

At Yale Law School, Hillary's politicization progressed rapidly. For a short period of time she was on the editorial board of the now-defunct *Yale Review of Law and Social Action*, an alternative legal journal which was dedicated, as its editors stated, "to the development of new forms of journalism which combine scholarship of the highest standard with reflections and recommendations based on experience and practice." The journal aimed to provide a forum for activists and community leaders as well as scholars. Its first issue featured a cover photo of national guardsmen in riot gear, and was followed by a second issue largely devoted to the Black Panthers.

Hillary Clinton recalls her years at Yale as a time of "trying to reconcile the reasoned, ordered world we were studying with what we saw around us." In a speech to her former classmates at a Yale Law School alumni weekend in October 1992, she recalled, "There was a great amount of ferment and confusion about what was and wasn't the proper role of law school education. We would have great arguments about whether we were selling out because we were getting a law degree, whether in fact we should be doing something else, not often defined clearly but certainly passionately argued. That we should somehow be 'out there,' wherever 'there' was, trying to help solve the problems that took up so much of our time in argument and discussion . . . those were difficult and turbulent times."

It was precisely the kind of hothouse atmosphere that she loved, the sort of tumultuous, complicated time in which her skills as conciliator and leader could thrive. Hillary Rodham would emerge from Yale with even greater negotiating skills and advocacy experience. She also would emerge a woman torn between love and the glories of professional life.

"And not only that, we grow the biggest watermelons in the world."

The words were to change the course of her life, though Hillary Rodham didn't know it then. She turned to look at their speaker.

"Who is that?" she asked a friend.

"That's Bill Clinton from Arkansas," the friend said, shrugging, "and that's all he ever talks about."

Well, *that* couldn't have been true. Hillary stole a glance over at the handsome, cheerful man with the voice oddly reminiscent of Elvis's.

Bill Clinton at Yale was a long-haired, bearded Rhodes scholar who had spent enough time in graduate school already to know when to study seriously and when to put things in perspective. He was a bit older than the average law student, and had more responsibilities. Although he had been fortunate enough to be chosen for one of Yale's few law school scholarships, the money was nowhere nearly enough to cover even the most meager costs of living. He was forced to hold as many as three part-time jobs at once to meet expenses. In the course of his years at Yale he taught in a small community college, staffed for a city councilman in Hartford, and worked for a lawyer in downtown New Haven.

Like Hillary, he had clearly not come to law school to prepare for a career on Wall Street. Politics ran in his blood. During his first three months of law school he worked full-time on a political campaign, starting to study for his classes only after the November election. He then amazed his worried friends by acing all his finals.

In many ways Bill Clinton was a perfect match for Hillary: attractive, high-energy, committed to public service. Like Hillary, he was a highly visible, unusual figure on campus as well. He as the only white student who dared break with lunchroom protocol to sit regularly at the all-black students table. Like Hillary, Bill Clinton also was a classic overachiever. In high school he was in the Key Club, was vice president of his class, in the Band Club. Never mind his role as senator in Boys Nation, through which he got to shake John F. Kennedy's hand.

"He had to be the class leader," Carolyn Staley, a high school friend recalled to Charles Allen. "He had to be the best in the band. He had to be the best in his class—in the grade. And he wanted to be at the top. . . . He wanted to be anything that put him at the forefront."

Bill Clinton and Hillary Rodham's first close contact came in a class they both took on political and civil liberties. It was a class neither attended very often, because the professor had written the textbook and was known to be better on paper than out loud. Bill followed Hillary out of class once, on a rare day when both had been present. He trailed her closely, but couldn't work up the courage to speak to her. He was shocked at himself; he'd never been shy before. Something about the woman with the thick glasses intimidated him.

"I could just look at her and tell she was interesting and deep," he told *Vanity Fair.*

A few days later, they happened to end up within staring distance in the Yale law library.

The story of that first meeting has become the stuff of legend. Both Bill and Hillary Clinton have told it countless times over the course of the campaign, and both say they can still see the spot where they spoke in the library in their mind's eye. The problem is that they both see different spots. The disparity has become a constant source of dinnertime debate, and both sides have been known to recruit Yale friends as witnesses in an effort to amass evidence for their position.

One thing they do agree upon is that on that fateful night, Bill Clinton was standing at one end of the law library, pretending to be involved in a conversation, and all the while he was staring at Hillary Rodham as she did pantomimed book study at a table at the other end of the room.

"This guy was trying to talk me into joining the *Yale Law Review* and telling me I could clerk for the U.S. Supreme Court if I was a member of the *Yale Law Review*, which is probably true. And then I could go on to New York and make a ton of money. And I kept telling him I didn't want to do all of that. I wanted to go home to Arkansas. It didn't matter to anybody [in Arkansas] whether I was on the *Yale Law Review* or not. . . . I just didn't much want to do it," Clinton told Charles Allen. "And all this time I was talking to this guy about the *Law Review*, I was looking at Hillary at the other end of the library. And the Yale Law School Library is a real long, narrow [room]. She was down at the other end, and . . . I just was staring at her. . . . And she closed this book, and she walked all the way down the library . . . and she came up to me and she said, 'Look, if you're going to keep staring at me, and I'm going to keep staring back, I think we should at least know each other: I'm Hillary Rodham. What's your name?' "

At which point, Bill Clinton has said, he drew a total blank.

In many ways Bill and Hillary Clinton were perfectly suited for each other. On an early date they held a discussion of diplomatic policy in Africa, and both came away enthralled.

They both were stars, with reputations to precede them. Hillary had started at Yale with a certain notoriety for her multiple wins for Wellesley College on the *G.E. College Bowl,* a popular television quiz show. Having had her picture in *Life* magazine hadn't hurt her reputation any either. She had already met some of the big names in Washington when she'd been invited, after receiving notice for her Wellesley speech, to a conference of young leaders sponsored by the League of Women Voters. There she'd met Peter Edelman, Robert Kennedy's former legislative assistant, and Vernon Jordan.

She had become, by the end of her freshman year, a bit of a campus celebrity. An image of her, sitting cross-legged in blue jeans on a huge lecture hall's stage, keeping order as students yelled and raged at each other all around her, has stayed fresh in her classmates' minds. No one is quite sure anymore just why that meeting had been called. It may have been about the Black Panthers marching through the building, or it might have been about Cambodia or Kent State or internal problems in the law school or myriad other things.

The trials of a group of Black Panthers, including Erica Huggins and Bobby Seale, who were accused of kidnapping and murdering another Panther, were going on just then in New Haven, in a courthouse problematically located right off the Yale green, and there were nonstop demonstrations going on outside it. The trials had divided Yale's law school between the faculty, who wanted to go on with business as usual, and the students who, unable to concentrate on contracts and torts—and failing to see their relevancy—talked of calling a strike. There was an internal trial going on in the law school too, over the case of a member of the Black American Law Student Association whom the law school faculty wanted to sue for damaging property. Whatever the cause, there was a meeting, a mass meeting, which drew a majority of the student body in the spring of 1970.

It was a bad time for New Haven and a bad time for Yale Law School. Downtown, in the streets running adjacent to the school, store owners had boarded over their windows, fearful of looters and rioters, when thousands of protesters came to the city to support the Black Panthers. A fire that had recently broken out in the International Law Library was thought by many to have been set in retribution for law school dean Louis Pollak's too reticent support of the Black Panthers.

In the general atmosphere of tension and potential danger, at Yale as in embattled cities across the nation, the students were angry and disturbed. Demonstrators had been tear-gassed on their own campus green. They were frustrated with "the system"—the government and institutions which, they felt, had no interest in justice—and they were frustrated with themselves for joining its ranks on such high levels by attending one of the nation's most prestigious schools for lawyers and politicians. Much of their anger jelled around Dean Pollak himself, who was called a "reactionary," and the Yale law faculty, who were seen by many students as out of touch with the concerns of the new generation of students.

In a contentious time, with passions running high, Hillary had the advantage of being the person with whom everyone on campus was still on speaking terms. She had been active in trying to figure out a constructive role that the law school could play during the Black Panther trials, and was known to both administrators and students as someone who would fairly represent their views and, hopefully, bring them past their current stalemate. She'd been seen out on the green helping coordinate marshals, trying to keep things in order so that the demonstrators wouldn't get gassed again. She knew how and when to keep calm. Carolyn Ellis, a friend from that time, has never forgotten the image of Hillary leading the mass meeting, her legs half crossed Indian-style on the stage and one leg swinging in impatience as a battery of male speakers droned in legalese around her. "None of us who were there can remember what the meeting was about—we can only remember we were awed by her," Ellis recalls. "She had complete self-possession."

After the mass meeting Hillary's reputation as a skillful conciliator stuck with her. She became the appointed spokesperson for the students with Dean Pollak, and continued to act as a bridge between them and the administration. As she had at Wellesley, Hillary became a sort of magnet for debate-addicted young women and now men. Her cafeteria table was always filled with friends and followers, who passionately flailed away at the issues of the day, while she sat at the center and mediated. "We'd just stay though the afternoon instead of going to the library where we should have been," recalls Kris

Olson Rogers, who accompanied Hillary from Wellesley to Yale, "and we'd sit around debating the issues and what we were going to do, what our roles were going to be."

Rogers also knew Hillary's lighter side. The two friends hung around together listening to Tammy Wynette and sharing stories. They giggled and whispered their way through anti-trust class. They made frequent pilgrimages to Clark's Dairy for milkshakes, which, Hillary swore, had a high nutritional value. To relax, she dragged Ellis off to the Yale gym to do calisthenics. "I was just horrified," Ellis recalls.

Little wonder that Bill Clinton was intimidated. But Hillary was undoubtedly a bit wary of him too. She was a serious, earnest person—at least in public. He was a happy-go-lucky guy all the time. In his first year at Yale, the year they met, he shared a four-bedroom beach house in Milford, Connecticut, with three other law students, most of whom had also already done some graduate work before coming to Yale. Since they were older, had studied more and seen more of the world, they tended not to take the law school grind quite as obsessively as many of his younger classmates.

"Bill, like many of us at that time who had come through long educational careers, wasn't as involved in the actual textbook learning as he might have been earlier in his education," his friend Alan Bersin recalls. "He spent lots of time on political activities, and there were occasional absences—on all our parts—from the law school."

As Bill Clinton and Hillary Rodham came together as a couple, the traits that would later define—and demarcate—them as political partners became apparent to their friends. Bill Clinton was a Southern populist; Hillary a product of the middle-class North. His heroes were Robert E. Lee and Franklin D. Roosevelt; hers were Abraham Lincoln and Martin Luther King, Jr. He as all easygoing, back-slapping, hand-shaking bonhomie. He emoted often and easily, especially in public. He liked to flirt, and liked even better to be flirted with. He had a seemingly endless well of sociability. He was equally warm and inclusive to close friends and acquaintances alike, truly democratic and egalitarian in his approach to people. Hillary was reserved, parsimonious in her affections. She liked who she liked and didn't suffer fools gladly.

Bill Clinton was a natural politician. He had a certain magnetism. Men and women flocked to him, and he made all of them feel that they had a place to shine in the reflected glory of his gaze. He had a look that devoured; when he spoke to someone, he had a special ability to make him or her feel that the two of them were the only people who existed in the world in that moment. He gave people the sense that he was absorbed in them and cared deeply about what they had to say. He also knew how to draw them out so that they ended up speaking of things close to their hearts. Hillary had that ability too, but she tended to feel her connection to people internally rather than wear it on her sleeve. She tended to mobilize her compassion into whatever idea she was forming or whatever project she was involved in.

Years later, as First Lady, shaking hands in rope lines or addressing huge crowds, she would amaze observers with her ability to focus in on single faces and individual stories and then later weave her memories of them into impassioned pleas for policy change.

Observers of Bill Clinton would also see his young adult personality mature into a political style. And in the long term friends would be somewhat less impressed with that development. For as everyone close to Clinton knew, the natural-born politician in him had its dark side. The democratic, all-inclusive impulse that would give such heartfelt egalitarianism to his politics made him something less than discriminating in his personal relationships. Clinton's ability to be, on a certain level, intimate with *everyone* debased the relationships that should have been the most intimate. The fact that Clinton felt *everyone's* pain made it rather doubtful that he felt anyone's with any real intensity.

"He's very interested in all different kinds of people, from welfare mothers to nuclear scientists, for what they can teach him about life, and he's got a wonderfully retentive mind and uses what they say to inform his thinking on social policy," says a friend of Hillary's who has known and at times worked with both Clintons since their earliest days as a couple. "He can ask a train conductor who he should select as vice president, and he'll listen to him with as much sincerity as he would Jimmy Carter or his college roommate or his mother," the friend adds. "But when he's talking to you, he's trying out something. He's not really engaged with you about what's in your life or what's coming next for you. He's sucking up what you have to tell him—but he's not giving it back and he's not vulnerable to you. He's not attached to people," the friend concludes. "Or rather, he's attached to people plural but not to people singular."

Opposites tend to attract—at first. And then, often enough, they start to find each other surprisingly familiar. Hillary Rodham must at first have been drawn in by Bill Clinton's considerable charm. The famous "contact high" reported by just about everyone who enters into his orbit. To bask in his attention, to enjoy the effusiveness of his praise, even to rue the excesses of his personality, must have felt like sheer bliss. It certainly would have been a change from home—from the miserly praise and emotional restraint of Hugh Rodham. But Bill Clinton would turn out to have one great similarity with Hillary's father: he could, in one sense, never be satisfied. Not by the love that Hillary could offer him—most probably not by the love that any one woman, any one mortal, could have offered him. And for strength Hillary would fall back on the self she'd constructed under Hugh Rodham's care: her inner core, her "groundedness," as her friends would call it—faith, hard work, self-determination. This self would keep her whole.

All that would, of course, become clear only later, both to Hillary and to the country at large. Yet even at Yale there were hints that hooking up with Bill Clinton wasn't going to be an easy ride. But then, neither was hooking up with Hillary. She was far from a typical helpmate: the mommy-cum-muse that ambitious men often marry to sustain their egos through better times and worse. Hillary had an agenda of her own. She was nothing like any woman that Bill Clinton had ever known.

His mother was "a gambler and a rogue," as one old friend puts it, but she worshiped the ground he walked upon. He'd had girlfriends and groupies and hangers-on galore—"beauty queen types" he thought of them, and he could talk circles around them. Hillary, on the other hand, he told a friend, had "brains and ability rather than glamour." This was more interesting, but also more dangerous. Hillary would love him—unconditionally, she would later prove—but she'd call him on everything. She'd take him to task. Much later, in the White House, she'd even berate him in front of staff: "How could you be so damn stupid?" as an aide recalled to Washington chronicler Elizabeth Drew. She would, in a certain sense, ignite the devouring insecurity and hunger for approval that always gnawed away inside him. "Sometimes you can see that Clinton needs this affirmation and Hillary doesn't give it to him," a source told Drew. "You could see her be aloof when he needed, at that moment, just a little warmth. . . . Hillary isn't the one to provide approval."

But that was a political lifetime away. At Yale, Bill Clinton and Hillary Rodham just knew that, in each other, they'd found something special. In a sense, they'd each met their match. Bill Clinton found a woman smart enough to outsmart him, see through him, and still love him. "She saw right past the charm and saw the complex person underneath," Yale classmate Harlon Dalton once said. "I think he found that irresistible." Hillary Rodham found a man smart enough to keep up with her, idealistic enough to dream with her, and difficult enough to provide her with a project worthy of her intelligence, energy, and ambition. She would help him direct his potential. She would help polish him into presidential material. Clinton would learn to sublimate his "free-floating" energies. The womanizer would be tamed. At the very least, it wouldn't be a life of quiet desperation.

Friends saw the potential for disaster. "They were both ambitious—both had aspirations to make their mark on the world," says Kris Olson Rogers. "And so we were all kind of holding our breath, wondering if it was going to work or not. But we knew that if it did work, it was going to be a dynamite partnership."

The dynamic duo had their first taste of team action when they both became involved in a Barristers Union prize trial. This was a clinical practice where people would team up and prepare for mock trials before a judge and jury of local people from New Haven. It was the sort of high-pressure competition that both Bill and Hillary have always loved.

Hillary Rodham and Bill Clinton as a team were rationality meeting intuition, though in their case the typical male and female roles were reversed. "Law teaches a form of reasoning," Richard Stearns, an old friend of the Clintons, sums it up. "Hillary absorbed it, I'm not sure Bill did. Bill is a more organic thinker, he tends to absorb information from all directions and mull it through, and I'm not quite sure how his thought process works—its more intuitive, though he often gets to the same result. Hillary's is more rational in the eighteenth-century sense."

For the Barristers Union, Bill Clinton's inchoate

brilliance and Hillary's rational coherency should have added up to a stellar team. They certainly prepared hard enough. And they certainly had enough fun. Kris Olson Rogers, who played key witness to the Rodham-Clinton legal team as they practiced for their mock trial, remembers how Hillary coached her to perfect her role as a "sultry, lying witness" whom Bill would destroy in cross-examination on the stand. "She really had the part down pat," Rogers recalls. "She was just cutting up. She could be a real ham."

The pair had a bad day, though. Hillary showed up in a bright red-orange dress which might have blinded the judges to the finer points of her argument. Bill, however, was dazzled. "He talked about how good she was when they were working on it and when it was over," Carolyn Ellis recalls. "He was incredibly proud of her."

After the trial there was no doubt in anyone's minds that Bill Clinton and Hillary Rodham were a serious couple. Daring to break the tacit Yale Law School rule against inter-student relationships, they lived together during her third year at Yale in a typical New England Victorian-style house with a pillared porch right off campus. But they remained ambivalent about their relationship. They were both consumed by career dreams and fearful of absorption into each other. They also knew that their relationship was deep, and real, and that frightened them. And there was always the issue of Arkansas.

Dorothy Rodham was perhaps more clearheaded than either of them. She saw very clearly that things had taken a serious turn when, the day after Christmas, Bill Clinton showed up at her door. Hillary had told her simply that a "young man" she had met at Yale was coming to stay a few days. The first encounter was, for Bill, rather harsh. He had driven the whole way from Little Rock in one stretch. That was the route that his father had taken, in the opposite direction, on the night he died. When he rang the Rodhams' doorbell, he was white with tiredness. He was nervous too.

Dorothy opened the door for him. She saw right away that her days with her single daughter were numbered.   .

"Hello, I'm Bill Clinton," he said hopefully.

"That's nice," she answered.

"The introductions were pretty chilly," Dorothy Rodham admitted to *Paris Match*. "To be honest, I sort of wanted him to go away. I knew he had come to take my daughter away."

Hillary was in her room on the second floor. Dorothy watched as Bill went up the stairs to find her. "It dawned on me to ask myself what kind of character he was," she remembered. "I knew nothing of him. But, I don't know why, I trusted him. He stayed a whole week. He slept in Tony's room. My husband and I made sure he stayed in there."

After a frigid first few hours the visit went surprisingly well. Dorothy Rodham's motherly concerns were no match for Bill Clinton's well-tested charm. On his second day in Park Ridge he came into the living room, where she was sitting reading philosophy for an extension course she was then taking at a local college. He asked her which thinker interested her the most. And then proceeded to deliver a short private lecture on the subject. Dorothy was thrilled.

She had long yearned for someone at home with whom to discuss philosophy. "He was brilliant," she said, "and from that moment on, I loved him right away."

Bill and Hillary spent the holiday week going out with friends and taking long walks in the park. They drove into downtown Chicago one night and went to the theater. Bill Clinton drew the Rodham family into card games, carefully keeping his competitiveness in polite check. The Rodham family welcomed his efforts.

Deep down, Dorothy Rodham knew that it was only a matter of time before Bill and Hillary were married. She also knew that it would be a tough decision for her daughter to make. She had asked Bill Clinton one day what his hopes for the future were after law school. Arkansas, he said. The answer less than thrilled her.

"Okay," she said, "you'll go back to Arkansas to realize your ideals, but what about my daughter?"

The question was unanswerable and they both knew it.

Hillary, meanwhile, was taking steps to move closer to her own ideal study of law in society.

In the spring of 1970, while picking through the notices on the crowded Yale Law School bulletin board, Hillary had seen one day a very small announcement that Marian Wright Edelman, a Yale Law School graduate and veteran civil rights lawyer, was coming to speak on campus. She had met Edelman very briefly once before, at the League of Women Voters' young leaders conference. She knew that Edelman had been the first black woman to pass the bar in Mississippi, and had read a short article about her in *Time* magazine earlier that semester. It had left her full of eagerness to meet the woman whose work seemed to parallel so many of her own dreams.

At the lecture Edelman spoke about her experiences as a civil rights lawyer, and urged the students in the audience to use their Yale degree on behalf of the poor. She was preaching to the converted as far as Hillary Rodham was concerned. After the talk she approached Edelman and asked if she could work during her summer break for the Washington Research Project, the public-interest group which Edelman had founded not long before. Edelman welcomed the chance to bring aboard an enthusiastic new recruit, but said she had no money to pay her. Hillary asked her whether, if she could figure out how to be paid, she could come and work for her.

Edelman said of course.

Hillary set her mind to finding some funds. She went to the dean's office and to the placement office, and discovered that the law school had something to offer called a Law Student Civil Rights Research Council Grant—a small stipend that supported law students who were trying to work in the area of civil rights law. Her first summer out of law school, while her classmates got their initial taste of lawerly corporate life, Hillary went to Washington.

Edelman sent her to work with Senator Walter Mondale's subcommittee, which was studying the conditions of workers in migrant labor camps. She did interviews with workers and their families, assessing the hardships their children suffered. She later studied the problems posed by segregated academies that were fighting for tax-exempt status under the Nixon administration. She returned to New Haven afterward with her interest in children now backed by professional experience and a sense of her own potential for accomplishment.

At that point Hillary sought out faculty members with whom she could further her interests in children's legal theory and increase her knowledge of child development. She began working with Yale professors Joseph Goldstein, a psychologist, and Jay Katz, a psychiatrist, both of whom taught courses on family law. Goldstein's course on children and the law fascinated her. Katz's family law course proved a particular thrill when, for four weeks of the semester, he brought in the famous child psychoanalyst Anna Freud, a co-founder of Yale's Child Study Center, and Sigmund Freud's daughter, to co-teach the class. Hillary as an avid participant in the course, a lecture which was run like a seminar. Her insights and enthusiasm stood her well.

Encouraged by her work with Goldstein, Katz, and Freud, and motivated perhaps in part by a wish to spend an extra year with Bill Clinton, who was a year behind her, Hillary applied to a law school program that allowed her to study children's rights under the law for credit at Yale's Child Study Center. There she worked with faculty member Sally Province on child development. She helped research a book, *Beyond the Best Interests of the Child*, which was published in 1973 by Freud, Goldstein, and Albert Solnit, then the director of the Yale Child Study Center, who is now commissioner of Connecticut's Department of Mental Health and Addiction Services. The point of the book was to set standards for evaluating the best interests of the child in regard to conflicts in custody placement.

Working with Anna Freud and other faculty members, Hillary participated in direct observations of children at play. She assisted the center's nursery school teachers, observed while diagnostic tests were conducted, and took part in a reading seminar on child-development literature. She applied herself to learning what she could about children's developmental goals and needs with as much rigor as she had earlier directed to the field of law. Her focus was particularly directed at normal childhood development and its variations. She impressed her instructors with her understanding of, and compassion for, the complexity and depth of children's lives.

Edelman remained a part of her life throughout this time. While Hillary was at the Child Study Center, her friend and mentor recommended her for a job doing legal research for the Carnegie Council on Children, which had been established by the nonprofit Carnegie Corporation in New York the year before to examine the conditions of children in America. While on the council she wrote a number of background papers on children's legal rights and collaborated on what became then council head Kenneth Keniston's important book, *All Our Children.* She helped assemble a chapter dealing with children's rights to education in the face of obstacles placed either by parents who refused to send their children to school or by schools which without good cause suspended or expelled problem children. The chapter also discussed children's rights to medical care, both in the context of problems posed by parents' refusing them medical care, as in the case of Christian Scientists, and of parents who needlessly subjected their children to experimental or extreme treatments like sterilization, shock treatments, or lobotomies. The work on Keniston's book placed her in somewhat of an ideological conflict with her earlier work for Freud, Goldstein et al., for Keniston has criticized *Beyond the Best Interests of the Child* as a white paper giving parents unquestioned final authority over their children.

Beyond the academy, Hillary was also gaining insight into the plight of unfortunate children in dramatic ways. Her work for the New Haven Legal Assistance Association involved her in the case of a foster child, born of black and white parents, who had lived with a foster parent, a black woman, while the claims of her parents were argued out in the courts. After a long hearing a judge decided the parents no longer had any rights over the child, and that the "best interests" of the child were not served by allowing the foster parent to gain custody, despite her long record of care, since she was fifty years old, single, and not prosperous. The court put the child in another foster home to await a better adoption.

Hillary's understanding of the complex issues of state intervention in custody grew even deeper when she worked trying to create rules for child-abuse cases with doctors at the Yale-New Haven Hospital. The issue of whether or not to remove an abused child from his or her parent was not, she saw, black and white.

"For some young children, abuse may be the only attention the child got, so when you remove it, there is an extraordinary guilt: 'I must have done something *really* terrible because now they do not even *want* me,'" she explained in an interview with Garry Wills. The standard of "least detrimental alternative," she was learning, was hardly a failsafe tool in practice.

Hillary also helped develop programs for children at Yale's then new Legal Services Organization. She also did work with Penn Rhodeen, a staff attorney at the New Haven Legal Assistance Association who was involved in legal battles with the state of Connecticut over the treatment of foster children.

By staying at Yale an extra year, Hillary graduated in the class of 1973 with Bill Clinton. Their lives were growing more and more intertwined—for the moment. In the summer of 1972 they had traveled together to Texas, where Bill had run George McGovern's campaign effort and Hillary had worked registering Hispanic voters for the Democratic party in San Antonio. Everything they did together now seemed to raise the issue of where they'd go next and what they'd each do. In Texas, Clinton and Rodham met Betsey Wright, a powerful woman who would later become his chief of staff and campaign manager. Wright had for a few years been active in Democratic politics in her native state of Texas. She was enormously impressed with Hillary, and began to harbor the hope that she would consider running for office. But Taylor Branch, the Pulitzer prize-winning author on the civil rights movement, who shared an apartment in Austin with the couple and co-directed the McGovern campaign in Texas, recalls that Hillary wasn't even sure if she liked politics. "Whereas his purpose was so fixed, she was so undecided about what to do," he told *U.S. News and World report.*

Ironically, the one most important thing that Bill and Hillary had in common—their dedication to public service—was precisely that which threatened to split them apart. In their first year at Yale, they did not interview with any law firms. Hillary knew that she wanted to work for the Child Development Fund, and Bill knew he was going back home. These choices distanced them greatly from the vast majority of their classmates, whose activist impulses seemed, upon reflection, to dry up as promises of lucrative offers grew near.

"There were a relatively small number of people who wanted to dedicate themselves to the idea of social change and therefore work outside of what was considered the establishment," friend Bill Coleman recalls. "There were people who did that in summer jobs, but when it came down to the short strokes, most people managed to come up with justifications to explain why, in the long run, it would make sense to go and work for a large firm. They'd say it gave you the skills you needed to go on and become an effective lawyer. It was economically in their interest, really. Everybody interviewed at the large firms except Bill—and Hillary."

Ambition seemed to mean something different to Bill Clinton and Hillary Rodham than it did to their peers, a classmate recalls. "Everyone was ambitious," she says. "But I see Bill and Hillary as driven by almost a religious purpose of some sort. They had the sort of late sixties sense of *we have to make the world better*. Not 'I have to make the world better,' but 'we,' all people, acting together.''

The stakes involved in Hillary Rodham's decision to pursue her career independently and alone, despite her love for Bill Clinton, were very high. She had worked so hard to get where she was, and the drag of forces weighing against her success had at times been very psychologically wearing. It hadn't been an easy time to be a woman at Yale Law School.

The thirty women who entered her class with her were considered an enormous influx, even after ten of them had dropped out. And those twenty remaining in classes were resented by some professors, who told them they were taking the places of more worthy men who were off fighting in Vietnam.

''Everybody assumed we were all accepted because they thought the class was going to be decimated by the draft,'' a classmate recalls. ''In fact, they just ended up with more students. So all the time people would come up to you and say, 'I've never seen a woman sit still and study for longer than an hour—I'm amazed.' And then the feminist group would ask you why you weren't more militant than you were. You were challenged all the time—from both sides.

''Hillary was considered an unusual bird,'' the classmate says. ''Lots of men at Yale Law School had never studied with women, so to see someone like Hillary, who was so competent and so committed, was new to them. It wasn't unusual to be a big man on campus like Bill Clinton, but it was for a woman to be as active and successful as Hillary was.''

Bill Clinton may have been one of the only men at that time who was able to appreciate Hillary's strengths without being at all threatened by them. He bragged about her, and claimed she'd shown him up at the Barristers Union. He didn't even mind when, in a particularly tough course on political and civil rights taught by the late First Amendment scholar Thomas Emerson, she received a higher class grade than he did. For some reason his fierce competitiveness seemed to thrive on hers rather than feed off it dangerously. Hillary appreciated this deeply.

She was attracted to him, she told Gail Sheehy in 1992, because "he wasn't afraid of me."

After graduation in 1973, Hillary Rodham worked as a staff attorney for the Children's Defense Fund in Cambridge for a few months. Then in January 1974 she got a call from John Doar, who had been hired as special counsel by the Democrats on the House Judiciary Committee to head their impeachment legal staff conducting an impeachment investigation of Richard Nixon. Doar was a good friend of Burke Marshall's at Yale. He wanted five young lawyers who were willing to work hard, and who didn't think they were above "grunt" work. Marshall recommended Hillary as well as four or five other students.

Bill Clinton was chosen too, but he turned down the opportunity. He was preparing to run for governor in Arkansas.

The decision to work apart was a tough one for the two young lawyers, but it was necessary. Hillary Rodham had not come as far as she had just to bury herself in a Deep Southern backwater. Neither had

Bill Clinton done so to sell out so easily on his Arkansan dream. And yet, for Bill Clinton at least, the match was made. Virginia Clinton had realized the importance of Hillary in Bill's future life during a visit he made to his hometown during a break from Yale Law School. They were sitting in the car at the airport, saying good-bye, when Bill turned to her and said, "Mother, I want you to pray for me that it's Hillary because if it isn't Hillary, it's nobody."

"He loved Hillary so much at Yale," Virginia Clinton told Charles Allen. "He was really concerned about whether she really would be happy in Arkansas or would even come. But he told her going in, he said, 'I promised myself a long time ago, if the people of Arkansas will let me, I'll break my back to help my state.' And he said, 'That's my life. And it's the way it has to be for me.' "

Hillary began work on the House of Representatives Judiciary Committee Impeachment Inquiry Staff in mid-January 1974. She was twenty-six, experienced only as a lawyer for the Children's Legal Defense Fund, and she was titled counsel, lowest on the professional scale.

The staff was headed by Special Counsel John Doar, a Republican appointee who had had an illustrious career in the South during the civil rights era. The Republican minority's special counsel, Albert E. Jenner Jr., was a Chicago attorney in his mid-sixties, a great Midwestern politico and party loyalist. The staff had been put together at the height of the Watergate controversy, after the Senate Watergate hearings had been aired on television. Their job as lawyers was to sift through information that had been compiled from many sources and tie it all together so that it told a coherent story. The staff began by investigating a broad range of accusations that had been made against President Nixon to see whether or not they were worth pursuing, and then to assemble and articulate the evidence against the president. There was considerable tension between Hillary's group and the permanent staff of the House Judiciary Committee, which was then chaired by Representative Peter W. Rodino Jr., a Democrat from New Jersey, as the lawyers on the House Judiciary Committee staff were not thrilled to see the historic occasion of a lifetime taken away and handed over to a bunch of outsiders.

The staff was supposed to be nonpartisan, to present facts and not to advocate any one outcome. "We were quite careful to try to avoid people who had taken positions with respect to Mr. Nixon's future," says Joseph A. Woods Jr., who was senior associate special counsel on the staff and is now a retired senior partner, of counsel, with the firm Donahue, Gallagher, Thomas and Woods in Oakland, California. "Our purpose was to conduct and be perceived as conducting a fair inquiry into the situation, it was to follow the trail where the trail led, and we didn't want doctrinaire people, we wanted open-minded people. That was very literally a requirement. We were particularly sensitive to not wanting anybody whose background contained anything that might ultimately embarrass the staff."

John Doar, a Republican with a great power base among Democrats, set an exacting standard of judicial objectivity from his lawyers. "It was reiterated to us time and time again that our job was not to be advocates, but rather to collect information and present it," says Fred Altshuler, a friend of Hillary's on the impeachment inquiry staff. "I was almost fired at the beginning because I made some comment that he interpreted as my taking an activist role."

To a surprising degree, the lawyers truly did remain true to Doar's standard. They were constantly reminded that Richard Nixon was still the president, and was to be treated always, even in discussions among themselves, with all the respect his position normally commanded. "Even today, eighteen years later, I automatically refer to it as being the president, and not Nixon, or Richard Nixon, or anything like that. That should give you some sense of the atmosphere," says Robert Sack, who headed a task force on agency abuse by the Nixon administration.

Hillary Rodham's main assignment was establishing the legal procedures to be followed in the course of the inquiry and impeachment. It meant handling subpoenas, making sure the proper legal steps were anticipated and followed in line with the Constitution. Her work ultimately led to suggesting drafting procedures to be followed by the committee in conducting the formal presentation aspects of its work, what sort of rules of evidence would be involved, a definition of the role of Nixon chief defense attorney James St. Clair, what sort of objections would be deemed appropriate or inappropriate, and the scope of cross-examination. It meant staying in the background, following Woods's lead, and being, above all, discreet.

"It was not necessarily the glamour assignment of

the moment," Woods, her supervisor, says. Hillary did at one point, though, get to work with the historian C. Vann Woodward, who was retained to advise on historical parallels or lack of parallels in other presidencies. She also got to listen to the *tapes*.

"I was kind of locked in this soundproof room with the big headphones on, listening to tapes," she told the *Arkansas Gazette*. "There was one we called the Tape of Tapes. It was Nixon taping himself listening to the tapes, making up his defenses to what he heard on the tapes. So you would hear Nixon talk and then you'd hear very faintly the sound of a taped prior conversation with Nixon, [his top aides Bob] Haldeman, and [John] Ehrlichman. . . .

"And you'd hear him say, 'What I meant when I said that was . . .' I mean, it was surreal, unbelievable. At one point he asked Manuel Sanchez (his valet), 'Don't you think I meant *this* when I said *that*?' "

On August 8, 1974, partly due to the committee's work, topped off by the damning revelations of the "smoking gun" tape, Nixon resigned. The lawyers felt a mixed sense of relief and anticlimax. They'd been under intense pressure, working eighteen-hour days, seven days a week, and the uncertainty about whether or not Nixon would resign or allow the impeachment proceedings to proceed had played havoc with their nerves. Most had left other jobs, sometimes families in other parts of the country, to come to Washington and play their part in legal history.

Hillary left her committee work an even more solid liberal, more firmly committed than ever to seeing social change and justice done through the American legal and legislative system. Her experience on the Nixon staff had taught her that the system *could* work, and that there was nothing more exhilarating than when it did. "Never have I been prouder to be a lawyer and to be an American than I was during those months," she later said. She was clearly destined to be a political player of some sort. But first she would have to let her relationship with Bill Clinton play itself out.

Chapter 3

~~~

"I Followed My Heart"

"Suppose I'd sat down and tried to map out my life," Hillary asked the *Arkansas Gazette* years ago. "Do you suppose I would have said I'd be married to the governor of Arkansas and practicing law in Little Rock? There is no way. I think life presents opportunities."

Hillary Rodham had expected that her work as counsel to the House Judiciary committee would continue well into the fall and winter of 1974. When Nixon resigned in August, she was left with a quandary. Her job with the Children's Defense Fund was still open to her, and it beckoned temptingly. But Bill Clinton had put in his claims too. He'd been down in Arkansas for more than a year now, and the strains of a long-distance relationship were wearing him thin. He begged her to come down and join him. Hillary had said no once before. "It was just as if somebody had asked someone to move to the moon," Carolyn Ellis recalls.

Now she missed him terribly, and she knew the relationship couldn't last forever as it was. But she was on the fast track, or better—she had played a role in history, and every option was now open to her. She had interviewed with a number of top-notch Washington law firms, and their offers were very tempting. The sense of her potential power, the thrill of her potential as one of the few women lawyers at the top agencies in Washington, was exhilarating. The idea of heading down to the second poorest state in the union, a backward state, a state with few legal services and no legal activism, seemed like shooting herself in the foot.

"It was not on her radar screen," Fred Altshuler recalls. "It was not the sort of thing that she had set out to do. Her expectations were of working at the Children's Defense Fund or doing litigation, and she was aware that this changed her horizons and her expectations, and she had to work through that."

In Arkansas the prospects really did look dim for Hillary.

"I remember Bill called me," says Brownie Ledbetter, a lobbyist for the progressive Arkansas Fairness Council and a long-term friend and friendly critic of Clinton's. "And he told me he'd met this incredible woman, and he wanted to marry her, and he said, 'You know, she's got to have a real job down here, not just some make-work thing, she's a feminist and she's just wonderful.' And he said, 'Do you know of something she could do, something in the line of what she does?' I said, 'What does she do?' He said, 'Children's rights.' And I said, 'Oh gosh, Bill . . .' "

After the Nixon inquiry came abruptly to an end, the judiciary committee's legal staff disbanded as abruptly as they'd been assembled. On their last night in Washington a group of four friends went to dinner in a small Italian restaurant not far from Capitol Hill. It was a bittersweet end to a difficult six months. Altshuler and Hillary had worked so tightly and so continuously together that they'd grown close, with the sort of intense familiarity that develops in unusually high-pressure situations. They were with two other young lawyers who had just arrived in Washington to start new government and public-interest jobs. Hillary laughed and joked with the rest, blowing off steam after the six months of hard labor and tension, but she was preoccupied. The three others were going on to new jobs where they knew they'd be doing exciting, socially significant legal work. She, on the other hand, had just about decided to give up a chance to work on important children's law issues and was instead heading off to an uncertain professional future in Arkansas. She was thoughtful and alternatively happy and sad, like a person being pulled in two directions by an ongoing inner argument. They teased her about missing the six months' stress, but they knew that wasn't it at all.

"You're going to Arkansas, aren't you?"

"I don't know what to do," she answered.

The next day she was en route to Little Rock.

Coming off her experience on the Nixon team, Hillary knew she was standing at a significant point in history. Legal activism was a new and growing field of specialty. The first women's advocacy groups were being set up, and her own field, children's legal theory, was only starting to take off. Moving to Arkansas was like taking a step back a decade, perhaps more. It would mean starting from scratch, with no professional support network upon which to fall back. She and Bill Clinton had had an ambivalent relationship almost from day one. They were wildly in love with each other, that much was clear, but their ambitions seemed utterly irreconcilable.

The debate over who was going to go where had started while they were both at Yale. While most of his law school contemporaries dreamed and schemed of clerking on the Supreme Court after graduation, Bill Clinton always planned to go back to Arkansas. It seemed a strange ambition to his fellow high achievers, not least of all to Hillary Rodham. Like her friends, Hillary saw Arkansas as a forgotten state, smack in the middle of the United States, known chiefly for its backwoods Ozark culture and its poverty. And for racism.

The one thing that every civil rights–minded Yalie knew about Arkansas was the story of Orval Faubus and the nine black students. In 1957 those nine students had attempted to enter the all-white Central High School in Little Rock. It was an attempt to test the state's commitment to desegregation in the years following *Brown* v. *Board of Education*. Arkansas governor Orval Faubus ordered the state's national guard to prevent the students from entering, prompting President Eisenhower to order the Army's 101st Airborne Division into Little Rock to protect the black students and see they were allowed to enter the school. The incident made Arkansas and Arkansans pariahs on the national scene. The state would not have presented itself to an up-and-coming young lawyer as an ideal spot for building a career.

"Arkansas felt to all of us, except Bill, like the end of the earth!" Kris Olson Rogers recalls.

Bill Clinton was the first person from Arkansas Hillary Rodham had ever met. He wasn't typical and he knew it. It was deeply important to him to bring her home, to the place that had nurtured him, to the little pond that had given him the big shot's self-confidence that had taken him to Georgetown University, Oxford, and Yale.

Hillary first visited Arkansas in 1973. Bill picked her up at the airport. His home in Hot Springs was only an hour's drive away, but he had bigger ideas for his intended than simply bringing her home to meet his mother. Like a self-appointed "one-man chamber of commerce," he was going to sell her on his state.

They drove for eight hours. Bill took Hillary to all the places he found beautiful: the state parks, the overlooks, the barbecue shacks. She ate something called "fried pie." By the end of the day she was dizzy.

To say that the sight of her future home less than enchanted Hillary would be a gross understatement. But she did take the Arkansas bar exam that summer. Ellen Brantley, a Little Rock judge and a contemporary of Hillary's at Wellesley, was surprised to hear her name said aloud in roll call when she showed up to take her own test.

"I was floored," Brantley says. "I knew she was from Chicago, and I couldn't figure out why she would be taking the bar exam in Arkansas. So sometime during the course of the test I asked her, 'What in the world are you doing her?' and she said that she had her job with the Children's Defense Fund and that she needed to be admitted to the bar of some state, that it didn't make much difference what state, and she had chosen Arkansas."

Hillary left it up to Brantley to puzzle out just why, of fifty potential state bar exams, Arkansas' would have been most attractive. She wasn't advertising her commitment to Bill Clinton then—perhaps not even to herself. But the symbolic gesture of laying down professional roots in his home state could not have been lost on Clinton. For the next year he asked her to come down and join him for good.

Friends fully expected her to stay in Washington. "The most likely thing I would have seen her doing over the long run was working with the Children's Defense Fund and doing something in politics," Carolyn Ellis says. "In my mind that did not mean Hillary would run for office, but that she would do something political—in the early seventies you did not think of women necessarily running for anything. Eventually she made an emotional decision. And she seemed so much more certain of herself once she went."

Many of her colleagues from the Nixon team and before thought she was throwing her career away. Betsey Wright, who was then working trying to mobilize more women to run for office at the National Women's Education Fund, certainly thought so.

"The center of my world then was getting more women elected to office, to get women to think of themselves as candidates," she says. "Hillary was as prime a candidate as stood in front of anybody. And yet I did have enough understanding of political realities to know that in the South in particular there was a very low tolerance of two-elected official marriages. But it wasn't like that was a choice she necessarily wanted. That was just my projection, and those were my dreams."

Finally it came down to a leap of faith. Caught between her head and her heart, Hillary says, "I followed my heart." Furthermore, she really wasn't sure of what she wanted to do—other than to change the world, which was a vague, if laudable, goal. Bill Clinton, at least, had plans. And the eighteen-hour days leading up to Nixon's resignation had left Hillary exhausted. She thought she'd coast for a while. When she had visited Bill at home in 1973 he had introduced her to the dean of the law school at Fayetteville, Wylie Davis. "If you ever want to teach, let me know," he had said. Now she took him up on his offer. "Are you serious?" she asked over the phone. "Well, I sure am," he answered. "I'll hire you right now."

Arkansas, she thought, would at least offer a respite from her high-pressure days and nights on the impeachment staff.

But taking it easy would have been out of character. By the third week of August, Hillary had taken up residence in Fayetteville. By the fourth week she'd learned that she was going to teach criminal law, to run a legal aid clinic and a project that sent students down to the prisons to work with prison inmates.

It wasn't going to be easy at all. Just before classes began, Hillary was invited to the local county bar association's welcoming cocktail party for the law school faculty. The president of the local bar took her around and made introductions. He approached a senior member of the Arkansas judiciary. "Judge," he said, "this is the new lady law professor. She is going to teach criminal law and run the legal aid clinic."

The judge looked down at Hillary. "Well, I don't have a use for either lady law professors or legal aid clinics," he said.

Bill Clinton, meanwhile, was quickly making a name for himself as Arkansas' new boy wonder. Twenty-eight-years old, a professor of law at the University of Arkansas, he launched a bid for Congress, running against an immensely popular Republican incumbent, John Paul Hammerschmidt, in the heavily Republican third district of Arkansas. Hammerschmidt was considered unbeatable. Clinton's beginnings were inauspicious enough. His campaign operated out of a little old house on College Avenue in Fayetteville. A green AMC Gremlin took him on campaign tours. Every day he drove around the district, shaking hands, making friends, collecting business cards and phone numbers, and then heading back to Fayetteville, to empty his pockets full of scraps of paper onto his desk. This pile was known as a "card file." Another pile—students' ungraded papers—accumulated in the hatchback of his little car.

All that changed once Hillary Rodham appeared on the scene. She joined the campaign at the point when Bill was running in the general election and became his unofficial campaign manager. Her talents as a campaign organizer appeared instantly. She organized the office, took charge, set the team to work. She emptied the office of the adoring girls who'd gathered to hang on every word of the aspiring congressman. She turned her back on those others who sniggered at her glasses and uncoiffed hair. Her whole family came to town to join in the effort, crossing the line to work for a Democrat for the first time. They also gave moral support to a daughter who was, at least as far as the local women were concerned, now working in hostile territory. While Hugh Rodham manned the phones, Tony and Hughie took up poster duty, combing the district, hanging up Clinton signs on any and every uncovered surface they saw—except trees. Hillary didn't allow them to pound nails into trees.

Although Bill Clinton did not ultimately defeat his Republican opponent, he did garner 48.5 percent of the vote—the greatest number of votes any Democrat had ever before drawn against the incumbent.

In the course of the campaign Hillary got to know Arkansas—and made herself known there—very quickly. And she found, much to her surprise, that she loved it.

"I had a lot of apprehension, partly because I didn't know anybody and did not know how I'd be received," she told Bill Clinton's Arkansas biographer, Charles Allen. But, she said, "the people were warm and welcoming to me. It felt very much at home. And it was a shock to me because I had never lived in the South or in a small place before. It gave me a perspective on life and helped me understand what it was like for most people."

Fayetteville is a hilly, tree-lined college town in the Ozark Mountains near the Missouri border. Back in the years when Bill Clinton and Hillary Rodham lived there, it was filled with big Victorian houses and had the small-scale, slow-paced street life of a small town combined with the intellectual vigor of a college town. The fraternity and sorority houses on campus and nearby Razorback Stadium brimmed with life, and people talked about books and ideas, and considered themselves, for Arkansas at least, quite progressive. The town spread out around the chief campus building, Old Main, a two-towered structure which dates from the turn of the century, and its hilly streets wove around the campus, with the names of college graduates engraved in the sidewalks around the university.

Once the initial shock of being known by name by virtually every person she passed on the street wore off, she thrived in the small-town atmosphere. She loves to tell the story of how once, when she was phoning a student and there was no answer at home, she called information to check the number and was told, "Oh, he's not home. I saw him leave this morning," by an operator who happened to live in the same apartment complex. She thought the law school, which had no air conditioning and was as hot as a sauna, was "fun."

At the University of Arkansas Law School, which had relatively few female students and fewer female faculty members, Hillary Rodham stood out from the start. It wasn't just her hippie clothes and Northern accent. She taught criminal law and criminal procedures her first year, and benevolently terrorized her students by running her classes in the Socratic method.

"She was highly intellectual, aggressive, blunt, very articulate, and fairly tough," Woody Bassett, a

Fayetteville lawyer and former student of Hillary's, recalls. "A lot of people initially weren't sure how they felt about her because she came on kind of strong. They were a little bit intimidated by her intellect and her personality. Some of the male students were not used to being taught by a woman with that kind of intellect, and I think it took some of them a little while to get used to it. But as time went on, people warmed up to that and got comfortable."

Unlike Bill Clinton, a warm and chummy teacher who taught his classes in a conversational way and tended to grade comparatively easily, Hillary kept a professorial distance from her students. She could be friendly and engaging in private, but did not, like Clinton, spend free periods hanging out in the student lounge, talking about classwork, or current events, or sports. Nonetheless, female students looked to her as a role model and sought her out during office hours for guidance and moral support.

Life went on for Bill and Hillary much as it had at Yale Law School. They worked long hours and were very intense about their work. They spent as much if not more time on outside projects—his campaign, her legal-service work—as they did on university-related duties. Evenings, and on the weekends, they spent time with a growing circle of friends, who included local political figures Bill had met on the campaign plus a good number of law school faculty members. Knowing that Bill worried that Hillary would be bored and lonely in Fayetteville, his friends obliged by welcoming her as warmly as they knew how.

"He wanted her to like Arkansas, he wanted her

to like Fayetteville, he was crazy about her and he wanted to marry her," Margaret Whillock, a friend who took Hillary under her wing at that time, recalls. "Bill loved to tell these Arkansas stories—we all did—and we used to eat a lot, sitting around in the floor of my living room, eating after ball games and talking till all hours." There were other informal dinner parties, a great deal of volleyball playing, football watching, charades, and, as always, debate. A facet of Bill Clinton's character, which would only get stronger over the years, made its first appearance to Hillary. He was fanatically competitive at games.

"Bill would get really into it, and if he gave a clue and Hillary didn't guess it, he'd go wild and scream," Ellen Brantley recalls. "He'd just go wild, and she'd sit there and look through a magazine and laugh at him."

After a year of living in Fayetteville, Bill and Hillary decided that if she was to stay there, they should get married. The time had come for a decision from Hillary: it was Bill or bust. They had been living apart in Fayetteville, where local mores frowned upon premarital cohabitation. The situation had to change one way or the other. Bill, in his best persuasive style, tried to talk her into a ring. But Hillary remained undecided. Arkansas was nice, but it wasn't Washington. Staying in the state, she knew now, would mean subordinating her political dreams to Bill Clinton's. She wouldn't have the mobility even to go where the action was, as subsequent presidential administrations took power. There would never be room for a two-elected official marriage in that

state. It was hard to imagine where she'd find a constituency, anyway. And what about seeing her
friends? Hillary decided she had to get a feel for
what she was missing. She flew to Park Ridge to see
her parents, then continued on to the East Coast to
visit her old college and law school friends. She traveled to Boston, to New York, to Washington.

The swing through the East pretty much decided
her—Hillary would return to Bill. "I didn't see anything out there that I thought was more exciting or
challenging than what I had in front of me," she later
told *Vanity Fair*. But the sight of the marshy, brown-
ish land stretching past as her plane made its descent
into Little Rock's little airport made her heart sink
again.

Bill came to pick her up at Adams Field airport.
Hillary was tired and wanted to go home. Instead,
Bill said, he had a surprise. "You know that house
you liked?" he said.

"What house?" Hillary answered.

While driving one day near the campus, Hillary
had mentioned in passing that she liked a cute
painted-brick ranch house with a For Sale sign on
California Drive. "Bill, that's all I said," she said.
"I've never been inside it."

"Well, I thought you liked it, so I bought it," he
said. "So I guess we'll have to get married now."

The house was a cottage, really, with beamed ceil-
ings, a bay window, and a screen porch on one side.
It had glazed brick and stone mortar work and was
situated on a hilly lot with a nice view. When Bill
and Hillary moved in, it had an antique bed with

Wal-Mart sheets that Bill had bought, and not much else.

Eight days before the wedding, Dorothy Rodham came to visit, and in desperation ran to buy the couple some household items as a wedding present. She also took Hillary to Dillard's department store to buy her wedding gown, a natural linen Victorian-style dress with lace at the elbow.

On Saturday, October 11, 1975, Hillary Rodham and Bill Clinton were married by Methodist minister Vic Nixon in the house Clinton had bought in Fayetteville. The wedding was a small ceremony attended only by immediate family and close friends, including Bill's mother, Virginia Kelley, Hillary's parents, and her brothers, Hugh and Tony Rodham. Roger Clinton, Jr. was his brother's best man. Hillary and Bill exchanged heirloom rings, and she kept her name. Bill was twenty-nine; Hillary was twenty-eight.

Later that day a larger wedding for friends was held in the home of Ann and Morris Henry, two of Bill Clinton and Hillary Rodham's best Fayetteville friends. Henry was then the local Democratic party chair as well as a lawyer, and, combining local friends, family, Yale, Georgetown, and Wellesley friends, Park Ridge and Hot Springs friends, Fayetteville faculty and political supporters, the wedding drew nearly three hundred people, among them Jim Guy Tucker, attorney general of the state of Arkansas. The wedding party, which was held early on a glorious October evening, spilled out of the Henrys' rambling house onto porches and yards and well into the family's surrounding two acres of property. The wedding cake had been baked by a local Fayetteville man with an artistic touch, and was simple and elegant—if huge—with graceful tiers, sugary white frosting, and light cream-colored sugar roses. As the child of another law school friend played background music on Ann Henry's baby grand piano, champagne was poured. The guests wandered from inside the house onto the wide screened porch and out into the moonlit night and back for charcuterie and sandwiches.

The mood, Ann Henry says, was ebullient. "We all loved Bill, and we had absolutely fallen in love with Hillary," she says. "We felt like we were lucky to have gotten her to come to live in Arkansas."

The poetry of Hillary's following her heart to Arkansas to roost was less resonant, however, for many of her friends. Bill Clinton's good qualities aside, they could hardly approve of Hillary's uprooting herself from the fast track for life in the slow lane of what they considered the Deep South. Her family too had some reservations—but for different reasons. Hugh Rodham was less than thrilled to see his daughter mixing family blood with a Democrat. He did come along, however, on the honeymoon to Acapulco. It was a Rodham family affair—Hugh and Tony, the parents, Hillary, and Bill Clinton—the brainchild of Dorothy, who, refusing to accept the argument that the couple didn't have time for a honeymoon, found cut-rate tickets and arranged the trip *en famille*.

By 1976 Hillary Rodham was making her presence known in Fayetteville. In March of that year she made headlines by urging that a coalition of women and prosecuting attorneys push for state legislation requiring that judges rule on the admissibility of evidence of rape victims' previous sexual conduct before it was presented to the jury. Despite her efforts, the bill died in committee. She started Fayetteville's first rape crisis center, and made an effort to educate the local population about sexual violence against women.

She also caught the attention of local journalist Paul Greenberg, a Pulitzer prize–winning columnist who has since proven to be one of her harshest critics, when she publicly opposed the state university's participation in the National Endowment for the Humanities, claiming, according to Greenberg, that those who accepted the grants would obligate themselves to the government instead of remaining intellectually free.

The Arkansas Law Association stood up and took notice when she spoke to their house of delegates to make a plea for start-up funds for a legal-aid program in the Fayetteville area. Addressing the all-male house of delegates, she spoke against a very popular, articulate lawyer who was opposed to the idea. She began with 90 percent of the delegates against her, and after ten minutes had three-quarters of the room won over to her side. Not just to her cause but to her. It was a double victory, for legal aid and for Hillary, for the exposure helped pave her way into the good graces of the legal establishment then holding forth in the state's capital.

She was also making great inroads in her legal aid service for indigents. In one case, when an Arkansas community tried to close a youth commune that had formed nearby, she took the unpopular stance of defending the commune.

"The judge *loved* the case," she told the historian Garry Wills. "It was the first time he ever wrote on *constitutional* issues."

In another case, a woman jailer called her during office hours before a hearing to report that a well-known and harmless wandering "preacher lady" was about to be committed to a mental institution in another Arkansas town.

"This is just wrong," the jailer said over the phone. "This woman is not crazy—she just loves the Lord." Hillary packed her student aides into cars and drove straight to the town. The judge threatened once again, that if the legal-services people released the woman from jail, it would only be a matter of time before he put her under lock and key once again.

Hillary talked to the woman, and learned she had family in California. "People need the Lord in California too," she told her. Wouldn't it be cheaper to buy a one-way plane ticket to California than to spend tax money supporting the unpopular woman in an institution in Arkansas? she asked the judge. He agreed, Wills relates, and the case at long last was closed.

Hillary has since said that her years in Fayetteville were some of the happiest in her life. She loved the slow pace of life, and the dinners and time for close friends. Idyllic as it seemed, however, it is unlikely that she and Bill Clinton would ever have been happy settling into the secluded lives of university professors. Ambition beckoned—in the form, for Bill Clinton, of his first statewide elected office, which he achieved in 1976, when he was elected the state's youngest attorney general at age thirty.

The new job necessitated a move to Little Rock. Hillary put down roots as best she could, but it wasn't easy. Little Rock was somewhat hostile territory to a woman with ambitious goals. There were no women in the major law firms. There were virtually no women lawyers at all. Fortunately, Hillary had met a few of the lawyers from the prestigious Rose Law Firm while she was still teaching in Fayetteville. They recruited her, and in 1977 she was hired—one of the first women in the state to join a mainline law practice.

The early years as a practicing lawyer were tough. Other women lawyers in Little Rock continued to be few and far between, and those she met tended to specialize in the more "feminine" field of domestic relations. Hillary drove to and from work in her little Fiat, wore frumpy clothes, and generally fell short of conforming to prevailing Southern standards of women's fashion. Hillary learned a partial lesson one day, though, when, having made the unfortunate choice of wearing orange pants to work, she was called in by a managing partner to meet an important client. She was mortified—and the memory stuck with her for years.

"Back in those days she was such an intellectual that she really paid very little attention to her appearance," a society writer for a local newspaper recalls. "That was not high on her list of priorities, and you'd see her around with her petticoats showing, and she just wasn't real put together. She was probably not as aware that people were noticing as she should have been. It takes you a while to catch on."

Her clipped, professional manner, agreeable by Eastern standards, proved at first a bit of a handicap. In the face of a woman, some clients read ambition as aggression, intelligence as arrogance, professionalism as unfeminine coldness. The word *pushy* came to mind. Despite the support of her colleagues, it could not have been an easy time.

There were some outside triumphs, however. In 1977 President Jimmy Carter appointed Hillary Rodham to the board of directors of the Legal Services Corporation, a Washington–based, federally financed independent corporation that provides federal funds to the nation's legal-aid bureaus. She had gotten his attention the year before, when she'd skillfully organized his presidential primary battle in Indiana. Now, with his help, she was edging her way back into Washington once again. That same year Hillary was active in the founding of the nonprofit Arkansas Advocates for Children and Families, the state's first children's legal advocacy group. The group's mandate—to help identify the problems facing poor children in the state: poverty, abuse, neglect, substance abuse, teenage pregnancy—was close to her heart, and was quite groundbreaking in a state whose rampant social problems tended to be dismissed with pious words and head shaking. As the group's first president she was involved in publishing reports on school dropouts, juvenile justice, and child care; in monitoring federal assistance programs; and in providing statistics on those programs to Arkansas' congressional delegation.

She also found a close ally in William R. Wilson Jr., a highly respected Little Rock attorney with whom she began to work on criminal defense cases. Wilson had first encountered Hillary Rodham when she had made her case before the Arkansas Law Association while still teaching in Fayetteville. He had been "doubly impressed," he said, by the way, as a lawyer, she could "appeal to your mind and your heart at the same time." The association with Wilson was a good break from the Rose firm for Hillary, for its corporate specialty had never been something close to her heart. Working with Wilson, she tried attempted-rape and personal-injury cases. She also began to make inroads into Little Rock's all-male legal establishment and, with Wilson's encouragement, to make herself known as a top, tough legal counsel for potentially skeptical clients.

"I remember one of the first things I told people when I litigated with her and against her was: she tries a lawsuit like a lawyer rather than like a woman," Wilson says. "At that point in time some female lawyers relied on their femininity, and sometimes didn't get down to the business at hand. It was a style for chauvinistic times, and Hillary didn't have it."

Hillary was, however, says Wilson, a particularly compassionate lawyer. When she and Wilson took on a domestic assault case which involved an obese client nicknamed Tiny, Hillary, immediately upon meeting him, asked him his real name, and proceeded to be the only person to use it throughout the entire proceedings. "It was obvious how pleased he was, just having been shown that human sensitivity,"

Wilson says. Hillary won the case for her client, who later reconciled with his girlfriend.

Bill Clinton proved to be a widely popular attorney general, and won the Democratic nomination for governor with sixty percent of the popular vote in 1978. The gubernatorial campaign that year, his first, found him with Hillary campaigning at his side, while he was deluged with criticism of his liberal views on gun control, marijuana laws, capital punishment, and women's issues. There were barbs thrown at Hillary for the use of her own last name too. That year, however, he had the momentum going to ride out all criticisms. He defeated his opponent, Lynn Lowe, by a nearly two-to-one margin. And on January 10, 1979, Bill Clinton was sworn in as governor of Arkansas.

At the swearing-in ceremony, the House chamber room of the Arkansas state capitol was packed. Smiling proudly behind her big glasses, Hillary Rodham held the Bible while her husband took his oath of office. The inaugural ball, held at Robinson Auditorium in downtown Little Rock, was billed as a "Diamonds and Denim" evening, to which the people of Arkansas were invited to come in formal clothes or Levi's or both. Beyond its democratizing call, the theme seemed designed to try to convey the message that the new Clinton administration would bring the state wealth and advancement without straying too far from down-home tradition. Prosperity would be, like the 4.25 carat diamond hanging around Hillary Rodham's neck, mined in Arkansas.

If the theme of the evening was state pride, Hillary's inaugural costume was like a pep talk. The

$20,000 diamond she wore had been mined at the Arkansas Crater of Diamonds State Park, the only site in the United States where diamonds can be found and long a source of special pride for Arkansans. Her dusty rose panne velvet gown was an all-Arkansas creation by Little Rock dress designer Connie Fails. Hillary had asked Fails to copy the basic pattern from her wedding dress, and then had asked her to embellish it with made-in-Arkansas millinery. A bit of scavenging produced some antique black lace, jet beads, and silk embroidery—all donations from dresses worn by Arkansas ladies of the nineteenth century. The beadwork on the dress, for example, had originally been worn by one Adeline Fullilove Weems, whose daughter Beatrice Weems Bulloch had preserved it. Beatrice Bulloch also gave Fails a belt, which she cut in half to form an armband, puffing the sleeves from shoulder to elbow and fitting to the wrist for an effect "something like a modified leg o'mutton," as a *Gazette* style writer put it.

The unfortunate analogy made clear some of the problems that the local press was having in dealing with the new first lady in print. It was difficult to write the run-of-the-mill "at home with" stories about her, since she was so very rarely at home. Even when Hillary did—as she tried very hard to do—perform a ceremonial function in grand style, the contrast between who she was in daily working life and who she was in gubernatorial dress-up was so great that it was hard not to wonder if her careful solicitude was real or if there was a sort of black humor behind it.

Although Hillary always made sure to express the requisite excitement over her domestic duties in the Arkansas governor's mansion, convincing Arkansans to look favorably on their first working first lady took some doing. The *Arkansas Democrat*, trying to help, ran an article by its Style editor headlined, "Ms. Rodham? Just an old-fashioned girl" in which it was explained to readers why Hillary had kept her last name, and they were told to rest assured that at heart she was just an "old-fashioned girl."

Though retaining her last name had clearly not been a decisive issue in that first gubernatorial campaign, it had nonetheless bothered some people in Arkansas. After the election Hillary was called upon for the first time to explain her decision. She told the *Democrat*: "I had made speeches in the name of Hillary Rodham. I had taught law under that name. I was, after all, twenty-eight when I married, and I was fairly well established."

It also, she said, made her feel like a "real person."

In 1979 Bill Clinton for the first time named Hillary Rodham to head a state board. As chair of the forty-four-member state Rural Health Advisory Committee, she helped develop a program to deliver adequate health care to people in small and isolated towns. The appointment was made without fanfare, and there were no public condemnations by partisan opponents. The Clintons, it seemed, were being given a chance to do things their own way. Arkansas was smiling on them for the time being.

One development that brought them goodwill was a joy to the couple as well: in late 1979 it became "official"—Hillary was expecting a baby. She glowed

with happiness. Bill was thrilled. They had been trying for a few years to have a child with no luck. The
pregnancy went as well as could be expected, given
the fact that Hillary was struggling under the worst
professional pressures of her life. She was competing
to make partner, putting in extra time on an agoniz-
ing child-custody case, and all the while suffering
from queasiness and fatigue.

The stress eventually caught up with her. On February 27, 1980, at 7:45 P.M., Hillary went into labor.
She was a three weeks early, and things didn't seem
quite right. She told Bill to rush her to the hospital.
Although the couple had worked together to learn
the Lamaze method of delivery, they did not get to
make use of it. After nearly four painful hours a decision was made to deliver the baby by cesarean section. Soon afterward the Baptist Medical Center staff
delivered a six-pound, one and three-quarter ounce,
perfectly healthy Chelsea Victoria Clinton. The name
had been chosen a year earlier while Bill and Hillary
were vacationing in London.

Bill Clinton emerged from the delivery room in
green scrubs, cradling his new daughter and claiming
to be engaging in paternal "bonding." "[Bill] was
amazed by fatherhood," Hillary later told *Newsweek*.
"He as overwhelmed by it. I've heard him say that
when he saw his child, he realized it was more than
his own father got to do."

Hillary Rodham made law partner later that
month. But she also made a vow with herself that
she would prioritize Chelsea above all else in her life.
Her mother had done that for her, she knew, and she
would always be grateful for it. That didn't mean, of

course, that she'd stay home. Neither did it mean she wouldn't worry about it.

"You never know in retrospect whether you did or didn't do exactly the right thing—stay-at-home mothers, gone-away mothers, all of us worry whether we should have done something differently than we did," she told *Newsweek*.

Rewarded for all her hard labors with child and with partnership, Hillary's star was on the rise. Meanwhile, Bill Clinton's seemed to have twinkled out. The 1980 gubernatorial campaign was a nasty race. Clinton had ruffled quite a few important feathers in Arkansas with his first term's valiant effort to take on the state's big industries and utilities companies. Now those concerns were backing his Republican opponent, Frank White. Many of his former supporters were too. They were angry about the fact that Clinton had quite substantially raised "car tags," or license plate fees, which for most people jumped from $15 to $30 in one year. They didn't care that the point was to repair the state's poorly maintained roads, which sometimes, in extreme weather or in isolated rural areas, became so impassable that emergency vehicles could not get through. It was the idea, the *nerve*. A lot of people were tired of Clinton's nerve. He had brought in his young, "long"-haired advisers, and they'd presumed to tell the state what to do. He'd let his wife go by her maiden name— even when their baby was born! He'd been too strident, too "arrogant," too out of touch.

The final straw was a bomb dropped by Jimmy Carter—a relocation of about nineteen thousand Cuban boat lift refugees into the federal compound at Northwest Arkansas' Fort Chaffee. Although Clinton had argued hard with Carter for more federal troops and fewer refugees, the president had said his hands were tied. Arkansans, fearful of reports of Fidel Castro's having emptied his jails and mental institutions, balked at the imposition. The state was in the midst of its worst drought in recent memory: chickens were dying, cows were starving, and tolerance was not running high. When the angry, detained Cubans—who had never wanted to come to godforsaken Arkansas in the first place—rioted on June 1, and about two hundred of them escaped far enough down Highway 22 to make an impending siege of Baring, Arkansas, look possible, it was as if the worst fears of the doomsayers had come true.

The image of rabid Cubans running through the streets of Arkansas past "good folks' " homes became a perfect rallying point for the campaign efforts of Clinton's opponent, Frank White. White let word fly throughout Arkansas that Bill Clinton had basically gone to Cuba, picked all the most violent and depraved criminals out of Castro's jails, and invited them to Arkansas out of the perverse kindness of his heart. Shamelessly playing to voter racism, White aired a commercial showing the detainees rioting and criticizing Clinton for not standing up to the president.

Bill Clinton first saw the commercial in the governor's mansion in late October, surrounded by old friends from Hot Springs and Fayetteville and, of course, Hillary. The images were grainy and flickering, like war footage: Cubans running down an Arkansas main street. Cubans holding sit-down strikes inside the federal fort. After Clinton watched the ad, he turned to the others in disbelief.

"Do people really believe this stuff?" he asked.

"Sure, they do," someone said. Heads nodded.

"See!" said Hillary, jumping up from her seat. "People believe what they see and hear, Bill. You can't just sit there and take it."

Hillary was doing what she could then to campaign, but, overwhelmed by work and busy with baby Chelsea, she had less time to devote to canvassing the state than she had had before. She'd become an issue for Bill Clinton, anyway. Her name, in particular. Letters had been pouring into the governor's mansion asking, "Doesn't your wife love you?" and "What's wrong with your marriage?" Eight percent of the voting population, it seemed, swore they would vote out Bill Clinton on the single issue of Hillary's keeping her last name.

Clinton's supporters were shocked. Hillary was shocked too. Just a year earlier women had been coming up to her in Arkansas and telling her how proud they were of her for keeping her own name. There were women all over the country by then who were keeping their own last names when they ran for political office. The problem was, Hillary was a candidate's *wife*. And the Arkansans who smiled by day had no qualms about stabbing her in the back by night. "She took us at face value," Brownie Ledbetter says. "The hostility was hard to understand because people would not show it. . . . People assumed that if Hillary kept her own name, she must be the boss, and therefore Bill was weaker, or not manly enough or something."

Everything was going wrong. Bill Clinton was stopped on a highway, going eighty miles per hour trying to make it to a YMCA library dedication in the midst of a statewide safe highway campaign, and people were enraged. He joked that he and Hillary should name their first child Hot Rodham. No one laughed. It was a sore point. Hillary's name was just the tip of the iceberg, but it was a very pointed and ship-sinking tip.

In November, Frank White won the election by a margin of 32,000 votes. He called it a "victory for the Lord."

Clinton, faced with his loss, wept openly. On election night he withdrew into himself, leaving Hillary to deal with reporters and well-wishers and to extend gracious words to the incoming Whites themselves.

For his farewell speech Clinton appeared before a joint session of the legislature in a crowded House chamber. Hillary was at his side, holding ten-month-old Chelsea.

"I'll take life a day at a time," he told reporters. "I can't really afford that, but that's what I plan to do." He said he would look for a new office. When asked if he would practice law, he uninspiringly said, "I don't know. Maybe."

A pall of gloom settled over the governor's mansion as Christmas approached. Clinton was inconsolable; friends struck attitudes of mourning as well. Hillary didn't take well to the passivist mood. Carolyn Staley remembers one occasion, at a mansion Christmas party, when Hillary's frustration surfaced, focusing briefly on the fact that she felt Staley, the piano player, was choosing too morose a selection of tunes.

"I didn't realize I was playing quietly and sort of softly—not funeral home music, but I wasn't playing upbeat 'Frosty the Snowman' and 'Rudolph the Red-Nosed Reindeer,' " she said. "I was probably playing 'Silent Night' and quieter things. And Hillary came over and said, 'Come on, Carolyn, pep it up. Pep it up. We've got to keep our happy face on.' "

Staley took the advice to heart. A few nights later she was at the mansion once again playing the piano. Bill Clinton was sitting morosely in the living room. As he stared off into space, a group of carolers showed up outside his window, singing "O Come, All Ye Faithful" in particularly forceful voices. Bill and Hillary opened the door—and a group of his classmates from Hot Springs High School walked in. "He sat down in one of those big wing chairs in the living room and tears just streamed down his face," Staley recalled. "He couldn't believe that his friends loved him that much. That was a kind of a watershed. After that he kept his chin up."

Bill Clinton took a position with one of Little Rock's most prestigious law firms, Wright, Lindsey and Jennings. The Clintons moved into a four-bedroom house in Hillcrest, a district where, Clinton knew, he had received 61 percent of the vote. It was a charming turn-of-the-century house, yellow with white trim, and an L-shaped porch, just around the corner from the stately stone mansions of Hill Road. It had beautiful hardwood floors and a library with floor-to-ceiling bookcases. It didn't console Bill Clinton much. Hillary's career was climbing to greater and greater heights. Bill felt himself to be sinking lower and lower.

It was a troubled time. A period of soul searching, some might say self-indulgence. For the next six months, friends say, Bill Clinton wasn't himself. He seemed aimless, depressed. For once he actually withdrew from people, drew into seclusion and introspection. It was as though he had been personally betrayed by every citizen who had cast a vote against him.

"It was just like he had been dislocated," says Staley. "And that Frank White didn't win on real issues of what his vision was for people's lives, but rather on negatives, like the Cubans in Arkansas, really hurt him. There was no tolerance, no compassion in that whole campaign. I think it just killed Bill that people had bought into that. He was truly unhappy, truly depressed, down. He had been split from his love, from the thing that gave him a reason to get up every morning, and practicing law just wasn't doing it for him."

Bill Clinton spent the second half of 1981 traveling around the state apologizing. He'd go up to people in supermarkets and say he was sorry he hadn't listened to them better. He virtually begged for criticism. "It was a masochistic exercise," Betsey Wright says. "He could pass no one without asking them to critique him. It was from the moment he was up in the morning until the moment he went to bed at night."

Hillary, Wright says, was somewhat disturbed by Clinton's excessive self-flagellation, but apart from a few offhand comments, kept her distance from that behavior. "It was her respect for what he chooses to do," Wright says. "They don't inject themselves in each other's behaviors. Her tolerance for some of his behavior just amazes me."

Bill Clinton sought absolution—and comfort—from anyone who would offer it. Many people have suggested that Clinton's infidelities started at this point. Or at least that a certain looseness in his behavior set in. It was axiomatic that the rumor mill would begin. News spread among reporters and gossips that Clinton was seeing another woman. In interviews in the 1992 campaign, Clinton did admit that the "trouble" he brought to his marriage began in this disaffected period. But he has never elaborated further. Neither has Hillary Clinton.

Betsey Wright, however, has frequently spoken of the "bimbos" and "groupies" who hung around him in those years—and afterward. "They were on the streets, sidewalks, in choirs, singing at his church," she says. "They were in the walls here. And nationwide! We'd go to a National Governors' Association meeting and there'd be women licking his feet. There were always so many women who were throwing themselves at him. And he was naive about that. They'd want to take photos, and he'd stand there with his arms around them and not understand that . . . that was naive. They'd go, 'Governor Clinton, I want to meet you,' and then the batting of the eyes and the silly gaze and the brushing of the shoulders would begin. When Chelsea and Hillary would both go out and do something together at night, or when they were both out of town, his idea of a really exciting thing to do was go to the movies by himself.

Well, we had rumors all over the place before the movies were out about how he was really there for some secret rendezvous or something sad like that. His attitude was: I don't care. I'm not gonna let people rob me of going to the movies by myself if I want to just because they want to make up stupid things.

"I think Hillary knew those women weren't important," Wright says.

Of course, the bimbo factor was nothing new. When Bill Clinton had been a teenager in Hot Springs, girls would find a thousand reasons to visit his next door neighbor, Carolyn Yeldell, just so they could look through the picture window at him. In graduate school, as a charismatic, bearded anti-war organizer, he was often surrounded by female groupies. Betsey Wright first encountered them in 1972 when Clinton ran McGovern's campaign in Texas. Paul Fray, an aide to Clinton's 1974 congressional campaign, has repeatedly bragged to reporters of how he would help Clinton usher one girlfriend after another out of the back door of the campaign office whenever Hillary was seen approaching. According to Clinton biographer David Maraniss, author of *First in His Class*, Clinton once said he'd tried to "run Hillary off" during this period, but "she just wouldn't go."

Bill Clinton liked to keep his eggs in different baskets emotionally. Perhaps he compartmentalized his love and his lusts, keeping competent Hillary in a "clean" space while giving big-haired, big-breasted women the lion's share of his baser desires. Hillary, he told friends, was the only woman he could imagine growing old with without becoming bored. She offered "brains and ability rather than glamour," he once told a friend, according to Maraniss. And that's what he wanted in a wife. That, over time, never changed.

The 1980 election brought other bad news for Hillary. Ronald Reagan's election in a Republican landslide meant the virtual evisceration of Jimmy Carter's Legal Services Corporation. Though Hillary fought hard to preserve it, and had the deans of all the most prestigious law schools in the country lobbying Congress behind her, it was hard to beat the Great Communicator when he was on a service-slashing tear. Reagan cut the corporation's budget by thirty percent, but, thanks largely to the lobbyists' efforts, stopped short of destroying it. He did, however, see Hillary Rodham, among Jimmy Carter's other appointees, unseated from the board.

It wasn't a good time for anyone. Tempers in the Clinton household flared. Carolyn Staley spurred an odd run-in with the Clintons when she visited their house on Midland Avenue to express concern over reports she had read in the newspaper about Bill's record on commuting sentences. In an effort to ease the prison population, Bill Clinton had asked the state parole board to recommend to him which prisoners had committed nonviolent offenses and had followed their recommendations in commuting some prisoners' sentences. The newspapers had reported, however, that he was responsible for commuting sentences of the state's most violent criminals.

"I went in and said, 'I'm sorry that that happened,' and Bill said, 'It's not true,' " Staley says. "And I said, 'It's not true? I mean, what's in the paper isn't true?' He said, 'No, it didn't happen. It's absolutely not true.' And I said, 'Well, I guess I just made a wrong assumption. It's reported in the paper and I assumed it was true.'

"And Hillary spun around and said, 'See, Bill!' She just screamed, 'See, Bill! People do believe what they read in the paper! Unless you come out and correct it, then people believe it's true, or if it wasn't, you would've fixed it.' "

Her frustration was that he had given the benefit of the doubt to the reader and thought, 'Oh, they're smart enough to know,' or 'People have a memory and they know I didn't do that.' "

It was a concept he had to get used to if he ever hoped to fight political foes effectively, Hillary told him. It was a theme that seemed to recur between them again and again. But facing opponents staunchly, standing up on principle, defending himself on views that were possibly unpopular, wasn't Bill Clinton's strong point. It was hers.

"When he first went in in 1979," Hillary told Charles Allen, "he was so excited about all of the challenges that the state posed . . . that he tried to do more than he had the support and understanding of the people to do. He didn't really lay the groundwork. He didn't give the kind of impression that he needed to give that he was really fulfilling an agenda that everybody held as opposed to imposing something on people. So they rebelled and defeated him."

Hillary talked Bill Clinton into his first act of defiant comeback. It was in April 1981, in the midst of his protracted funk. Local journalists were preparing to produce their yearly lampoon show, "The Farkle-berry Follies," which usually featured a well-known person as a "mystery guest," delivering a funny monologue and then revealing his identity at the end of the show. That year the show was titled "Cubans and Car Tags." Clinton was asked to appear and, not surprisingly, said no. Go ahead, Hillary urged him. Make them laugh. Make them laugh, and you'll see they love you again.

Clinton appeared in a skit where a bunch of bum-bling Cuban hijackers attempted to take over a small commuter airplane. He wore a leather pilot's helmet covering his face. At the end he whipped off the helmet and delivered a speech in which he poked fun at himself and at Frank White, who was seated before him, front and center. The crowd loved it.

"You could see the change occurring in Clinton. You could see his face light up," Leroy Donald, busi-ness editor of the *Arkansas Gazette* and producer of the show, told Allen and Portis. Bill Clinton's star was on the rise once again as he declared his candi-dacy for 1982. And Hillary was helping shine the way.

She had her own personal difficulties to overcome, though. Campaigning on behalf of her husband again as Hillary Rodham, she received somewhat chilly ap-plause as she faced audiences around the state. Now that voters had a traditional, more palatable first lady in Gay White, who, as her husband liked to brag, was a "full-time first lady," they gave full vent to their feelings of antipathy toward Hillary. The hostil-ity toward her from many quarters was palpable—and cruel. When the Rose Law Firm moved to its present downtown location, in a renovated old YWCA building, and held an open house to show off its new elegant offices (swimming pool in the basement not included), Hillary was rudely rebuked by a client when she stepped forward to welcome him to the reception. As she stuck out her hand and said, "Hi, I'm Hillary Rodham," the man began forcefully poking her shoulder where her name tag was, saying loudly: "That's not your name! That's *not* your name!"

The Clintons both took leave of their law firms in 1982 to devote themselves to full-time campaigning. At a press conference that February, announcing the official campaign kickoff, Hillary also let drop the unexpected news that, while she would continue to practice law as Hillary Rodham, she would campaign and introduce herself "in non-professional capacities" as Mrs. Bill Clinton.

When reporters, understandably intrigued, pounced on Hillary Clinton with questions about the name change, she bristled. Cradling two-year-old Chelsea in her arms, she said, "I don't have to change my name; I've been Mrs. Bill Clinton since the day we were married." As reporters pressed her further on the name change, she admitted that she had not legally changed her name and that she was still registered to vote as Hillary Rodham.

As much as Hillary tried to disown it, the name change was news. She was forced to go on the record discussing it. She told an *Arkansas Democrat* reporter that she had kept her maiden name when she married because it was "important to me that I be judged on my merits and that Bill be judged on his merits," but added that she had been "not at all prepared about the concern people expressed about this decision which we had made personally." Her name had "interfered with people's perceptions of the kind of job Bill did," and, she said, "I did not want to have made a decision which would impact adversely on what he had chosen to be his life's work. After thinking about it a lot and seeking a lot of guidance, I became Hillary Rodham Clinton."

Although Hillary *Clinton* disavowed any great pain in the giving up of her maiden name, her friends thought otherwise.

"You have to wonder what her options were," Ledbetter says. "Her options appear to me to be either to have changed her name or to have left Bill. Or to have in some way endangered, or at least be accused of destroying his career—as she regularly was.

"The horrible thing," Ledbetter continues, "was that once she did change her name, many of the people who were incredibly critical immediately flipped over and were so overwhelmingly positive about her, and many kept saying that she would be a better governor than Bill."

It was true. After Hillary's name change the local paper was suddenly proclaiming: "Biggest supporter is asset to Clinton," and was charitably enough describing her as "an Illinois native, perhaps a little brisker, a little more outspoken than the traditional Southern governor's lady. . . . The name change indicates that she's working at softening her image a bit. . . . And succeeding, apparently."

Hillary began to see local crowds warming to her.

Local journalists and political pundits started to take notice. There were calls for more, not less, of Hillary in the 1982 campaign. The differences between her and Bill Clinton's styles became apparent, and many judged they liked her way of addressing issues better. Word was that though she was as articulate and persuasive a speaker as Bill Clinton, she cut to the chase and hit the bottom line much quicker. People felt they could tell where she was coming from, and what she was leading them to. They trusted her. Ironically, they started to like her.

Even though, with Chelsea just a baby, her time was limited, Hillary maintained a back-breaking speech-making campaign schedule for Bill Clinton. In a few months' time she won him more goodwill than a whole bevy of political aides could have hoped to achieve. She sat in on all the strategy sessions for the new gubernatorial race. She plugged Bill Clinton's programs in her speeches and explained them. She repackaged him. When necessary, she played "bad cop" to complement his often too-accepting manner with campaign staffers. Her role would prove a prototype for her work on the national stage a decade later.

"When she saw a problem with the campaign structure, or when she saw people weren't producing, or when she saw things weren't going as well as they should be, she was the one who always brought it to Bill's attention, and always made sure he tried to do something about it to correct it," says Woody Bassett, who was active in the campaign.

Hillary had, of course, by now changed more than her name. It was also discovered, at the February press conference, that her formerly wild hair had been cut straight, curled primly under, and lightened. She had finally discovered contact lenses that worked for her, and she started wearing them.

Bill Clinton too had made some changes. He'd cut his hair so that his ears now showed in photographs, a point of character considered important to Arkansas voters. He changed the look of his staff, exchanging his bearded young aides for clean-shaven middle-aged men.

The 1982 gubernatorial race bore some eerie similarities to the 1992 presidential campaign. Hillary Rodham *Clinton* was a hot political issue. Frank White, running for reelection, made every effort through innuendoes to run her against his stay-at-home wife. The man who had won his 1980 election on racially charged images of rioting Cubans now told the state's Republican convention in September that "you can't wash the spots off a leopard. It's still Hillary Rodham and Bill Clinton."

Presenting himself as a traditional family values–defending man, from an older and more wholesome generation, he made every effort to suggest that Clinton's character was weak and his liberalism morally suspect. Clinton was moved to retort that his cosmetic changes had been made to better present his true face to the public and stated for the record that he had not cut his hair—yet another bête noire of his later candidacy—but started combing it back over his ears at his wife's request. He continued to assert that Hillary Rodham Clinton had always used his last name socially. In fact, on a 1977 listing of guests for a White House dinner, the attorney general and his wife had been listed as Bill Clinton and Hillary Rodham.

Hillary and Bill Clinton learned a great number of lessons that campaign year. Hillary, in particular, received an education in Southern politics. You can't, she found, ever trust a smiling face.

Chapter 4

◆

"Happy Days Are Here Again"—The Clinton Decade

By Election Day 1982, Arkansas was ready to hand the governorship back to Bill Clinton. The prodigal son had been chastened and could now be welcomed back home. Many voters in 1980 had simply wanted to scold the young upstart. They hadn't expected him to lose. They had kicked themselves the next January when the new right-wing Republican regime had taken office, and they'd waited eagerly for the chance to get back their state.

"There were so many people who regretted the day after that they'd made the wrong decision," Ann Henderson, an old friend of Clinton's and campaign staffer, says. "Back in 1980 there were a lot of good Democrats who just got aggravated and decided they'd teach him a lesson and that one vote less wouldn't make any difference, and woke up the next morning and were absolutely shocked."

The 1982 return to office was a triumph. The Clintons rushed their possessions back into the governor's mansion, and staked out their former home with an avidity verging on vengeance. Hillary Rodham Clinton made a ripple-free return to first ladydom. In her two years out of the mansion she had studied the flawless acts of First Lady Gay White so well that her public appearances were now picture-perfect in their graciousness. This time around, although she and Connie Fails were becoming close friends, she chose a dress by a New York designer. The *Arkansas Democrat* went into paroxysms of joy at the sight of it. The dress was hailed as a "feminine creation . . . which relies on a pleasing set of feminine contradictions to state its case . . . innocent . . . yet sophisticated . . . soft and wispy." It was a floor-length gown of chantilly lace in an overdress ("pure innocence") with a satin underdress "in that intriguing gray called taupe." Hillary wore with it the Kahn Canary diamond, set this time as a solitaire in a simple ring setting.

A record crowd turned out for the inaugural ball, which was held at the State House Convention Center, while an overflow of nine hundred people shuttled over into the grand ballroom of the new Excelsior Hotel. Betty Fowler's Orchestra, performing that evening, played "Happy Days Are Here Again" as the Clintons entered the Governors Exhibition Hall. After Clinton delivered a short speech welcoming his supporters to his "nice little intimate party for a few friends," he and Hillary danced to "You'll Never Know." It was like the formal wedding they'd never had. Virginia Kelley and her husband were there, as well as Roger Clinton and all the Rodhams except Hillary's father, who, earlier in the day, had been rushed to University Hospital with chest pains.

Hillary's transformation into perfect first lady was so complete that old friends found her nearly unrecognizable. Kris Olson Rogers first saw her again, after about a six-year hiatus, when Hillary came out to her new home state of Oregon to speak to a teachers group.

She was shocked, she said, at the changes in her friend. "We went and picked her up at the airport, and she had this Southern accent," Rogers remembers. "I really did a double take; I wondered if this was the same woman I knew, because she had acculturated so quickly. I was really taken aback, wondering if this was a surrogate or the real person. But then that's Hillary; she had made up her mind to do that and had to go all the way. She sank herself into it heart and soul."

The astuteness of Hillary's style overhaul became clear when, in 1983, Bill Clinton appointed her to head his Arkansas Education Standards Committee. Although aides warned him the appointment would bring him charges of nepotism and possible scandal, Hillary by then had become so acceptable that none were raised.

When the Education Standards Committee was formed, students in Arkansas were scoring far below the national average in standardized reading and math tests. A new report, "Nation at Risk," had just come out from the National Commission on Excellence in Education, and had warned of a "rising tide of mediocrity" in the nation's schools. Clearly, there were lessons to be learned in Arkansas. None of the state's 371 districts were requiring students to take all the subjects that the commission said a high school education should cover. Hillary said her committee would place its study of Arkansas' schools in the context of the national report. With that framework provided, she was ready to begin.

The first problem Hillary Clinton knew she had to tackle was attitude. Students in Arkansas suffered from a terrible sense of inferiority—and many of their parents and teachers, who had grown up with the same attitude, showed a stoic aversion to change. She had seen the damning effects of that combination of factors in the lowered expectations that many of her law students in Fayetteville held for themselves. They got by, no better. Hillary knew that if the state's brightest, best minds were so poisoned, then the state's average and weaker students had to be floundering even more.

"There are advantages to smallness so long as smallness is accompanied by excellence," Hillary told people. At a Pulaski County PTA Council Founders Day luncheon, she said, "We expect nothing but the best from our athletes: discipline, teamwork, standards. I wish we could translate the same expectations and standards we have for athletics into the classroom. I wish we could give teachers the same support and praise for teaching children to read and write as we do those who teach them to throw a ball through a hoop."

In a lengthy interview with the *Arkansas Democrat* she elaborated: "One of the principal problems we face in our state and apparently in the country is that we are not expecting enough of ourselves, our schools, or our students. We have an obligation to challenge our students and to set high expectations for them. Rather than setting minimum standards, we should set expectations and urge schools and districts to aim to achieve those expectations and not to be satisfied with meeting some artificial minimum."

A key element in education reform, Hillary believed, would have to be accountability. It would have to work in both directions. Third, sixth and eighth graders would have to pass minimum skill-competency exams before being promoted. Schools where more than fifteen percent of the students failed their exams would have to participate in a state-sponsored improvement program or face the loss of accreditation. Teenagers would have to stay in school until age seventeen. At that time they were able to stop at age sixteen or after eighth grade.

The committee's goal was to draft a set of new standards by the 1983–84 school year so that comments could be solicited from the public and written into the final draft. Hillary Clinton began to conduct county hearings, traveling from town to town. She stressed that improving education was a consumer issue: that parents had the right to demand the best teaching possible for what they were paying for with their taxes.

Some of the committee's recommendations—like a call for smaller classes in kindergarten and elementary schools—were easily accepted. A proposed requirement that high schools offer more courses, including English, math, science, social studies, and fine arts, sat well with adult voters if not with teenagers. Others, like a demand for statewide teacher testing, were less well received. The testing proposal created a torrent of hate. The teachers union geared up for war. One school librarian was cited calling Hillary Clinton "lower than a snake's belly." A principal told her he didn't want the children in his district to get an education. The National Education Association fought the test in court but failed.

The governor's legislative package that year included a proposed $180 million tax increase for education. The revenues were to come from a highly controversial sales tax increase. The teacher test, which was popular with parents if not teachers, was a way to make the people of Arkansas feel they were "getting" something—accountability—for their hard-earned tax money. Clinton said he felt "it is a small price to pay for the biggest tax increase in the history of the state and to restore the teaching profession to the position of public esteem that I think it deserves."

In speeches around the state, and even a daring venture into a hostile conference of the American Federation of Teachers, Hillary rallied public opinion around the idea of testing teachers to weed out the "incompetents." The public perceived that many classroom teachers were incompetent, she argued, "and whether it was fair, whether it was accurate or true, we were going to have to come to terms with the perceptions that they were," Hillary said. "The problem and the perception had to be dealt with together." Hillary also appreciated the pragmatic need of using the tests to help voters accept their first sales tax increase in twenty-six years.

Eventually, Hillary won the public over to her proposal to administer standard tests to pupils. Students, she argued, had the right to a good education—and they also had a duty to repay the state for their schooling through good performance. It made for a convincing argument. The teacher-competency tests remained more controversial. The first series were dismissed by critics as laughably easy. They suggested that spending state funds to promote the idea of responsible performance was more important to the committee than actually bringing about change.

With a feeling of having had an insult piled on to injury the Arkansas Education Association attacked the teacher-testing law. Association representatives also attacked Bill Clinton, Hillary Clinton, the press, and anyone else who supported the standards. What was to become a long, protracted feud began. At one hearing, where Dr. Kai Erikson, executive secretary of the AEA testified, Hillary rolled her eyes, picked up her coat, and left.

On March 23, 1985, Arkansas' more than twenty-five thousand teachers took the competency test. Just the day before a state court judge had ruled against a suit deeming it unconstitutional. A threatened teachers strike did not materialize. But just before the test was to be administered, there were allegations that copies of it had been leaked in advance. The Arkansas Department of Education ended up having to release a statement saying that no compromising practices had taken place.

Ten percent of the state's teachers failed the test. For the most part, they failed the writing portion, which required them to compose two-hundred-word essays on various themes, such as a letter to be sent home to a parent or a memo to colleagues that explained a new teaching technique.

Black teachers failed at a much higher rate than did whites. Some Arkansas critics charged that the test was blatantly racist—a tool to devalue and oust black teachers or intimidate them into quitting or failing without having to identify that goal by name.

"It was a way to appeal to the segregationists by using another symbol for race," a critic says. "When they said they were testing for teacher competency and would get the incompetents out of there, people's heads saw black teachers. And then ten percent of the black teachers were gone after that test, and that test was a joke. It was true that some of them had had difficulty, but mostly it was such a zonker emotionally that they were afraid of it."

The criticism was forceful enough that Bill Clinton was moved to make an appearance on the CBS news program *Face the Nation* to say that the test was not discriminatory.

"I don't think he expected it to be," the critic says. "He wasn't thinking about that at all. He was thinking about getting his damn sales tax passed."

Hillary took the ten percent failure rate as a vindication of her committee's efforts. "Nobody should have failed our test," she said to the *Washington Post*. "The fact that ten percent failed is very significant. Those ten percent touch thousands and thousands of children's lives."

Not all educators were won over, however, by Hillary's fire and rhetoric. Linda Darling-Hammond, a nationally respected educator, called Arkansas' test "a quick-fix political measure" which was "at worst, counterproductive." As she addressed the American Federation of Teachers, Darling-Hammond, unlike Hillary, was treated to uproarious applause when she made the point that Arkansas ranked fiftieth among the states in education spending, and that the average teacher salary then in some of the state's districts was $12,000 per year.

Despite lingering criticism—and lawsuit threats by the National Education Association—the Arkansas test was followed by similar efforts in Georgia and Texas. In Texas scores of teachers union volunteers combed the state tutoring teachers to help them pass. In Arkansas the state provided opportunities for remedial instruction to the teachers who failed. The tests, it was then ultimately argued, served the purpose of increasing teacher education. Eventually, Hillary's program for "in-service" education of teachers was backed by the teachers union that had booed her in the first place.

By March 1984 Hillary Clinton was able to proudly say, "We've turned the corner on attitude." It was a good year. She and Bill Clinton made that year's "Esquire Registry": a list of 272 people the magazine called "the best of the new generation." Also in March she received the Public Citizen of the Year award from the Arkansas chapter of the National Association of Social Workers. In May she was chosen as Woman of the Year in a poll of *Arkansas Democrat* readers.

Hillary had achieved what had once seemed impossible: she had found a cause, right in Arkansas, and she had used all her skills and her strengths to see something done that would better people's lives. She had built up the constituency her law school friends had hoped she would find. She'd made a lot of new friends too, great political allies. And now a stream of projects, offers to chair boards and foundations, was coming her way. She was hitting her stride. After ten years in Arkansas she had fully come into her own. Now the state was changing itself for *her*.

Or maybe the two were just growing together. By 1986 Hillary was a pillar of the Little Rock legal establishment and a fully assimilated member of the city. She had mastered a Southern-professional look that worked so well that in pictures from the period she is almost unrecognizable. Her hair was short and loosely curled, brushed back from her face, like a fuller, softer version of Nancy Reagan's. Her legal career had raced along over the years. At a firm where two-thirds of the partners had earned their law degrees at the University of Arkansas, Hillary easily stood out. She developed the firm's intellectual-property and patent-infringement practice. She gained renown for being the first trial lawyer in the state to conduct the examination by satellite of a witness who was unable to travel to the trial. In 1989 a survey of Arkansas' top lawyers named her one of the best business-litigation attorneys in the state.

The first half of the decade wasn't all triumph, however. There were always, in election years, periodic claims that Hillary Clinton's name helped the Rose Law Firm gain state business. That was undoubtedly true—though in her defense, Hillary countered that under the terms of her partnership, she shared none of the money the firm earned from state contracts and received no fees from representing bond underwriters. In any case, the proximity of business and government was so common in Arkansas that her work raised few eyebrows. After all, Hillary's partner Webb Hubbell had actually served as mayor of Little Rock from 1979 to 1981. Arkansas had its own rules, and anybody who played by them was usually safe from censure.

The old Arkansas rules, however, wouldn't play well in Washington when they came under scrutiny a decade later. And there were other events in the mid-1980s that portended more serious problems to follow.

In 1984, during Bill Clinton's second term as governor, a colonel of the state police called his office to say that Roger Clinton, the governor's twenty-seven-year-old stepbrother, had been seen selling cocaine and was now under surveillance. They were planning to arrest him, but wanted the Governor's approval. Bill Clinton approved. It was perhaps the most painful decision of his lifetime.

Roger Clinton served more than a year in prison. After he was off cocaine, he discovered that his real problem was alcoholism, like his father. Bill, Roger, their mother, and occasionally Hillary were called in for intensive family therapy. They discussed codependency. Hillary took a leading role in the discussion, and was quite astute at pointing out patterns and weaknesses to the assembled family.

"That was incredibly cathartic for them," Kris Olson Rogers says. "Hillary was really one of the first to open up and talk about what she saw as some of the vulnerabilities of that family. She's very good at capturing what's going on in people's hearts and minds, sometimes saying it for them better than they can themselves. I think she does that for Bill a lot."

Both Bill and Roger Clinton, looking back years later, saw it as a period of great leaps in self-knowledge and growth. But it was painful at the time, and often unpleasant. It was hard for Hillary too. She had to walk the fine line of telling the family things they didn't want to hear without stepping on too many toes. Though he was grateful afterward, it probably didn't always endear her at the moment to her husband.

A first encounter with psychotherapy, and the ghosts of the past, can be extremely destabilizing. Therapy forced Bill to look inside himself at the darkness that so often threatened to trip him up. Like many extremely friendly, outgoing people, he was unused to that kind of introspection. Friends of the Clintons have said they believed that the period of soul searching destabilized Bill Clinton a bit excessively. Printed reports have suggested that it threw his marriage, for a short while, into the balance. Turning forty was rough territory, as it is for many men.

"I was forty when I was sixteen" is a statement he has made many times to explain his eruption of adolescent-like behavior at the later date. Perhaps it was that the arrest of his half brother, the making public of trouble in his family, marred the patina of calm he had maintained for so many years and made old wounds gape open. Perhaps facing up to the troubles in his life made him give in to them. Friends have said that Bill Clinton began to see himself as a failure around this time, that his mood fell and he became self-destructive. Once again the rumor mill started up with stories of adulterous affairs.

Clinton's family and close friends did their best to close in around him, shielding him from the public eye. Kris Olson Rogers retains the impression that therapy actually pulled Bill and Hillary Clinton more solidly together. "That was one of the real watersheds for them," she says. "I think it made her feel closer to Bill."

In 1986 Hillary received a grant from the Winthrop Rockefeller Foundation to develop a program that would help "at risk" children with social, psychological, or economic problems improve their chances in school. In November of that year she was named to the William T. Grant Foundation Commission on Work, Family, and Citizenship to compile a study on "Youth and America's Future." She was also that month appointed to the board of directors of Wal-Mart, Inc. of Bentonville. Meanwhile, Bill Clinton was running yet again for governor. There had been a contested primary, against Orval Faubus, among other opponents. Frank White was running on the Republican ticket. He had won his last race through personal attacks on the Clintons, and the 1986 race promised to be ugly as well.

Chelsea was too big now to be counted on not to hear campaign slurs on TV, too little to understand where truth and lies met, but old enough to know that mudslinging hurt. Hillary and Bill Clinton decided they had to begin to educate her in the seamier side of political life.

"When I saw we were going to have a primary campaign in 1986, Bill and I talked to her at dinner, telling her that sometimes in political campaigns people say mean things and untrue things about other people. And her eyes got real big, and she said, 'Like what?' And I said, 'Why don't you pretend to be

your daddy?' She was six years old. 'Why should
you be governor?' And she said, 'I should be governor because I've done a good job.' And I said, 'Okay,
but somebody running against your daddy will stand
up and say, Bill Clinton has done a terrible job, he
doesn't care about anybody, he's a bad person.' Her
eyes just got huge. And she said, 'Why would they
say that?' And I said, 'Because they want people to
vote for them,' " Hillary told the *Washington Post*.

Frank White's wife, Gay, and Hillary were pitted
against each other. Mrs. White accused Hillary Clinton in the local press of being a first lady who
"shamelessly uses" her "vicarious role." Frank White
accused her of conflict of interest because she benefited financially from bond business done with the
state by the Rose Law Firm. On a morning talk radio
show he claimed she had made $500,000 on work on
the bond issues. The Rose Firm had served as either
bond counsel or underwriter's counsel on every bond
issue by the Arkansas Development Finance Authority, an agency which played a key role in the governor's economic development program, since 1983.
Clinton acknowledged his wife had benefited financially but denied a conflict of interest problem. Calcu-
lations based on figures provided by the ADFA
showed that the entire Rose firm had received only
$159,000 for serving as bond counsel on six of twenty
bond issues for the three years proceeding, the *Democrat* reported.

Finally, Hillary Clinton challenged Frank White to
reveal his own earnings from state-related business
while employed at Stephens, Inc. the major investment banking firm located in Little Rock, saying she

would release her own earnings from bond business. She and the Governor offered to disclose their tax returns, but Frank and Gay White refused.

To counter the Whites' negative campaigning, Clinton based much of his campaign on extolling the work that Hillary had done in education since 1983. The phrase "two for one" was first used in reference to Bill and Hillary Clinton just after that election, as many voters told reporters they had voted for the governor because it would mean getting his wife too. In his victory speech Clinton thanked Hillary for standing by him so staunchly. "I'm proud that she made this walk with me tonight," he said to applause which seemed to surpass that which he himself had received. "I think when the history of our state is written . . . no one will prove to have done more to advance the cause of our children and the future of this state than she has."

This was the golden age of Bill and Hillary Clinton's reign over the state of Arkansas. They were frantically busy. Hillary's typical day, after work at the law firm, might include a conference, a cocktail reception at the governor's mansion, a museum exhibition opening and a dinner party, with her first meal after a vending machine lunch eaten at nearly ten o'clock at night. Often for dinner she merely sneaked hors d'oeuvres in the kitchen during an official reception. Time with Bill out of the public eye was hard to catch. Hillary might wait up late at night for him, if she could. Otherwise they saw each other riding together in the limousine between events.

They made every effort they could to find time together to relax and reconnect. Making personal time was essential to Hillary. It was so easy to be devoured by the governorship, to have no time left for a married life, a personal life, a social life.

"Our social life is almost nonexistent," she told the *Gazette* in 1986. "We love going to friends for a visit, but we seldom do it. Maybe once a month, if that often."

She always, however, made time for Chelsea. Chelsea was a pleasure. When she began school, Hillary drove her in the mornings, savoring the time spent together. She kept mementos and little presents that Chelsea made her—like a plastic bead necklace of beautiful "jewels" she had fashioned once in Washington after seeing the shining jewelry many of the other wives had worn. Hillary wore the necklace to a formal lunch the next day. If the limousine driver had thought anything odd about it, he didn't say. Chelsea was very proud.

Hillary Clinton was asked in 1986 if she had any plans of her own for political races any time in the future. She'd said that she had no personal political ambitions. "I'll let Bill do that. I value being a private person too much," she told the *Gazette*. What she didn't say was that Bill Clinton was considering running for president. It was the dream of his lifetime. As 1987 dawned and spring passed, it seemed it was about to become a reality.

The preliminary campaign machinery was set in place. Phone calls were made, advisers considered. Hillary braced herself for what she knew would be a messy race. She braced Chelsea. She was excited, though, and pleased. She was going to have a shot at being First Lady.

A press conference was called in Little Rock for July 15, 1987. All indications seemed to read that Bill Clinton was about to announce his candidacy for the presidency. There were subtle and not-so-subtle clues. The Clintons had recently bought a condo for Hillary's parents in the Cantrell Road area of Little Rock, presumably so that they could keep a close eye on Chelsea while the Clintons were out on the road.

Dozens of reporters and guests of the governor's flew into Little Rock. Some had come for his scheduled announcement luncheon at the mansion. Others brought their gear to cover the press conference. Everyone was ready and raring to go. The news conference had been scheduled eight days earlier, and the general belief was that Clinton would use it to announce his formation of an exploratory committee for the election. The grand ballroom of the Excelsior Hotel was filled to capacity, jammed with network TV crews and people from all over the country. But then something went wrong. When the governor and his luncheon guests walked in, they looked like they were in the grip of a powerful emotion—a bad one. It turned out that over chicken salad in the mansion dining room, Clinton had made the announcement that he wouldn't be running. He and Hillary had discussed the fact that they knew the campaign would bury them in rumors of his infidelity, he had said, and they had decided it wasn't worth it, not then.

Tears rising in his eyes, Bill Clinton officially announced that he would not seek the nomination. "My heart says no," he said at an hour-long news conference. "Our daughter is seven. She is the most impor-

tant person in the world to us and our most
important responsibility. In order to wage a winning
campaign, both Hillary and I would have to leave
her for long periods of time. That would not be good
for her or for us."

As he spoke of his promise to himself, "a long,
long time ago . . . if I was ever lucky enough to have
a kid, my child would never grow up wondering
who her father was," Hillary Clinton brushed a tear
from her face.

He had changed his mind, he said, seven days
earlier, but had delayed the announcement until
the Tuesday news conference because it would
"give me enough time to change my mind, if I
could change it."

"It was shocking and it was very moving," says
Max Brantley, editor of the *Arkansas Times*. "The
room was jammed with network TV crews and people from all over the country. And most of the people
and friends of Bill's and political associates in the
room fully expected him to announce that he was
running for president. It was one of the most moving
talks he had ever given. He didn't speak from notes,
he spoke from his heart. It seemed a really genuine
performance. It seemed regretful on his part and
deeply felt, and it seemed that he had a high purpose. I guess it was the picture of a politician for-
going a chance to do something that clearly, from the
day I met him, I knew he was destined to do. It
seemed like a selfless kind of decision."

That night a group of Bill and Hillary's friends
threw a party. Carolyn Staley made a banner reading
"Welcome Home, Bill" and had a professional sign

maker color it red, white, and blue. She hung it on the front of her house to welcome the Clintons back home.

Both Bill and Hillary delivered measured, intellectualized statements afterward about not running. Hillary made the most of a bad situation by calling the media coverage of Gary Hart and other politicians' private lives a "return to an assessment of values." Expanding on one of her favorite themes, she called the issue a "symptom, an indicator of a large question," involving people "casting about looking for models and examples. We've really lost our way," she told the *Democrat*. "It's very tough to lead a satisfying life these days. . . . And so I see all these stories or allegations, or whatever they are, as desperate attempts on the part of the press, frankly, to really figure out what's going on underneath. . . . What's really going on is . . . people deciding to spend more time with their children . . . to gain some balance. . . . What's going on is real interesting, but no one is writing about it. Nobody understands it yet."

The rambling explanation did little more to hide her pain than Bill Clinton's blunt admission to the *New York Times*: "It hurt so bad to walk away from it."

Bill Clinton had spoken to Gary Hart on the phone that summer. The depth of attention the candidate had received, and the extent of the probe into his personal life, had deeply shaken him. Afterward, watching one of Chelsea's softball games with Max Brantley, he sadly shook his head.

"You know," he said reflectively, speaking almost to an invisible audience somewhere out in the ball field before him, "is there a point ever in a person's life, a political person's life, when the things you've done in the past are forgotten? There's nobody in the world who hasn't done things they were embarrassed about. Aren't you ever forgiven? Aren't they ever allowed to be in the past?"

In the context of a conversation about Gary Hart, it seems fair to assume that Bill Clinton was talking about absolution by the public, by the country. But with hindsight, one can't help but wonder whether he was speaking just as much about Hillary.

That the Clintons had quite severe marital difficulties at that time appears to be confirmed by Bill Clinton's statement to Steve Kroft on *60 Minutes* in 1992: "If we had given up on our marriage . . . three years ago, four years ago, you know . . . If we were divorced, I wouldn't be half the man I am today, without her and Chelsea." What really happened in private, in discussions between Bill and Hillary Clinton at that time, as in 1984 and 1980 and 1998, will never be known. Hillary Clinton's commitment to preserving a "zone of privacy" in their lives is unswerving, and the few friends with whom she discussed the difficulties will never betray that trust. Hillary is, furthermore, extremely circumspect, and has confided fully in very few of her friends.

As she told *Newsweek*: "What is important to us is that we have always dealt with each other. We haven't run away or walked away. We've been willing to work through all kinds of problems. You have hard times because people overwork and they get short-tempered. Marriages go through rough times because you have problems with family members

like we've had. It's very stressful. There are all kinds
of things that happen. And I think it is inappropriate
to talk about that. I don't believe in all of that confessional stuff, because from my perspective you begin
to undermine the relationship when you open it up
to strangers. We don't talk about this kind of stuff
in our marriage with family and friends. It's the way
we are and how we live. And I think it's the way
most people live."

Even if Hillary Clinton had spoken to friends, it is
unlikely that her confidences would have been detailed, personally involved anecdotes full of emotional outpourings of grief. "Hillary has a great
ability to take her personal feelings and put them in
a soft cushion and set them back in the back of her
head while she goes on and not let them interfere,"
Betsey Wright says.

After the painful summer of 1987, life went on for
the Clintons much as before. In the fall Hillary was
active in working as a member of a special committee
appointed by U.S. District Judge Henry Woods to
find a way to eliminate racially identifiable schools—
schools with enrollments of 75 percent black or
greater. Also that year Robert MacCrate, a retired
partner with Sullivan and Cromwell in New York
and then president of the American Bar Association,
appointed her as the first chairman of the newly created twelve-member ABA Commission on Women
and the Profession. In 1988 the Clintons jointly received the National Humanitarian Award from the
National Conference of Christians and Jews. Mayor
Andrew Young of Atlanta spoke in praise of them at
the Little Rock meeting and said that their partner-

ship, based upon a commitment to public service and
to each other, was a model other couples would have
to emulate if marriage was to survive in the future.
The last word—if not the last laugh—on their marriage, it seemed, would belong to the Clintons.

As the 1990 campaign year began, Hillary Clinton
was mentioned as a candidate for Second District
representative for Congress. She was supported by
former Democratic representative from that district
Jim Guy Tucker. "It could be very helpful to Bill's
eventual ambitions," he said. That same year a flood
of rumors circulated saying that Hillary might run
for governor instead of her husband the next year.
In August, Bill Clinton told local newspapers that his
wife would be "wonderful," "unbelievably good,"
and "terrific" as governor. But he wouldn't say if she
was willing to run if he decided not to run for reelection. "I'm not going to speak for her," he told reporters. "That's not my business." He said that if Hillary
was willing to run, "that would have a big impact
on my own decision" about whether to seek the governorship again.

That Hillary Rodham Clinton could ever have won
an election in Arkansas is rather doubtful. Although
her work on educational reform and health care was
extremely popular in the state, there was always a
certain degree of resistance to her and some hard-
core opposition as well. Bill Clinton's natural detractors
repudiated her, and the state's rather powerful religious right viewed her marital role as flying in the
face of Scripture. "A rare, small, and nutty number"
made it their personal campaign to take her on, Max
Brantley says. Other opposition was more mundane

but more widespread. "Outspoken, aggressive women who can stand up on their own two feet and get along in the world just leave some people cold," says Brantley. "She's friendly, she's accessible, but she doesn't project the same puppy dog warmth that Bill does. She was threatening to a lot of people in Arkansas."

It was certainly true that in the course of her varying campaigns, Hillary Clinton acquired a reputation with some people for being pushy, arrogant, and domineering. This criticism flared in 1990, when she crashed a press conference being given by an erstwhile friend and political opponent Tom McRae.

While Bill Clinton was in Washington to deliver a report by the Delta Commission, McRae, a top challenger in the Democratic primary, called a news conference to criticize him on some points that he said Clinton hadn't adequately answered: teacher salaries, the Vertac dioxin contamination in Jacksonville, clearcutting of timber, and whether he planned to seek higher office during his next term if reelected. Arkansas, McRae reminded the crowd, ranked last among states in teacher pay seven years after the Clintons pushed through the school standards and an accompanying one-cent sales tax increase to pay for them.

"Those are the four issues that I would raise, but since the governor is not here, I would give him at least an opportunity to respond," McRae said, pointing at a cartoon of Clinton, clothes scattered at his feet, with the caption: "The Emperor Has No Clothes." "Since the governor will not debate me, we are giving our own answers," he said.

Hillary Clinton, who claimed she just happened to

have been at the capitol "to pick some things up," shot out from the background. She was looking very telegenic, in a houndstooth tweed blazer and turtleneck, with pearl earrings and a big Clinton button on her lapel.

"Do you really want an answer, Tom? Do you really want a response from Bill when you know he's in Washington doing work for the state? That sounds a bit like a stunt to me."

McRae claimed that Clinton had refused to debate him one-on-one.

"Tom, who's the one who didn't show up at the debate in Springdale—give me a break," Hillary countered.

McRae claimed a scheduling mix-up had made him the only one of five Democratic candidates to miss a debate there two weeks earlier.

As cameras swung from McRae to her, she pulled out and began quoting from a four-page prepared statement listing excerpts from reports from the Winthrop Rockefeller foundation, a public policy institute, that had been issued during the fourteen years McRae had presided over it. Many of the excerpts praised Clinton on the same issues McRae had lately criticized him for, including the environment, economic development, and educational reform. Hillary Clinton had served with McRae on the foundation's board.

"I went through all your reports because I've really been disappointed in you as a candidate, and I've been really disappointed in you as a person, Tom," she said.

McRae acknowledged he had approved or authored the reports. He said Clinton's record was in fact good in many areas.

"The issue is not whether he's done good things," McRae finally said. "The final issue is, shouldn't somebody else be given a chance to try? If the best he can do is last, then it's time for someone else to give it a try."

Hillary ticked off Clinton's record of progress. She admitted that problems remained but added, "For goodness sakes, let Arkansas stand up and be proud."

McRae remained at the podium, but he was flustered. Clearly the news conference had gotten out of hand. The cameras kept swinging back and forth. McRae kept smiling. Hillary Clinton did not. She was furious, she said later, about the fact that McRae had displayed a caricature drawing of her husband, nude, with his hands positioned over his crotch.

Hillary later admitted that she might have heard about McRae's planned news conference when she had spoken at a lunchtime civic club with two other Democratic gubernatorial hopefuls. She claimed, however, to have forgotten about it until she showed up at one-thirty at the capitol—coincidentally—and a reporter brought it to her attention. She said the notes she had with her were background information she had brought with her to an appearance before the North Little Rock Sertoma Club.

After the McRae-Clinton confrontation, Representative Tommy Robinson, who had unsuccessfully sought the Republican nomination, said that Hillary had been the real governor of Arkansas for ten years. As former director of public safety during the governor's first term, he told the *Gazette*, he had "had to put up with her tirades before."

"She had no right interrupting his press conference," he told the *Democrat*. "If my wife did what Hillary Clinton did," he said, "she and I would have a private discussion."

Robinson had little to fear on that score, however. His wife did not mince words in her opinion of Hillary Clinton's actions. "I hope that I would not do that," she told the *Arkansas Gazette*. "I would hope that I would be able to contain my feelings. I think it's more tasteful to do that."

Columnist Meredith Oakley of the *Arkansas Democrat* suggested that Bill Clinton lacked "not only . . . fire in the belly but steel in the spine," and accused him of sending his wife "to do his dirty work." Two days later, however, Oakley, reputedly a feminist, expressed a grudging admiration for the way Hillary Clinton "set out to eat McRae's lunch and didn't stop until she'd finished off his dessert."

"If it were a man," Hillary Clinton told the *Gazette*, "they would probably say what a great, strong person this fellow is, how commanding he is and all the rest. . . . I'm not reluctant to say what's on my mind, and if some people interpret that one way instead of another, I can't help that."

During the 1990 campaign for governor, rumors about Clinton's marital infidelities were once again on the rise. The Gary Hart fiasco had left the media hungry for stories about the sexual lives of politicians, and Bill Clinton was a prime target. The question of whether or not he could risk a presidential campaign haunted him. Max Brantley recalls a conversation he had with Bill Clinton in the early summer of 1991, when both men were at the airport seeing their children off to summer camp. Clinton, he said, was on the verge of a decision about whether or not to run for president in 1992. Hillary, Brantley says, was strongly pushing him to run. "I don't think they were thinking so much of actually winning in '92 but of using the election for the future, for building up recognition," he says.

It was a tense time, though Hillary's friends would never have known it. Connie Fails, who wanted to adopt a baby girl from Thailand and bring her to the United States, called Hillary in desperation when her arrangements started to fall through. She needed a letter of recommendation from someone high-level immediately. She called Hillary with an urgent request for a letter of recommendation to the adoption agency. She was told that Hillary as out of town. She left a message saying it was urgent. She had thirty-six hours before the child was going to fall out of her hands forever.

Hillary called back as soon as she got the message.

"I have to get the best and biggest letters I can, recommending us as parents," Connie said. "There's another family that wants the child."

Tell me about the child, Hillary said.

She's four years old, Connie Fails said. She's in an orphanage in Thailand.

And, she said, she doesn't have any arms.

There was no response for a moment from the other end of the line.

Where are you? Connie said.

"I'm at a pay phone in the Kansas City Airport, crying," Hillary responded.

"Don't cry for this kid, she's really tough," said Connie.

"I just love you so much," Hillary said.

The letter was ready and waiting at the governor's mansion the next morning.

"I later found out," Fails says, "she was in the middle of the biggest trial of her entire career. It was ten days before Bill announced his candidacy. And she never said anything."

Later that summer Hillary wrote a letter to her old Wellesley mentor, Alan Schechter. "We are about to start a great adventure," it said.

The word would prove inadequate in the extreme.

Chapter 5

⟨✦⟩

The Hillary Problem

January 1992 was the best and the worst of times for Hillary Rodham Clinton. For her husband's presidential campaign, the campaign she had poured herself into, body and soul, things could not have been worse. Bill Clinton was under constant assault, his integrity and Southern style assailed both by Jerry Brown and his youthful followers and by Paul Tsongas, the principled New Englander whose stoic appearance could have made anyone with some style seem slick by comparison.

Clinton, whose status as a front runner was then held by only shaky and uneven leads in the polls, had for a long time known that his campaign was built on quicksand. The rumors that had dogged him throughout the 1980s, and surfaced with particular nastiness in the 1990 campaign, were not likely to die. Arkansas itself was a political liability when its vital statistics were turned against him by his Democratic primary opponents. The state he loved was gaining renewed renown as the poorest and allegedly most corrupt state in the union, with a highly conservative, backroom-operating legislature, and a poorly educated, mostly rural, politically unsophisticated voting body. Everyone knew that the governor and state legislators of Arkansas were in the hands of the state's poultry and timber industries, it was argued; it was hardly a place expected to produce inspiring, principled politicians. As the New Hampshire primary loomed ahead, the Clinton campaign had a month to cloak "Slick Willie" in respectability.

Campaign director James Carville, deputy campaign manager George Stephanopoulos—and Hillary Clinton—went to work putting together a strategy. Keeping the campaign going would mean anticipating stories before they leaked, plugging up the leaks with watertight denials, or turning them around with positive "spins" before they could turn into an avalanche of catastrophic proportions. They would repackage Bill Clinton as a good-natured, well-intentioned "Bubba" and tone down the wily aspects of the "Willie" problem. No one was more centrally involved in that repackaging than Hillary Clinton. She had given up her natural hair color, her glasses, and her maiden name to help remake the governor in his 1982 election bid—and it had worked. For the presidency she was ready to go for broke. And at first, it seemed, going for broke wasn't really all that bad.

When the stories of Clinton's marital infidelities started circulating nationwide, Hillary was quickly on the case. At her prodding, way back in September 1991, he had faced the press—even before declaring his candidacy. It was a move reminiscent of the television ads he had purchased during his two years of disgraced banishment from the Arkansas governor's mansion when, before he had even declared he would run again, he had apologized to the state's voters for the errors he agreed he had made during his first tenure in office. Bill Clinton had learned some solid lessons from that experience ten years earlier, and he had also paid close heed to the error of Gary Hart. Polls had shown that 39 percent of voters would have reservations about voting for a candidate who had been unfaithful to his wife. They further stated that that number would diminish considerably if the wife knew about the infidelity and had accepted it.

So, at a Washington breakfast with reporters that fall, with Hillary at his side, Bill Clinton had admitted that his marriage hadn't been perfect. He and Hillary had worked hard to stay together, he said, and they were proud of their union.

"We are committed to our marriage and its obligation, to our child and to each other. We love each other very much," he said. "Like nearly anybody that's been together twenty years, our relationship has not been perfect or free of difficulties. But we feel good about where we are. We believe in our obligations. And we intend to be together thirty or forty years from now, regardless of whether I run for president or not."

After a pause, he concluded, "And I think that ought to be enough."

It all worked. Having survived the grilling of Washington's top journalists, Clinton was crowned "most electable" by the national press. Hillary was recognized too. At the end of the meeting, just before she left to return to Little Rock, where Chelsea had a school open house, the reporters asked her if she herself would have made a good candidate for president. They then asked Bill Clinton for comment.

"If she would run," he said, "I would gladly withdraw." Having her at his side would thereafter prove indispensable.

As the campaign year began, Hillary became a star in her own right. She was articulate and politically savvy—"far better organized, more in control, more intelligent and more eloquent," the candidate said, than he was. As things heated up, she gained strength. The worse things looked, the better she did. Standing resolutely by his side, Hillary seemed to give weight to Bill Clinton's often fragile-seeming campaign. Perhaps it was in part subliminal: if Bill Clinton could be supported, believed in—even loved—by such a formidable woman, how could the average voter not follow? Hillary was a person who would not waver, or "waffle," as the Republicans later delighted in saying about Bill Clinton. She was, many wagered, the better politician. Accordingly, in the early days the campaign gave her free reign.

"Two for the price of one!" was the offer Bill Clinton made in those early weeks. "Buy one, get one free!" he exclaimed at his fund-raisers, Hillary close by. "If I get elected president," he said, "it will be an unprecedented partnership, far more than Franklin Roosevelt and Eleanor. They were two great people, but on different tracks. If I get elected, we'll do things together like we always have."

The wide smile rarely left Hillary Clinton's face in those early months of the presidential campaign. Her eyes, however, did keep a guarded look. She responded to talk of her possible appointment as vice president or attorney general with a verbal shrug: "I'm not interested in attending a lot of funerals around the world," she said. But the suggestion of a high-level administration post did not seem entirely beyond the realm of possibility. "I want maneuverability . . ." she said. "I want to get deeply involved in solving problems." If she couldn't quite see herself in the cabinet, she did not rule out the possibility of work as an all-around adviser.

The campaign was not foolhardy. They knew the American public would probably not rush to embrace a first lady who admitted she had her eye on a high-level administration appointment. In reality, due to the Postal Revenue and Federal Salary Act of 1967 (also called the Bobby Kennedy law, passed in response to his appointment as attorney general under John F. Kennedy), that would have been illegal. But they didn't publicize that fact very forcibly— or didn't know it. They let the public feel its way around the issue. They planned to build Hillary Clinton up gradually. They planned to show her slowly to the American people, let them warm up to her, and then allow them to claim her as one of their own.

But the press wasn't playing the game. In early January the *Star*, a supermarket tabloid, decided to run with the story of a long-term affair between Bill Clinton and a nightclub singer with the unlikely name of Gennifer Flowers. "My 12-Year Affair with Bill Clinton," the front-page headline read. On January 16, James Carville was in New Hampshire, holed up in a motel with a score of post-adolescent staffers and candidate Clinton when the story came over his fax machine. His first phone call was to Hillary.

"How's Bill?" she asked. Her voice registered no sign of distress, he later told *Newsweek*. She grilled him, and he answered her questions, grateful for the steady focus her words gave him. This was a battle, Hillary reassured him, that she and Bill would fight, once again, together.

She said she wanted to nip the thing in the bud, to go public. Ted Koppel had already contacted the Clinton campaign and offered the Governor time to respond to the *Star* on *Nightline*. The campaign first said yes and then said no. Respond to the *Star*? It seemed absurd. But some kind of damage control was clearly necessary. It was time to bring out the Hillary 'n' Bill show for another round in the Coliseum.

There were logistical problems, however. Hillary was busy campaigning in Atlanta, Bill enmeshed in New Hampshire pre-primary electioneering. They would rendezvous that night in Little Rock, but there was no way they could unite to prepare and deliver a response for that evening's newscast. For once, though, the fates of press scheduling fell in their favor. The Gennifer Flowers story didn't make the evening news.

An execution was scheduled to take place in an Arkansas jail that day. Bill Clinton arrived at the governor's mansion and waited for Hillary to come home. When Carolyn Staley called, he came to the phone.

"I guess we've had two executions today," she said.

When Bill Clinton answered, he spoke so softly and slowly that she had trouble understanding his words. "I gotta go," he said then, breaking off. "Hillary's home."

Working late into the night, they hammered out a position and prepared their respective scripts. In the end, it all came down to a simple proposition: go public or give up. One thing a Clinton candidacy could not sustain was evasiveness or half-truths, which could be read as a sign of dishonesty. Faced with a choice between minimum damage containment and an all-out frontal attack, the Clintons, hoping for a repeat performance of their September success, chose to stand and fight. The vehicle they finally agreed on was as risky as any could be: a special episode of *60 Minutes* immediately following the Super Bowl. It was a scary prospect: Viewers, hyped from an afternoon of vicarious skirmishing, would kick off their evening with a visit from the first family of Arkansas, airing the worst of their collective dirty laundry.

Not surprisingly, Bill Clinton was squeamish about the idea. It was one thing to go public before an audience of two hundred largely jaded journalists, leaving it to their deadpan prose to translate his feelings into newspaper inches, and quite another to discuss marriage and infidelity before the zoom lens of prime-time television. His face tended to be very expressive, his feelings close to the surface. How well would he be able to control his emotions? *60 Minutes*, unlike *Larry King*, could not be counted upon to provide a sympathetic sounding board for his peculiar sort of public apologies. He and Hillary would have to wing it—and put their trust in the empathy of the nation's viewers.

Hillary had some reason to think they might empathize. On January 18, at a campaign rally in Bedford, New Hampshire, when someone had asked her if marital fidelity should be a campaign issue, she had faced the four hundred-strong crowd, Bill Clinton by her side, and responded, "In any marriage there are issues that come up between two people who are married that I think are their business." The crowd applauded for almost half a minute. "From my perspective," she said, "our marriage is a strong marriage. We love each other, support each other, and we have had a lot of strong and important experiences together that have meant a lot to us." She was proud of her family, Hillary said, and added in conclusion that she thought that what should matter to New Hampshire residents was how their own families were doing. The barb was met with uproarious applause. Clearly the public taste for Gary Hart scandals in a recession year was less than the Republicans might have hoped for.

On January 26, in a crowded anteroom of the Clinton's suite at the Ritz-Carlton Hotel in Boston, the campaign staff stood frozen to a TV monitor as CBS reporter Steve Kroft taped his forty-five-minute interview. "I have acknowledged wrongdoing," the Governor offered into the camera. "I have acknowledged causing pain in my marriage." For aides who had been with Clinton since his 1982 reelection bid for Arkansas' governorship, there was an eerie sense of déjà vu. Once again the boy wonder was asking Mom and Dad if he could come in from the doghouse. Would humble pie play on national TV? the aides wondered. And, they asked each other, crossing their fingers and saying prayers, could a confessional Clinton remember to play by the new rules devised for him?

Before the interview the campaign had decided that Bill Clinton's only hope of not falling into an endless quagmire of questions about the history of his marriage was to refuse to speak specifically about any single alleged affair. But the governor was not a very wily interviewee.

"I am assuming from your answer that you're categorically denying that you ever had an affair with Gennifer Flowers." Kroft, aiming to force Clinton to make a specific admission, carefully set his trap.

"I've said that before," the governor said, taking the bait. "And so has she."

The seeds of prime-time disaster were ready to bloom.

"You've said that your marriage has had problems," Kroft pressed on. "What does that mean?"

"I don't me—" Clinton stopped.

"You were separated?" broke in Kroft. "Does it mean adultery?"

Clinton paused again. Hillary's gaze on him was sharp and intense.

"I think the American people, at least people who have been married for a long time, know what it means," Clinton said defiantly.

Voices rising slightly, Clinton's temper visibly shortening, the governor and the journalist continued their verbal volleying. Finally, Hillary Clinton broke in:

"There isn't a person watching this who would feel comfortable sitting on this couch detailing everything that ever went on in their life or their marriage," she said. "And I think it's real dangerous in this country if we don't have a zone of privacy for everybody."

Message: *That's enough.*

"I-I-I couldn't agree with you more," Kroft stumbled. "And I think—and I agree with you that everyone wants to put it behind you."

"We've gone further than anybody we know of," she said, "and that's all we're going to say."

The *60 Minutes* interview, it was generally agreed, was a success. Hillary, many said, had saved the day. Some who witnessed the odd event went so far as to say it was Hillary's day.

She had stared into Bill's face as he spoke during the interview, not with the vulture-eyed glare of a Nancy Reagan (or even a slowly simmering Barbara Bush), but rather with an intent concentration that conveyed a sort of indulgence—indulgence and rapt attention. If Bill didn't make his point clearly enough, Hillary slipped in. When Bill seemed poised to waffle, Hillary cut him off.

Hillary came so close to dominating the *60 Minutes* interview that the CBS team found themselves rationing her sound bites to keep her from burying Bill. Yet despite the careful editing, Hillary nonetheless emerged as the more articulate, the more forcefully secure Clinton. She had incontestably made the *60 Minutes* appearance a success. In the popular imagination, the word of a graciously groomed married woman carries much more weight than that of a showy nightclub singer. Daunting as she was as a lawyer and campaigner, Hillary also proved that she was a force to be reckoned with as a wife. Soon, she was an even more dominant figure in Clinton's campaign.

Her new strategy: attack the attackers. Turn the spotlight on the press. James Carville soon was denouncing every reporter he saw as a "cash for trash" journalist. At a New Jersey fundraiser, surrounded by reporters and TV cameras, he ranted so much that after about five minutes a confused rookie interrupted to ask if he was in fact with the Clinton campaign. "Yes," Carville retorted, "and I'm a lot more expensive then Gennifer Flowers."

Hillary equated the Gennifer Flowers story with "a conversation with Elvis." Speaking with Sam Donaldson on *Prime Time Live*, she said, "We know that this woman has admitted that the Republicans offered her money to change her story and implicate my husband after having denied it repeatedly. And we know that the former Republican gubernatorial opponent has been out beating the bushes trying to stir this up for as long as he could since he was defeated. . . . If somebody's willing to pay you $130,000 or $170,000 to say something and you get your fifteen minutes of fame and you get your picture on the front page of every newspaper and you're some failed cabaret singer who doesn't even have much of a résumé to fall back on, and what's there she lied about, you know—that's the daughter of Willie Horton as far as I'm concerned."

In a move that only reinforced the campaign's view that she was a fake smoking gun for hire, Gennifer Flowers eventually gave an in-depth—illustrated—interview to *Penthouse*.

Whether in response to revelations that the *Star* had

paid Flowers, or due to Carville's quite impressive histrionics, the media began to cool to the Clinton-Flowers connection. Flowers—and the *Star*—were too easily discreditable. It came to light that one of the sources of the infidelity stories was a local food vendor named Robert "Say" McIntosh, a political gadfly, who sold sweet potato pie from a truck and handed out rather lurid handbills on the streets of Little Rock accusing Clinton of extramarital affairs. McIntosh had frequently been heard to say that he was willing to spread his allegations if someone would pay his expenses. *Newsweek* reported a series of six inconsistencies in Gennifer Flowers's story. They included the fact that she had said she had worked on the TV show *Hee Haw* but had not, and had stated that her first meeting with Clinton took place at the Excelsior Hotel in 1979 or 1980, two years before it opened. The *New York Post,* having learned that Gennifer Flowers had tape-recorded other lovers, ran a front-page story headlined, "She's Done It Before."

There was one last notable press conference, in which Gennifer Flowers, standing alongside a blow-up of the *Star* story, said Clinton's denials of their affair had hurt her deeply. The crowd of reporters showed little pity. Things degraded rather rapidly.

"Did the governor use a condom?" one reporter shouted while the others hooted with laughter. They laughed even harder when Blake Hendrick, Gennifer Flowers's attorney, threatened to end the news conference "if there are any further questions that are degrading in my opinion."

Hillary and Co. had brought Bill Clinton back from the all but dead. Clinton's favorable ratings had by now risen to 67 percent, and his negatives hung in the low 20s. The campaign's all-out frontal attack, the tactic Hillary had learned in the early 1980s was indispensable, had saved Bill Clinton's candidacy. Her aggressive defense of him, everyone agreed, had been their best weapon of all. The problem was that in the process she had put herself in the line of fire.

Very shortly after Hillary's impressive appearance on *60 Minutes*, a virulent backlash began. In the brief period when the attacks on Bill Clinton receded, a new attack machine cranked into gear. And this time the rocks flew not at Bill Clinton's head, but at Hillary's.

In the first week of February reporters began to ask Bill Clinton if he was concerned about being up-staged by his wife. The questions didn't put him off at all. "I've always liked strong women," he said at a February 7 rally. "It doesn't bother me for people to see her and get excited and say she could be president too."

Richard Nixon, however, gave the Clintons quite a different spin. Observing the couple's progress as "co-candidates," he acridly observed that a strong wife "makes the husband look like a wimp."

"Hillary pounds on the piano so hard that Bill can't be heard," he said. "You want a wife who's intelligent, but not too intelligent."

Other men in the media soon seemed to feel the same way. A normally expressionless Tom Brokaw, looking south for Super Tuesday, expressed shock when, at a rally after the votes came in, Hillary victo-riously rushed past her husband, rose to the podium, and grabbed the microphone first. While Bill hopped up and down in the wings, she slowly worked her way through an introduction in which she referred rather sparingly to her husband—and then only as "the messenger." She concluded, "We believe passionately in this country, and we cannot stand by for one more year and watch what is happening to it!" After her wind-up, minutes later, Brokaw observed, over the din of audience applause, "Not just an introduction, this is a *speech* by Mrs. Clinton."

After Clinton's victory in the Illinois primary, the networks switched to campaign headquarters for a reaction from the candidate and tuned into the same scene: Hillary delivering a long and proud introduction, while Bill lingered eagerly in the back. "Like a hanger-on hungering for home-baked cookies," William Safire described it. Brokaw and Peter Jennings once again seemed miffed. Safire accused Hillary of "usurpation of a candidate's strength."

Safire had written on the female usurpation theme before. He had similarly attacked Nancy Reagan in 1987, saying that because of her "interference," Ronald Reagan was being "weakened and made to appear wimpish and helpless." Then, as in 1992, his words would have a singularly damaging impact.

Accordingly, by late March public opinion of the candidate's overachieving wife was starting to turn. The 65 percent approval rating she had garnered earlier in the month was swiftly falling. The same thing that her friends said proudly—that Hillary was "tougher" than Bill—was now being used against her. Even her headband was seen as a sign of malevolence.

"There's something a little scary, a little Al Haigish about her," a close observer was quoted as saying in *Vanity Fair*.

If the mainstream press was now having trouble with Hillary's untraditional ways, the journalists of the right were in the throes of an all-out war. A sympathetic article by Garry Wills in the *New York Review of Books*, which detailed Hillary's legal writings and speeches from many years earlier, provoked a tidal wave of right-wing outrage. William F. Buckley's *National Review* featured a cover with a photo of Clinton captioned "Stop—Or My Wife Will Shoot." The *American Spectator*, in an article entitled "The Lady Macbeth of Little Rock," compared Hillary to Eva Peron and called her the "Winnie Mandela of American politics." The article tore apart Hillary's legal theories, said she endorsed the right of children to sue parents "to solve family arguments," and accused her of having channeled illegal financial support to an assortment of left-wing causes while acting as the head of federally funded agencies. Soon a widely circulated right-wing fund-raising letter was calling Hillary "a radical feminist who has little use for religious values or even the traditional family unit."

More bad news was on the way. In early March a story surfaced that in 1978 Hillary and Bill Clinton had invested in an Ozark vacation-property deal with a friend, James B. McDougal, who went on to become a Clinton administration appointee—and the owner of an Arkansas savings and loan institution. That institution, which at some points subsidized the real estate venture, later failed (at a cost to taxpayers of about $60 million)—and was represented by Hillary Clinton and her Rose law firm when it became subject to state regulation. Hillary quickly acknowledged that she had done legal work for the savings and loan, Madison Guaranty, but stressed that it had not been related to the S&L's dealings with state regulators. She stated, furthermore, that she had refused to accept her share of earnings from any state business the Rose law firm might have earned since 1978, when Bill first attained statewide office.

It turned out that the Clintons had improperly deducted at least $5,000 on their personal tax returns in 1984 and 1985 for interest paid on a portion of at least $30,000 in bank loan payments that the real estate company, Whitewater Development, made for them. The deductions saved them about $1,000 in taxes, but since the error had been made more than three years earlier, the IRS did not require the Clintons to pay. Lawyers for the Clintons said these were honest errors, made due to confusion over who really owned a certain piece of Whitewater property and who was responsible for the loan taken out to buy it.

Many other questions could not be answered, because Whitewater's records could not be found. McDougal said that at the governor's request they had been delivered to the mansion years earlier. The Clintons said many of them had simply disappeared.

The story, which was a bit too abstruse to make tabloid headlines, might have been temporarily forgotten if not for former California governor Jerry Brown's suggestion that Hillary and Bill's business connections were tantamount to "corruption." Hillary counterattacked by charging Brown with striking a blow at all struggling two-career couples, and attributed his remarks to "pathetic and desperate" mudslinging.

"You've got to remember," she said on a campaign stop in a Chicago bakery, "that I have tried the best way I know how to be as careful as possible. Now, in hindsight I suppose people can say 'You should have done this, you should have done that.' I didn't presume that anybody would presume anything other than that I was trying to do the right thing all the way down the line."

Then she made the comment that would haunt her for the rest of the campaign: "I suppose I could have stayed home and baked cookies and had teas," she said. "But what I decided to do was pursue my profession, which I entered before my husband was in public life."

She was clearly enraged. She had taken particular offense at an offhand remark Brown had made which she felt was an insult to her as a working wife. "In response to a question about his father's law firm doing business with the state when he was governor, he said, 'Well, I don't control my father,'" she said on *The Today Show*. "And you know, it wasn't very subtle, and I was trying to point out that his attitude seemed to be that I should have only confined myself to the ceremonial role of a first lady."

Barbara Bush clearly appreciated her anger, and spoke out against Brown's attack and in favor of Hillary Clinton's right to a career. But the public did not prove sensitive to Hillary's sense of outrage.

Hillary had already, on *60 Minutes*, offended people with her line "I'm not some little woman standing by her man like Tammy Wynette." For that she had had to issue an official apology, after Wynette, "mad as hell," had sent her a letter which read, "Mrs. Clinton, you have offended every woman and man who loves that song—several million in number. I believe you have offended every true country music fan and every person who has 'made it on their own' with no one to take them to a White House."

Hillary's unapologetic intelligence, her combativeness, her refusal to do anything other than speak her mind, for some weeks now had been wearing on the nerves of America's change-wary voters. The "cookies and tea" comment was just too much. Hillary had touched a nerve. She had crossed a line that was to many still sacred. Millions of women who had never worked outside the home read Hillary's statement as a contemptuous insult. Overnight, their indignation inflamed by the press, they turned on her.

The Arkansas Travelers, friends of Bill and Hillary's from home who helped out on the campaign trail, encountered voters who said they wouldn't vote for Bill Clinton because they baked cookies, because their daughters baked cookies, because they were "afraid" of Hillary. "I feel like she's the power behind the throne." "I think she's a very aggressive woman, and she's overly ambitious." "She has no use for us, we have no use for her," average Americans were quoted saying in April.

One week after the infamous "cookie" line, William Safire coined the phrase the "Hillary Problem." In an op-ed piece published in the *New York Times*, he accused Hillary Clinton of "elitism in action," and attributed her two major gaffes—the "cookie" line and her politically incorrect sneer at Tammy Wynette—

to a severe case of "foot-in-mouth disease." Mocking
self-help jargon, Safire proposed a "six-step solution"
to the Problem of Hillary, which suggested, among
its more salient features, that she be banished from
taking the podium for victory statements or conces-
sion speeches.

Such censure came as a shock to Hillary. As a lawyer, she was so used to choosing her words carefully
that to have been caught in a blooper felt like a blow
to her character. She insisted her words had been
taken out of context. They'd become, she said, a
"misconstruction." Her choice of phrase, which once
again lacked the warmth and softness she needed,
was hard like armor, and its unconscious brittleness
betrayed the fact that she was truly hurting.

Though the public might soon have been ready to
let the issue pass, the media was not about to let a
situation rife with such dramatic possibilities die. All
throughout March, Hillary made headlines and cover
stories. Soon it seemed that the more page spreads
and column inches were devoted to the "Hillary
Problem," the greater that problem became. The *New
York Times*, for example, ran an article which promi-
nently quoted the views of two elderly, anti-Hillary
homebodies. Having resolved among themselves
whether to identify themselves as "retired homemak-
ers" or "housewives" by settling upon the latter term
("Is that word O.K. by Hillary?") they opined that
Hillary was up to no good.

"She's only interested in being with a winner,"
seventy-one-year-old Bernadine Elliott said. "And believe me, if he doesn't get elected, she's going to
dump him. Mark my words."

"That's right. She'll dump him," sixty-nine-year-old LaRoux Tanner agreed. Although dozens of other voters interviewed for the article voiced positive views of Hillary, the Elliott quote was the one picked up and repeated in the weekly news magazines.

There were other ethics charges too. In late March the *Times* reported that Bill Clinton had supported an ethics and disclosure law for public officials but with his advisers had altered it before it was approved by voters in 1988 so that he and other public officials were exempt from disclosing potential conflicts of interest, such as questions related to state dealings with the Rose law firm. The deletion occurred during a private drafting session, with participants including Clinton, close political aides, allies, and Webb Hubbell, a senior partner at Rose, the *Times* said. Clinton and Hubbell denied it.

Hillary, understandably, was getting bitter—and the tension was starting to show. Her "vamp" image was improved not at all when, in an article to be published in the May issue of *Vanity Fair*, she complained to Gail Sheehy about the "double standard" in the press, which had long focused so much on her husband's infidelities and ignored a long-rumored, long-term affair between George Bush and Jennifer Fitzgerald, a loyal staffer now employed in a senior position in the State Department. Referring to a conversation she had held with Anne Cox Chambers, the chairwoman of Cox newspapers, Hillary said: "She's sittin' there in her sun room saying, 'You know, I just don't understand why they think they can get away with this—everybody knows about George

Bush's carrying on, all of which is apparently well known in Washington.' "

By referring to George Bush's purported affair, Hillary had dared what no Washington reporter had ever pulled off in print. Once again she had crossed a sacred line. The newspapers were quick to castigate her, their glee barely contained behind shocked banner headlines: "Hillary's Revenge," "Hillary Goes Tabloid," and "Bill's Wife Dishes the Dirt." Even Barbara Bush was moved to make a public statement of outrage.

Hillary had no choice but to backpedal—fast. It was three days before New York's Democratic primary, and scandal was not something the Clinton campaign needed in a then lukewarm state. Borrowing a technique from the Bush campaign—attack and "repent"—on April 4 Hillary apologized. Campaigning for her husband at the College of St. Rose in Albany, she said, "It was a mistake. People were asking me questions at the time and I responded, but nobody knows better than I the pain that can be caused by discussing rumors in private conversation."

Bush's "Jennifer" did not make as much of a splash as the Clinton campaign had probably hoped. But the accusation—a poor strategic call on Hillary's part—did help drive another nail into the coffin of her good standing. Hillary's name was quickly becoming a buzzword in the popular mind for everything that was a bit too cold, a bit too opportunistic, a bit too mean about successful working women. One cartoon in the *New Yorker* showed a woman asking a sales clerk for a jacket and saying "Nothing Too Hillary."

At the time of the New York primary in early April, polls found Hillary Clinton's approval rating down to around 35 percent. While a minority of respondents still said they found Hillary strong and inspirational, the overwhelming majority now seemed to have swung over to the Richard Nixon school of gender relations. More and more, voters who otherwise had admired the candidate's wife's strength and candor now worried that her power pointed to Bill Clinton's impotence. "What does it tell you about a presidential candidate if people say: 'His wife will back him up. His wife will run the White House?'" one voter rhetorically asked in the *New York Times*. "I want the President to be President."

The unpleasant task of telling Hillary that she had to make a change fell to Clinton's pollster, Stan Greenberg, Carville, and media consultant Frank Greer. In April they presented the candidate and his wife with a carefully researched interim report. Its conclusion: voters saw Hillary Clinton as "being in the race for herself," "going for the power," and being intent on "running the show," and they didn't like it one bit. The consultants told the Clintons that they needed to act the part of a warmer, more simple, and more loving couple. Why not, they wrote, arrange "joint appearances with her friends where Hillary can laugh, do her mimicry," and perhaps even stage an event where "Bill and Chelsea surprise Hillary on Mother's Day"?

Hillary may have gagged—but she took the hint. After the New York primary she retreated very briefly from the national stage. When she reappeared, in late spring, she was a new woman. She cut ribbons at openings of new campaign headquarters and read stories like "Chicka Chicka Boom Boom" to children in preschool classes, against a backdrop of plastic ironing boards and stoves. She let a bit of an Arkansas twang into her voice, talked much about Chelsea and her interest in education. Her photo opportunities were designed to have her surrounded by small children. As she looked more warm and maternal, her headband now seemed more schoolmarmish than like the velvet crown of a yuppie conqueror.

Most important, she worked hard to reassure voters that Bill Clinton wasn't a wimp. "He has a real core of toughness," she said at one rally. She reiterated his new promise not to offer her a cabinet post: "That's not going to happen, and I wouldn't take it if it did." She swore she would not sit in on cabinet meetings—"I never did that in Arkansas, and I'm not going to start now." And she demurred on the question of becoming a radical, pioneering First Lady— "I don't think so; I hope I'm going to be myself." The Clinton campaign insisted that Hillary wouldn't have any special influence in the White House, and that she herself would insist upon taking only an unpaid job.

In a conversation with David Frost in late May, she dismissed a reference to one of her husband's earlier statements that the Clintons' reign in the White House would be an "unprecedented partnership," greater than that of the Roosevelts, as "very nice hyperbole."

She even, though somewhat disingenuously, tried to sidestep the label of "feminist" she had proudly claimed for so many years. She believed, like Bill, in equality, she said, but added that she rejected some of what the term has come to mean today.

"I don't think feminism, as I understand the definition, implies the rejection of maternal values, nurturing children, caring about the men in your life," she said. "That is just nonsense to me."

Though Hillary wasn't about to give up the feminist mantle altogether, she wasn't flaunting it either. Instead she was drawing comparisons between herself and Barbara Bush. "We're both very committed women. We care very deeply about our families, and we're supportive of our husbands."

The effort to sustain a spiritual link to Barbara Bush was never clearer than when, on Memorial Day weekend, Hillary Clinton addressed the graduating class of Wellesley College. Barbara Bush had been asked to speak two years earlier, and her selection had touched off a storm of controversy on the highly feminist campus. About a fourth of the graduating class said that they believed that Mrs. Bush, someone who had dropped out of college to marry, was a poor choice, and had been invited only because of her husband. In accordance with her new "kinder, gentler" image, Hillary made a point of praising women who decide to stay at home to raise families as well as those who choose careers.

"You may choose to be a corporate executive or a rocket scientist; you may run for public office, or you may stay home and raise your children," she said. "You can now make any or all of these choices, and they can be the work of your life." She delivered a pointed attack on Dan Quayle's "family values" crusade: "Women who pack lunches for their kids or take the early bus to work, or stay out late at the PTA or spend every minute tending to their aging parents do not need lectures from Washington about values. They don't need to hear about an idealized world that never was as righteous or as carefree as some would like to think." But she also made sure to add that her daughter, Chelsea, "has been the joy of our life."

She told graduates that she had made her life's work helping children and said that in their future lives there would be many ways to do so too. "You can do it by making policy or by making cookies," she said to applause.

Walking the fine line between "feminist" and the Democratic version of "family values," Hillary Clinton entered the summer with a damagingly low approval rating of 29 percent. The Democratic National Convention was approaching; it was time for even more serious action. On the day of the California primary, she was taken hostage by her good friends, the actress Mary Steenburgen and the producer Linda Bloodworth-Thomason, who brought over her three top production stylists, Christophe for hair, Charlie Blackwell for makeup, and Cliff Chally for wardrobe, along with a trio of salespeople from Ron Ross, a Studio City designer boutique. Hillary spent the day in a bathrobe, trying on clothes. The result was that Christophe cut five inches off her hair and recolored it "honey blonde," and Hillary showed up at the convention in New York with a newly revitalized, more glamorous wardrobe. The night of Bill Clinton's acceptance speech at Madison Square Garden, she wore a pastel yellow silk suit. That night she grabbed Tipper Gore by the wrist and led her in a dance, looking "like 1960s teenyboppers recovering their lost youth," as Bill Clinton said to *W.*

Chelsea was pulled out of privacy and marched around to prove to the doubting public that the Clintons did in fact have a child. Swallowing her distaste, Hillary allowed *People* magazine to run a profile of Chelsea (without her daughter's participation), and shared opinions for that story on issues ranging from ear piercing to questions on the facts of life.

Child rearing, dessert recipes, and the Fourth of July became Hillary's topics of the day. She tolerated reporters' queries on her clothes. She made news in the days before the Democratic convention by promoting her chocolate chip cookie recipe in a reader's choice cookie bake-off between herself and Barbara Bush. The competition was sponsored by *Family Circle* magazine, which had seized the opportunity provided by Hillary's unfortunate cookie comment to combine a recipe feature with some timely current events.

She promoted her cookies with an energy and enthusiasm attributable only to a colossal act of sublimation. "Join with me in the first real effort of the election year," she implored supporters at a preconvention tea. "Try my cookies. I hope you like them, but like good Democrats, vote for them anyway."

Whether Hillary actually took the time to bake a batch of her cookies for the convention-time bake-off is unclear. The cookies at the tea were baked by Powell Weeks, a cook who worked for one of Mrs. Clin-

LEFT: Hillary Rodham, the "Goldwater Girl," in her 1965 Maine Township High School South yearbook picture. (Peter Frahm)

BELOW: Seventeen-year-old Hillary Rodham, front and center in this picture of National Merit Scholarship finalists, was voted "most likely to succeed," a high school classmate recalls. Hillary Rodham's childhood home at 235 North Wisner in Park Ridge, Illinois. (Peter Frahm)

LEFT: Wellesley College Government Association president Hillary Rodham made *Life* magazine with her commencement speech calling for a "more immediate, ecstatic, and penetrating mode of living." (Lee Balterman/*Life* magazine)

BELOW: An "adoring look" worthy of Nancy Reagan. Hillary Rodham, with the infamous "frizzy" hair and thick glasses, holds the bible as her husband is sworn in as Governor of Arkansas. (*Arkansas Democrat-Gazette*)

LEFT: The 1979 inaugural ball. The first lady's made-in-Arkansas dress is now a museum piece. (*Arkansas Democrat-Gazette*)

BELOW: The Clinton couple on the campaign trail in 1982. Hillary Rodham *Clinton*'s infamous "makeover" is a success. Even the "comeback kid" had to cut his hair. (*Arkansas Democrat-Gazette*)

The triumphant return to the governor's mansion in 1983. "Innocent . . . yet sophisticated." Second time around, the chastened first lady's inaugural gown used "a pleasing set of feminine contradictions to state its case," the *Arkansas Democrat* said. (*Arkansas Democrat-Gazette*)

A mother-daughter portrait with four-year-old Chelsea, named for a Judy Collins recording. (*Arkansas Democrat-Gazette*)

Hillary Clinton, in a rare show of emotion, wiped a tear from her eye as her husband announced he would not run for president in 1988. (*Arkansas Democrat-Gazette*)

The nation met Hillary Clinton—headband-clad—as she stood by her man on "60 Minutes." (AP/Wide World Photos)

On January 26, 1996, Hillary Clinton became the first First Lady ever called to testify before a grand jury. (AP Photo)

The Inaugural Gala, January 1997: The worst was yet to come. (Globe Photos)

Chelsea Clinton, here at her high school graduation, has emerged from her trying White House years an intelligent and grounded young woman. (Sharon Farmer, Official White House Photograph supplied by Globe Photos)

Building the Global Village: Hillary Rodham Clinton and Ghanian First Lady Mana Rawlings on a visit to a day care center in Accra, Ghana, March 1998. (AP Photo)

In the darkest days of the Monica Lewinsky scandal, the Clintons went on vacation to Martha's Vineyard. (AP Photo)

Hillary, standing with Sammy Sosa and Tipper Gore, appeared unfazed as Bill Clinton delivered his 1999 State of the Union address inside the very walls where, hours earlier, senators had debated his impeachment. (Brad Markel/Gamma Liaison)

ton's friends, Norma Asnes. Other friends from around the country baked and brought them too, and would, in a uniquely feminine show of support for Hillary, have passed them out on the floor of Madison Square Garden had not the Garden's management ruled that health regulations made that illegal. At the last minute the Soutine Bakery was hired to deliver six thousand cookies.

In what was undoubtedly one of the silliest moments in Hillary's political life, she appeared cum recipe, in an article in the *New York Times'* Living section, formerly known as the Ladies' Page. "My friends say my recipe is more democratic," she was quoted as saying, "because I use vegetable shortening instead of butter." Hillary's cookies, made with oatmeal and vegetable shortening, were deemed more politically correct—and lower in calories too—than Barbara Bush's butter-laden ones, according to food writer Marion Burros. The article was capped with a picture of Hillary and Tipper Gore taking time out from their busy cookie campaign to have tea at the Waldorf.

Aides said afterward that Hillary's cookie promoting comments were meant to be tongue-in-cheek. But the press didn't take them that way. She just didn't have the right touch. Miming traditional femininity was just not her forte. Everything sounded so fake that it was hard to tell what, of Hillary's new wide-eyed, down-home comments, was meant to be taken seriously. "I almost have to pinch myself to believe I am going to New York to see my husband nominated for the presidency of the United States," she said before the New York convention. "I am an old-fashioned patriot. I cry at the Fourth of July when kids put crepe paper on their bicycle wheels, so this is, like just incredible, it's so extraordinary to me," she enthused, in a locution worthy of Monica Lewinsky.

Many observers found it an appalling spectacle. The *New York Times'* Joyce Purnick begged the Democrats to "Let Hillary be Hillary." Republican consultant Roger Ailes noted that "Hillary Clinton in an apron is like Michael Dukakis in a tank." After the convention, *Newsweek*'s Eleanor Clift lamented, "today's Hillary is a burned-out, buttoned-up automation compared with the vibrant woman who strode purposefully onto the national scene last January."

Having brought Bill Clinton "back from the dead," what life was there left in Hillary? Her three transformations—from wounded wife to campaign crusader to perfect political wife had taken their toll. Her battering by the press had too. "I'm not in this to win personality polls. I'm trying to effect change in people's lives," she had told Carl Sferrazza Anthony, author of numerous books on American first ladies, who met with Hillary early in the campaign and answered her questions about the political power of past first ladies and the balance of power in presidential marriages. "I'm a big girl," she had said. "If I get criticized I can take it."

But she'd made a vital miscalculation. Hillary had thought that criticism would focus on her ideas. Yet she wasn't the candidate; she was the wife. There was no political platform for which she could be criticized. There was only herself, her very self. That was much worse. As she put it to the editors of Grand

Junction Colorado's *Daily Sentinel:* "You feel like you're standing in the middle of a firing range, and sometimes they come close to hitting you on the top of the head."

The media "they" were the enemy. This was a certainty Hillary Clinton would not lose throughout her years in the White House. The media would never, she was convinced, try to convey the truth about her marriage or her political views. (Even the cookies business had been a scam. *Family Circle* had asked Hillary for a recipe without telling her it was to be used in a bake-off against Barbara Bush. And Barbara Bush's recipe had been reprinted from a 1986 article in *McCall's.*) The media would never care as much about her political positions as it did about her hair and clothes. It would never pay attention to her policy statements. In the run-up to the general election, it was ignoring her speeches—and running instead with reports that she'd been "muzzled"!

She was furious. She shut down. She stopped giving long interviews and allotted reporters only small portions of time during short car rides to and from campaign events. She sidestepped personal revelations, even avoided saying "I." With odd formality, she referred to her husband as "Bill Clinton."

Hillary's self-assurance, so striking in the early days of the campaign, had taken a bad blow. She could not make sense of the censure she'd gotten for her few slips of tongue on the campaign trail. She'd never gotten over the fallout from her "cookies and teas" comment. It never, really, made sense to her.

It was a bit as though she'd been tried for a crime she was only half aware of having committed. There is a picture hanging in the study of the governor's mansion in Little Rock: she and Bill pictured as farmer and wife in a spoof on the painting *American Gothic.* In the picture she casts a sidelong "there you go again" look at Bill. Now would the roles be reversed? Could their marriage, their sense of themselves, stand such a reversal?

Hillary appeared on the daytime television show *Home* and fielded questions with a group of other mothers during an advice feature called "Club Mom." She continued to take time out on the campaign trail for long, quiet conversations with Chelsea. She prayed: "Dear Lord, be good to me. The sea is so wide and my boat is so small."

And, for once, it was Bill Clinton who kept her afloat.

Chapter 6

Trial by Fire

On the morning after the election, Bill and Hillary Clinton woke up early and exhausted in their bedroom in the Arkansas governor's mansion. They turned to look at each other and burst out laughing. Despite the years of dreaming, the long months of anticipation, victory—the White House—still didn't seem real. They couldn't believe it had happened to them. "It's like the dog that keeps chasing the car and all of a sudden catches it," Hillary reflected.

The elation of the first weeks after the election felt like a second honeymoon. The Clintons were in fact enjoying their "honeymoon period" with the American media and public. For a short, sweet while they could do no wrong. The partisan politicking of the campaign year had ended, and with it, the demonization of Hillary Clinton seemed miraculously to have vanished. Instead, in its typically schizophrenic fashion, the American public now canonized her. In late November the *San Francisco Chronicle* commented that Hillary's enthusiasts had elevated her to a status "somewhere between Wonder Woman and Cinderella." The *Washington Post* suggested that a "Hillary Cult" might be in the making. Even the Little Rock

Airport Commission briefly considered rechristening the state's major airport, Adams Field, in her name.

The sudden rush of adoration terrified Hillary. She knew that the higher she was placed on the pedestal of national opinion, the harder she would eventually fall. She retreated to the Arkansas governor's mansion and hid out with a few close friends. She buried herself in the familiar comforts of her book-lined study and read every book she could on the lives of her predecessors. The lessons of history were less than encouraging. Strong first ladies tended to be reviled by the public. Their strengths underscored their husbands' weaknesses. Eleanor Roosevelt, who traveled around the country serving as Franklin D. Roosevelt's "eyes and ears," had been criticized for drawing attention to the fact that the president was confined to a wheelchair. Rosalynn Carter's travels to Latin America made her husband Jimmy's "malaise" seem all the more debilitating. Nancy Reagan's influence in White House hirings and firings gave greater credibility to reports that her husband Ronald was showing the early symptoms of senility.

Using the past as a guide, there was every reason to think that Hillary, embarking on first ladydom as the avowed "co-president," would soon flounder miserably. But the received wisdom of the hour held that for her things would be different. Eleanor Roosevelt, after all, hadn't even been to college. Nancy Reagan was a Hollywood wife who consulted regularly with a psychic. Rosalynn Carter was a woman of another generation. Hillary was the first First Lady to have a professional status equal to her husband's. She was the first to have a long history of political activism and a considerable power base in Washington. Why, she deserved to be a member of Clinton's cabinet—might even have been one if only her husband hadn't been the President.

Bill Clinton, at least, seemed to think so. The election was now over; he'd had enough of trying to domesticate Hillary for the sake of public opinion. His wife, the President-elect now made clear, would be his top adviser, with a hand in his major appointments and policy statements. When asked by *Time* magazine whom he needed to have in the room when he made his most important decisions, he answered, without hesitation, "Hillary." She participated in Bill Clinton's first meeting with congressional Democrats. "Stayed the whole time, talked a lot, knew more than we did about some things," the President bragged afterward. He made no secret of the key role she played in his cabinet choices. It was Clinton & Clinton at work again, or "Billary," as Beltway regulars were starting to call them. The public was almost unimaginably quiescent. In January the Clinton-hostile *Wall Street Journal* found Hillary's approval rating at 57 percent, twenty points higher than it had been the previous summer. Seventy-four percent of respondents said that she was a positive role model.

By inauguration week the whole country seemed to be caught by the spell of youth and joyous populism emanating from the Clintons. The press gushed over the glory of the inaugural proceedings. On inauguration day Hillary was forgiven the unfortunate choice of a garish blue hat worn with a fuscia and gold suit; those few journalists who stooped to comment were immediately rebuked for their callousness.

If she looked distinctly unnatural one evening on TV, as she sang and clapped self-consciously with the puppet Kermit the Frog on her shoulder, no one commented—and if she had to fight to keep Chelsea awake during the most solemn inaugural proceedings, no one noticed. And though it was rumored that Hillary had "muffled" Bill Clinton's mother, Virginia Kelley, and troublesome brother Roger by forbidding them to speak to the press, no one criticized her for it. For one suspended moment she was golden.

Then the party ended.

Hillary dropped the first bomb herself when she announced during the inaugural proceedings that she would heretofore be known nationally by the name she'd long used professionally: Hillary Rodham Clinton. Then, as the country worked its way around that idea, the White House announced that the first lady's office, traditionally located in the East Wing of the White House, would be moved to the West Wing, one floor above the Oval Office and right next to Clinton's senior staff. Hillary's chief of staff, Maggie Williams, would match Clinton's chief, Thomas F. "Mack" McLarty, in power and influence. Five members of her staff were assigned presidential-assistant rank, making her aides more powerful than those assigned to Vice President Gore.

The symbolic importance of the office move was enormous. In the popular imagination, the public-domestic split between the realms of president and first lady was sacrosanct and solidified by the separation of their spheres of influence between East and West wings. First ladies through the centuries had marked the breadth of their influence by their choice of working quarters. Edith Roosevelt and Grace Coolidge had worked only in sitting rooms. Lou Hoover had spread her paperwork out on her bed, as did Mamie Eisenhower, who placed a small tray upon her pink bedspread and scheduled her meetings around her favorite soap opera. Lady Bird Johnson, Pat Nixon, and Barbara Bush had set up shop in a dressing room. Nancy Reagan's office was strategically placed midway between West and East wings, neighboring her gymnasium, her cosmetology room, and twelve double-door clothes closets.

Hillary's office choice pushed the bounds of acceptability. Soon enough the role she would play in the new government did too. Five days after the inauguration Bill Clinton announced that he had named Hillary to chair a special committee charged with drafting a proposal for legislation to overhaul the nation's health care system. "She's better at organizing and leading people from a complex beginning to a certain end than anybody I've ever worked with in my life," Clinton said, adding that he believed that putting his credibility on the line in appointing his wife to the post was the best way he knew of demonstrating to the American people how serious he was about health care reform. "I want it done—now," he said.

No president had ever before taken such a risk. Franklin Roosevelt had made sure to distance himself from Eleanor's views on such issues as women's rights and racism, disassociating himself from her more unpopular causes and basking in her glory only when the public approved. The fact that the Roosevelts had been estranged while in the White House, and that Eleanor, employed by Franklin as an emissary and information gatherer, was never invited to participate in policy decisions, meant that Roosevelt and his administration were quite well sheltered against attacks on the first lady. Clinton would have no such security. By naming Hillary to such a central role in his administration, he permanently tied his political fate to her success or failure. This, as the disastrous 1994 congressional elections proved, would turn out to be a major mistake.

Reforming the nation's health care system was just about the most ambitious project that Hillary could have been assigned. In 1993 health care accounted for seven percent of the U.S. gross domestic product. Health care prices, allowed to flourish in an unregulated free market environment, were rising four times faster than the average salary. The cost of immunizing children alone had increased over 1,250 percent in the public sector between 1981 and 1991, and the U.S. record on childhood immunizations was the third worst in the Western Hemisphere, followed only by Bolivia and Haiti.

As many as 36.6 million Americans had no health insurance at all. Many others had partial, often inadequate insurance packages which cost them thousands of dollars annually. People who became sick were denied coverage if their insurers could prove their illness were attributable to a "preexisting condition." A job loss or even a job change meant a loss of health insurance for the employee's entire family. Americans were losing their insurance at a rate of a hundred thousand people per month.

Hillary traveled up and down the Eastern Seaboard, visiting schools and hospitals and factories, and speaking to doctors, nurses, hospital administrators, clinic operators, ministers, insurance companies, union leaders, and small business owners. People told her of losing their health coverage after becoming ill, and then of being saddled with astronomical bills. Hard-hit heads of families said they had considered quitting work and applying for welfare as a way to receive Medicaid, state-supported health care for the nation's poorest.

In Tampa, Florida, she heard the story of a union carpenter who had been forced to go without health insurance rather than take a cut in salary. A forty-six-year-old cancer victim told of the prospect of facing a new round of extensive chemotherapy treatment without health insurance. A lawyer spoke on behalf of a thirty-one-year-old mother of three who had been paralyzed in an automobile accident and left with medical costs that reached a million dollars a year. In New Orleans a steel worker told Hillary of taking his wife to the hospital for eye surgery and being billed for more than his annual salary.

Health care reform was an issue that affected everyone, and that touched upon the most basic of American political beliefs. Talk of reform through a single-payer nationalized network like France's or Canada's sparked cries of socialism. Proposals for price controls raised complaints of big-government interference. The medical and insurance industries, two of the most powerful lobbying forces in Washington, inveighed against government regulation as though the whole American way of life were at risk.

And in a sense it was: the health care reformers were daring to challenge America's survival-of-the-fittest mentality. They were trying to sell the country on the idea of health care as an inalienable right.

The problem was, the Clinton administration didn't have the courage to follow through on its convictions. It tried to stake out a middle ground between the goals of idealists like Hillary Rodham Clinton and the political realities being put forward by the President's Wall Street–oriented economic advisers. Because that middle ground was a fiction, a never-never land that no one believed truly existed, that compromise position had all the staying power of quicksand.

The Clinton administration's stated goal was to guarantee to all Americans a legally enforceable right to a standard package of health care benefits. It said it would try to control the skyrocketing costs of medical care by creating a more competitive marketplace through a scheme called "managed competition," in which networks of doctors, hospitals, and insurance companies would operate within the framework of a national budget for all health care spending. This approach, which drew the strong support of the country's major insurance companies, would seek to control costs without excessive government regulation or restrictions on free market competition. In other words, it was relatively industry-friendly and unchallenging to the interests of doctors, insurers, and hospitals.

Nevertheless, there was considerable grumbling on the part of these special-interest groups, doctors in particular. From the beginning, the makeup and ac-

tivities of the health care task force had been cloaked
in secrecy. The committee held all its informal meetings in private, hoping not to be waylaid by public
pressures and outside influences, and the White
House refused to release the names of the people
involved in the process until late March, when the
publication of a partially incorrect list in the *Wall
Street Journal* forced the administration's hand. After
the American Medical Association, one of the richest
and most powerful lobbying forces in the country, in
March requested a bigger role in the reform process
and was rebuffed, the campaign to force the opening
of Hillary's committee meetings heated up. Two
groups of doctors and health-policy advocates, with
the gleeful support of many Republicans, filed a lawsuit, invoking a 1972 law that requires federal advisory committees to conduct their business in open
meetings, but makes an exception for committees that
are composed wholly of full-time officers or employees of the federal government. The plaintiffs said that
Hillary's group did not qualify for exemption because she held no job in the government; the administration countered that she was "the functional
equivalent" of a government employee. In the end,
the judge deciding the case, a Reagan appointee, was
surprisingly generous to the Clinton administration.
He ruled that the committee had to make all sessions
where it collected facts and information open to the
public but said it could meet in private when formu-
lating its recommendations to the President.

Though the judge's ruling was a relative triumph,
the lawsuit nonetheless drove home the fact that the
honeymoon period was over for Hillary Rodham

Clinton. The power, both real and symbolic, that she'd been given by the White House was starting to make some people nervous. Americans didn't like the idea of unelected officials making policy. And the Clintons had overlooked one unfortunate truth that had emerged in new poll data about Hillary. This was that half of the people who had told pollsters they viewed Hillary as a positive role model had also warned that they didn't think she should play a role in major decisions. Now she was doing just that— and the public was growing antsy.

People were growing suspicious too about the ideological influence Hillary seemed to be exerting over the President. Clinton had been elected as a conservative Democrat—the closest thing to a Republican that the Democratic party could produce. He was a churchgoing Southern Baptist, personally ambivalent on abortion rights, warm to the death penalty, hot on free enterprise and "individual responsibility." The first measures taken by his government—to protect abortion clinics, offer women paid maternity leave, and challenge armed forces rules barring gays and lesbians, looked, to both his opponents and some supporters, like unadulterated old-fashioned leftism. Hard-core, big-government, bleeding heart Hillaryism. Her plans for more government control of health care just fed the fire.

As her role in advising Clinton on cabinet appointments continued, and word leaked out that she was pushing for bringing greater gender and racial diversity to the cabinet, critics began calling her a "quota queen." She was instrumental in bringing Donna Shalala, chancellor of the University of Wisconsin and a friend from the Children's Defense Fund, to the position of secretary of health and human services. She saw that women were named to the posts of chief domestic adviser and energy secretary. She and her friend Susan Thomases, Clinton's former campaign scheduler who had stayed on for the transition, ran the search for an attorney general. Critics soon said they were running a "diversity jihad"— screening out highly eligible white men in favor of less qualified women. Thomases, a New York corporate lawyer with a shock of gray hair and an abrasive manner, seemed to many worried observers like Hillary Clinton's evil twin, the ugly feminist within.

With Thomases suspiciously omnipresent, Hillary's old friend Bernard Nussbaum named White House counsel, her Wellesley pal Eldee Acheson nominated for a senior policy-making job at the Justice Department, and friend Margaret Richardson named director of the Internal Revenue Service, it was all too easy to accuse the President's wife of cronyism. Especially once her old Rose Law Firm partners Vincent Foster, Webster Hubbell, and William Kennedy landed jobs in the White House counsel's office. And particularly since Hillary's friends (or FOHs—Friends of Hillary—as they were called) weren't, in some ways, quite ready for prime time. Hubbell, Foster, and Kennedy were members of an all-white golf club. This was normal enough in Little Rock; it was unacceptable in Washington. Acheson also belonged to a country club that had no black members, and she hadn't paid her Social Security charges on a housekeeper until shortly before she was nominated.

Hillary had virtually unseated Vice President Al

Gore. The White House denied it—but when an official at the cabinet swearing-in ceremony in late January had to correct himself when he inadvertently started to announce Hillary's title as "Vice—" the impression stuck. By all accounts, Hillary was the unofficial number two in the government. Candidates for high office had to meet not just with the President and his advisers but alone with the First Lady as well. Sometimes they spent more time with her than him; sometimes they never met him at all. Some felt that their candidacies had been derailed permanently by a bad interview with Hillary. When the secretary of education and his deputy went to the White House to review proposed education legislation, they met not with the President but with the First Lady. An administration official was prompted to say, "Of course, she's in the loop; she *is* the loop."

Hillary's presence, critics said, bogged the administration down considerably, worsening the time-wasting effects of its already considerable disorganization. White House staff members said they were afraid of her. She was a redoubtable presence at the policy meetings she attended every day: sharp and cutting, impatient and often caustic. Clinton might have a hot temper, but he always forgave, and you could, at the right moment, bring him bad news. Hillary had a chillingly ferocious tongue. If you fell on her bad side, you never had any hope of setting things right ever again.

Bill Clinton had insisted that his administration's attempt to foster gender and racial diversity be carried out in the spirit of real egalitarianism and not as a feel-good exercise in "bean-counting," as he put it. But when it floundered, it was easy for critics to call the White House's efforts to foster diversity a poorly conceived quota system—a superficial and at times even shoddy attempt at packaging the administration in political correctness.

The overlong and bungling search for an attorney general was a case in point. The job was generally understood to have been set aside for a woman. And, everyone felt, for a woman more or less from Hillary Clinton and Susan Thomases's social and intellectual world. The first two candidates were perfectly sympatico: corporate lawyer Zoë Baird, a $500,000-a-year overachiever from Connecticut, and New York judge Kimba Wood. There was just one problem: both women had broken the law, employing illegal aliens as domestic help. "Nannygate," as the ensuing embarrassment was dubbed, turned into a class-based scandal, as low wage–earning working women complained that these top-ranking women believed themselves above the law. In the end, and after months of painful wrangling, the matter was resolved when a woman with no child-care entanglements in her past was named to Robert Kennedy's former post: unmarried state attorney Janet Reno of Dade County, Florida.

The clumsy identity politics at work in the selection of an attorney general spilled over into an even worse fiasco once it came time to fill lower-level posts in the Justice Department. For the assistant attorney general for civil rights slot, both Clintons had effusive praise for their candidate, civil rights lawyer Lani Guinier. Guinier had the perfect profile: she was progressive, black, part Jewish, and female. And she happened to be an old friend of Bill and Hillary's from Yale Law School. But another side of Guinier surfaced during the scrutiny that followed the announcement of her candidacy.

It turned out that her dedication to seeing civil rights theory put into action went beyond simple notions of "one man-one vote" electoral politics, which Guinier called "simple-minded notions of majority rule." Minority voters, she believed, should have the right to exert special veto powers to contradict the will of the majority. And their voting power should be supplemented by using forms of proportional representation to give them "super-majorities." In one of her most controversial articles, Guinier questioned whether some elected black leaders were "authentic representatives of the black community" and said that blacks elected by a predominantly white voter pool might not serve the interests of their ethnic community. She intimated that Virginia Governor L. Douglas Wilder was this kind of public servant-cum-Uncle Tom.

To many critics this looked like American leftism at its worst, seeped in the poisonous political correctness that raged unchecked in the early 1990s. Guinier's theories seemed to them to objectify citizens by their ethnicity. Guinier's supporters objected that this was precisely the opposite of what Guinier was all about, and indeed her verbal statements and past political stands seemed to prove them right. Still, the written word was the written word—and when Clinton read Guinier's (as he hadn't prior to her nomination), he got cold feet. Soon even his political supporters on Capitol Hill were letting him know that they weren't willing to go to bat to defend Guinier. "The word was coming back from the Senate floor: 'I'm going to vote for the lesbian but not the black radical,' " a legislative aide confided to political reporter Elizabeth Drew, whose 1994 book, *On the Edge*, chronicled the first eighteen months of the Clinton administration.

As far as identity politics were concerned, what went around came around—rebounding usually in more venomous form. The fact that Bill Clinton hadn't even read Guinier's writings before her nomination made the whole nominating process look like a sham. Hillary looked like she was more interested in finding jobs for her friends than in promoting serious and politically viable candidates. "Her attitude was typical of the baby boomers," a witness to the selection process told Hillary Clinton biographer David Brock. " 'I'm going to do it my way, and if the world doesn't like it, fuck the world.' "

As such embarrassments accrued, the Clintons' aides—the hot young things who had only recently been photographed in evening wear by the magazine *Vanity Fair*, whose amorous exploits and Diet Coke consumption were earning them fame among teenyboppers everywhere—were starting to look lazily ignorant. Their inexperience and cocky arrogance had already turned off the Washington press corps. Their casual dress and pizza habits had horrified the permanent staff of stewards and secretaries who served in the White House from administration to administration. Many of these staffers had grown loyal to the spiffed-up Reagans and patrician Bushes during their collective twelve-year tenure. They were less than fond of the young women in casual pants who worked in the cluster of offices that had come to be called "Hillaryland." Hillary herself, working off-hours in the West Wing, uncoiffed and without makeup, offended them. She used her favorite Little Rock stylist to redo a number of White House rooms, and her penchant for bright colors and contrasting plaids struck the staid social secretaries as tacky. As a couple the Clintons seemed utterly incomprehensible. And they weren't doing much to enhance their image. In fact, they were indirectly making it worse.

In the months since the election, they had managed to alienate most of the otherwise sympathetically inclined members of the Washington press corps. Hillary's distrust of the press, her insistence upon maintaining a "zone of privacy" for her family, had begun during the Clintons' darkest days in Arkansas. It had worsened during the 1992 campaign, hardening, once the Clintons took office, into something that bordered on paranoia. This was a bad call politically. Because the new Clinton White House was—and would remain—so very tightlipped as far as the Clintons' private life was concerned, even mainstream journalists ultimately felt constrained to run with lurid stories planted by the Clintons' enemies.

The amateur-hour aspect of the early Clinton White House didn't help. George Stephanopoulos, Clinton's baby-faced first communications chief, became famous for his rudeness to would-be interviewers. Reporters complained of being kept waiting for hours, only to be received by Stephanopolous with his feet on his desk, and to be dismissed summarily when the communications whiz's attention span fiz-

zled out. Young and lively press secretary Dee Dee
Myers was more accommodating, but always seemed
to be out of the loop. At Hillary's urging, the passage
linking the White House press room to the communications office was for a time sealed shut. Symboli-
cally, the move was a final slap in the face to the
press corps.

The ultimate result was that the Clintons alienated
the core group of Washington insiders best positioned to help them. After all, like the Clintons, most
high-level Washington journalists were baby boomers. Over 85 percent had voted Clinton into office.
The women identified directly with Hillary. They
wanted to see her succeed. But in the name of protecting their privacy, the Clintons created an information vacuum—and their enemies were all too ready
to fill in the blanks. All the journalists wanted was a
little access, a few benignly pithy column inches.
When they didn't get it, they ran with what they
could.

Stories of unsavory behavior by the Clinton couple
started leaking out of the White House almost immediately, all of them denied by the White House. The
first couple slept in separate bedrooms, it was whispered, and their conversations degenerated into
screaming fights. A Secret Service agent even alleged
that Hillary had once thrown a lamp at Bill during
an argument. She was so work obsessed that, a story
soon making the rounds in Washington alleged,
when Chelsea needed permission at school to get as-
pirin, she told her school nurse to "Call my dad, my
mom's too busy." Fearing hostile spies, the Clintons
managed to remove the Secret Service detail outside

their living quarters. But the public relations problems continued.

A hungry press turned relatively minor public relations incidents into fiascoes. There was the time that *Air Force One* tied up traffic for over an hour at the Los Angeles airport while the President sat inside getting his hair cut by Christophe of Beverly Hills. That $200 haircut—reportedly the first truly costly coiffure of the President's life—occupied the radio call-in shows for days. It grew worse when a story floated that Hillary and Chelsea were tagging on with a presidential flight to New York just for haircuts and to attend the ballet. There was also plenty of snickering about the overnight visits from celebrities—Barbra Streisand and Hillary's friend Mary Steenburgen and the singer Judy Collins. The Clintons were starstruck in the early days. They loved being able to meet anyone they wanted, whenever they wanted—and they missed being able to leave the White House to socialize. So they overdid the invitations to glitsy guests—all the while neglecting to hold an official state dinner until they'd been at the White House for a full eighteen months. Georgetown society was furious. And out in the heartland the "people" felt betrayed.

It was "Travelgate" that gave the press its first chance to nail the Clintons, and Hillary Clinton in particular. It was a story that never should have been—a pure creation of the cronyism and provincialism that the Clintons had brought with them from Arkansas melded with the aura of suspicion and fear that had come to settle around Hillary Clinton. Simply put, it went like this: four months after Clinton took office, seven long-term White House travel office employees were summarily fired on charges of financial mismanagement and poor accounting procedures. After the firings an FBI investigation was hastily mounted to provide justification. An independent audit did find financial misconduct—but that almost seemed beside the point once the news broke that the new travel team was headed by a cousin of Bill Clinton's and that the new travel agency they would work with was run by a former business associate of Hillary's. The press, which had long enjoyed the favors of the old travel employees, went wild. When a memo later emerged placing the blame for the firings upon Hillary, her critics had a field day.

But there was worse. On July 20, 1993, as the Travelgate scandal brewed, Vince Foster's body was found in nearby Fort Marcy Park. Foster was found with an antique Colt .38 revolver in his hand. He'd died of a single bullet wound to the head.

"No one can ever know why this happened . . . what happened was a mystery about something inside him," a devastated Bill Clinton said the next morning to the White House staff. Few people stopped to think about the fact that Clinton had just lost one of his closest childhood friends. The word *mystery* was what stuck in their minds. And the image of foul play endured tenaciously even as inquiry after inquiry concluded that Foster had, in a moment of overwhelming despondency, taken his own life.

It turned out that he'd recently started taking antidepressants. The names of two Washington psychiatrists were in his pocket when he died. It seemed that the cruel pressures of Washington had proven too much for him. He'd felt battered by a stream of negative press questioning his actions as the Clintons' private counselor and casting aspersions on the qualifications of the whole Rose Law Firm contingent. The reaction to Travelgate in particular had pushed him over the edge. Foster was mortified that his old friend William Kennedy had been reprimanded in connection with it. He felt that he should have been better able to protect his friends and colleagues and, at best, to have kept the scandal from happening. He was a man who valued his reputation and integrity beyond all else—as straight-laced a character as Bill Clinton was slick. "Before we came here, we thought of ourselves as good people," he told *Time* magazine's Margaret Carlson shortly before he died. "I made mistakes from ignorance, inexperience, and overwork," he wrote in what appeared to be a suicide note, found nearly a week after his death in twenty-seven torn pieces in the bottom of his briefcase. "I did not knowingly violate any law or standard of conduct . . ." he wrote. "The public will never believe the innocence of the Clintons and their loyal staff. . . . I was not meant for the job or the spotlight of public life in Washington. Here ruining people is considered sport."

Despite the overwhelming evidence, Clinton critics on the right refused to accept Foster's death as a simple suicide. Some said that he had been killed and his body moved and his suicide staged—perhaps by none other than Hillary Clinton. Others said he had killed himself because of Hillary—either in desperation at not having been her lover or in terror that a longtime affair was about to be revealed. No one who had known the Fosters and Clintons in Arkansas ever gave much credence to the affair theory. Everyone knew that Vince and Hillary had been very close friends. They lunched together. They worked late nights together. They confided in each other. But as journalist James B. Stewart revealed years later in *Blood Sport: The President and His Adversaries*, the warm friendship between Foster and Hillary had chilled in the White House. He'd taken to referring to her in his notes as "the client." And she allegedly had come to treat him like someone whose time she owned.

Hillary soldiered on. In the fall of 1993 she launched the administration's health care reform plan. She presented Congress with a bill that was 1,342 pages long—a distillation of the thirty three-ring binders full of findings that the health care task force had assembled. The plan pledged universal coverage by 1998 and would have made insurers unable to deny benefits to patients with "preexisting conditions." In addition, it would have made it illegal to charge higher benefits to people who were ill or revoke benefits if a person changed jobs or got sick.

Those were its strong points. Unfortunately, the plan had many weak points as well. For one, because it promised a generous package of benefits, it was likely to cost consumers more than their current policies. For another, it was virtually incomprehensible. Polls had shown that people wanted radical reform of the health care system overall but didn't want any change in their own health care. They wanted security for the middle class, and didn't particularly want to hear about providing coverage for the poor. So Hillary's plan, which started out as a revolutionary reform effort, ended up stressing how much things would stay the same. It proposed keeping down costs by organizing individuals and companies into health care "alliances" run by the states. These alliances, which would be overseen by a federal agency, would force insurance companies to compete for their business and, in the process, pressure them to keep premium costs down. There would be price controls on some prescription drugs and quotas set to encourage medical schools to churn out more generalists and fewer specialists and to send them to work in poor and undeserved areas of the country. Employers would be required to cover 80 percent of the cost of their employees' premiums, and the government would pay for the poor and the unemployed and subsidize the cost of health insurance for the working poor and small businesses.

The plan pleased no one. The left critiqued it as pro-industry and argued that too much power was being handed over to health maintenance organizations, which were then notorious for skimping on quality in the interest of cutting costs. Conservatives attacked the plan as an example of big, bloated government. Critics on all sides of the political spectrum pointed out that because the plan encouraged people to use HMOs and penalized them if they didn't, it effectively curtailed their free choice of doctors.

In the end, it was just too complicated—too academic. One influential congressman likened it to Star Wars. Other critics pointed out that the plan's numbers were based on guesswork: estimates of the "cost of waste" within the system, for example, were little more than intellectual exercises.

The country was overwhelmed by the complexity of the health care bill. And it had no real champion. Hillary's erstwhile allies in Congress had abandoned her when she refused early on to work with moderate Democrats and Republicans on a less ambitious but more politically plausible reform effort.

Hillary and her allies did the best they could to sell the health plan to the public. But their opponents' arguments were so much simpler and commonsensical than the plan that they won the war of words without contest. "The health care reform bill was not meant to be accepted as written," says a member of Hillary's staff. "It was meant to be the beginning of a legislative process." But by now, it seemed, there was no one willing to carry this process forward. The final blow came when the Health Insurance Association of America launched a series of television ads showing a couple discussing the health plan over breakfast. The couple, "Harry and Louise," shook their heads over the plan's complexity, worried aloud about Big Government, and prayed for the status quo. Soon the whole country was following their lead.

Before long the press had a much juicier Clinton story to cover than health care. It broke over Christmas vacation—a Christmas marked by the absence of Hugh Rodham, who had died the previous spring. The Clintons were holed up in the White House with Chelsea, both mothers-in-law and, perhaps most unfortunately, each other. The story wasn't the kind that anyone would have wanted to discuss over

Christmas dinner. Four Arkansas state troopers who had previously worked on the Clintons' private security detail had come forward to speak to the *American Spectator* and *Los Angeles Times*. They had provided a detailed account of debauchery and deceit in the Arkansas governor's mansion. Bill Clinton was portrayed as a man of devouring sexual appetites (except where his wife was concerned), endless energy for making new conquests, and nonexistent scruples. He was accused of having used the state troopers to shuttle him back and forth to secret liaisons, to procure women for him, and to cover for him with Hillary. He was supposed to have smuggled women in and out of the governor's mansion while Hillary slept. Hillary, for her part, was painted as a foul-mouthed harpy who tolerated her husband's sexual indiscretions because she believed he'd lead her to the White House. The troopers insisted she'd been having a very open affair with Vince Foster.

None of the stories were corroborated. The troopers were easy to discredit—they were out for a lucrative book deal and being represented by Cliff Jackson, a Little Rock lawyer and longtime Clinton enemy. Years later, *American Spectator* journalist David Brock cast doubt upon his own story. Even at the time it seemed too salacious to be true. The depictions of Hillary in particular sounded like the overheated fantasies of a misogynous fourteen-year-old boy.

But as the years passed and more stories about Bill Clinton's philandering emerged, some of the details of the early "Troopergate" smut began to ring eerily true. "[Clinton] told me that he had researched the subject in the Bible and oral sex isn't considered adultery," trooper Larry Patterson told Brock in 1993. A bizarre bit of rationalization and perhaps false— but all too similar to the reasoning Clinton would allegedly use four years later with Monica Lewinsky. That was always Clinton's problem: amid the mass of outrageous stories that swirled around him, something always rang true. You could just about always count on him to have tripped up just enough to make anything seem plausible.

Most respectable newspapers wouldn't run the trooper allegations at any length. To compensate, they ran with another story, and they made it sound as juicy as possible. It concerned some papers that had been moved from Vince Foster's office after his suicide.

Apparently, after Foster's body was found, Justice Department investigators had showed up at the White House and been barred by counsel Bernard Nussbaum from inspecting files in Foster's office. Later a Clinton aide took the family's papers up to the White House residence. One of the files removed from Foster's office, it was rumored, was marked "Whitewater." All winter the *Wall Street Journal* led the pack of the national press in screaming cover-up. Nussbaum was replaced—the second Friend of Hillary eliminated from the White House in a year. After a great deal of internal debate, which pitted a reticent Hillary against many of her own friends and the president's closest advisers, the White House called for a special prosecutor to look into the Whitewater affair. Coming clean, the Clintons advisers assured them, would clear their names for good.

It was all too much for Hillary Rodham Clinton. Her first twelve months in the White House had been the worst year of her life. Vince Foster was dead. Her father was dead—victim of a stroke that had sent Hillary back to Little Rock to sit by his bedside for weeks, while a rapacious press sat in wait outside the hospital doors. Health care reform was dead. Her reputation lay in tatters. Whitewater was becoming an obsession in the press. In October it was reported that the Resolution Trust Corporation, which acquired and disposed of the assets of failed savings and loans, had asked the Justice Department to conduct a criminal investigation of Madison Guaranty, the failed savings and loan run by the Clintons' former business partner, James McDougal. The referral included questions about whether Madison funds had been used to pay off a Clinton campaign debt from the 1984 gubernatorial race. There were also, the newspapers said, questions raised about Whitewater.

A majority of Americans now said they believed that Hillary was lying about Whitewater and her work for Madison Guaranty. *New York Times* columnist William Safire called the First Lady a "congenital liar."

The combination of professional failure and personal scandal was a shocking blow to a woman whose whole self-image, her entire life, had been based upon a sense of integrity. Hillary knew how Vince Foster, another highly principled, some might say rigid, person, must have felt. She wished she could have protected him better. She knew she hadn't done anything to cause Foster's death, but could she have done something to save his life? The question tortured her. And she couldn't shake her sense of responsibility for having brought him to the snake pit of Washington in the first place.

She sobbed for days after Foster committed suicide. "Remind me," she asked an aide as scandal brewed after Foster's death, "have I ever done anything right in my life?"

Her conviction that a right-wing conspiracy, aided by a complicitous press, was gunning to bring the Clintons down was quickly turning into an obsession. But how could she strike back? Battle-weary, Hillary retreated into her East Wing offices. Her faithful aides built a great wall of silence around her. She stayed away from the West Wing and out of the public eye. She watched as a Republican majority led by Newt Gingrich swept into Congress, toting a "Contract with America" that aimed, in large measure, to dismantle the covenant that Hillary believed linked government and governed together. She shut her ears to media commentary that blamed the Republican victory on her own botched attempts to reform health care. ("My husband and I never watch the news. We consider it part of our mental health routine," she joked.) And, thinking hard, regrouping, retooling, she nursed her wounds.

It was Hillary's time in the desert, and, like Bill Clinton in 1980, she took her personal failures very much to heart. She embarked upon a period of deep reflection, of serious self-questioning. What a pity, she'd say to friends, that the position of First Lady didn't come with a job description. What was she supposed to do? Who was she supposed to be? She had assumed that the people of America had known what they were getting into when they'd signed on for the Clinton & Clinton two-for-one ticket in 1992. But somehow they hadn't. And they didn't understand what Hillary in particular was all about. They thought she was power-mad at best, a lying schemer at worst. They believed the stories drummed up by her husband's political enemies. They seemed not to take anything she said at face value.

For this, to a large extent, Hillary blamed the media. But she also, as time passed, came to understand that she had in part to blame herself. She had taken on too much with health care reform. She had acted too much like a government official. She didn't have the mandate for that—and perhaps, it had to be admitted, she didn't really have the skills. She was a talented advocate, with decades of experience behind her. She wasn't a trained politician. Maybe, she came to think, public opinion was actually on target. Maybe her place wasn't in the halls of Congress. Maybe the best place for her to get her message across wasn't in the Beltway. Maybe the best way to use her talents and her position was to go to the people directly. To transmit their concerns to the President and his to them—and hers too, along the way. After all, she was the First Lady; when she spoke, people listened. She had never really been comfortable bearing the mantle of the First Lady title before. Now perhaps it was time to stop trying to be all the things she was *not* and take advantage instead of being who she *was*. Not as an ego trip, not to gain personal power, but to *get things done.* "Hillary never wanted to be a symbol as such," says a close associate. "But with time, she learned the kind of symbolic efficacy that comes with the position." And once she figured it out, she had the job all sewn up.

She would, like her heroine Eleanor Roosevelt, be the president's eyes and ears. And she would give a new twist to the meaning of "First Lady"; she'd become the country's premier advocate for women. It was a good way to come back to her roots, to come back to herself. And it was a good way to fight the Republican revolution.

Hillary went on the road. She met children in foster homes and awaiting placement by adoption agencies, and advocated legislation to make adoption easier, quicker, and freer from prejudice. She urged Congress to allocate funds for programs to help adolescents "aging out" of foster care learn to make it on their own. Horrified by speaker Newt Gingrich's remarks in favor of placing children from troubled homes in orphanages, she struck back, piously: "I recently heard a sermon in which the minister related a story in Leviticus about the ancient Israelites who annually placed all of their miseries and sins on the head of a goat. And then sent the goat off into the wilderness. And when the goat reached the wilderness, the tribe felt cleansed of all problems, all evils, all sins. That, unfortunately, is an apt parable for what is happening in America today. In today's society, the scapegoat is poor children and their parents." Her remarks were addressed to guests at a dinner for the Legal Aid Society, a grantee of the Legal Services Corporation, which was now once again under attack by the Republicans. Her comments were well received.

Hillary picked up steam and took her message abroad. She traveled to Denmark and admired the workings of its child-care system. In Copenhagen she announced a new ten-year, $100 million girls and women's education initiative that she had actively developed with the organization U.S. AID. "Where women prosper, countries prosper," she declared. She traveled to India, the first country to benefit from the new grants, and delivered a speech devoted to the need for government investment in girls and women. She read from a poem that had been handed to her not long before, written by an Indian teenage girl. It began: "Too many women in too many countries speak the same language—of silence."

She preached self-sufficiency and self-respect for the world's women. She advocated women's self-reliance and economic independence. She became the administration's most outspoken advocate of micro credit. She loved to tell of a visit to Bangladesh, where she'd met with the female beneficiaries of $15 and $25 loans from the Grameen Bank. She was told that the community she planned to visit was a village of Hindu untouchables and that no one ever went there. When she persisted in going, a nearby village of Muslims asked that she visit there too. Time didn't permit; so, for the first time ever, the Muslim women came to the Hindu village. They sat together on benches waiting for the American First Lady. "Then as they talked, I could not tell any difference in their aspirations or their hopes for themselves and their families," Hillary later reported to officials of the World Bank in Washington. "And as I talked with them individually about what they had spent their loans for, I heard the same stories from Hindus and Muslims alike: buying a milk cow, buying a second milk cow, buying a rickshaw for a husband to make a living. . . . All that I heard reinforced my belief that providing this kind of opportunity was not only a bridge to economic prosperity, but at least a hoped-for bridge across many other divisions that keep us apart from one another."

Hillary's speeches were now much more than the dutiful reporting of a goodwill ambassador. They were starting to form the core of a political philosophy. "Women's rights cannot be separated from human rights," she said in a speech to the Women's Foundation of Colorado in July 1995. "Women do most of the work in the world. They have the responsibility for raising our children in the world. They are the backbone of the vast majority of families and communities." She took her philosophy with her in September 1995 to the United Nations World Conference on Women in Beijing, a historic meeting that aimed to produce an agenda for action by governments around the world on improving women's health, education, economic equality, and political power. And there, against the backdrop of a storm of criticism at home and with punishing rains coming down outside, she gave her politics their most ardent and articulate expression. "If there is one message that echoes forth from this conference, it is that human rights are women's rights—and women's rights are human rights," she declared.

Without naming names, she lobbed bomb after bomb at the human rights record of her host nation. "Let me be clear," she said. "Freedom means the right of people to assemble, organize, and debate openly. It means respecting the views of those who may disagree with the views of their governments. It means not taking citizens away from their loved ones and jailing them, mistreating them, or denying them their freedom or dignity because of the peaceful expression of their ideas and opinions."

She blasted the authorities on behalf of the nongovernmental organizations that the Chinese government had exiled to a separate forum in Huairou, thirty-five miles away from the U.N. conference in Beijing: "Let us not forget that among those rights are the right to speak freely—and the right to be heard. . . . For too long the history of women has been a history of silence. Even today there are those who are trying to silence our words." She attacked the Chinese one-child policy: "It is a violation of *human* rights when women are denied the right to plan their own families, and that includes being forced to have abortions or being sterilized against their will." She attacked discriminatory cultural practices that went unpunished by the Chinese authorities: "It is a violation of *human* rights when babies are denied food, or drowned, or suffocated or their spines broken, simply because they are born girls."

Many in Washington had urged Hillary Clinton not to attend the Beijing conference. Some of China's most ardent critics had argued that her attendance would undercut efforts to condemn the country's atrocious record of human rights abuse. They urged Hillary not to dignify the country with her presence. Diplomats warned that one false step could expose a fatal fault in the already shaky ground of Chinese-American relations. But after the conference media commentators hailed Hillary's speech as the most forceful human rights declaration ever made by a prominent American on Chinese soil. The *New York Times* called it "her finest moment in public life." A *Times* editorial writer said: "Mrs. Clinton's unapologetic affirmation of American values is a departure from the bland and euphemistic rhetoric of other recent United States diplomatic visitors to Beijing. The Clinton Administration should follow her good example."

Hillary's handlers were thrilled. The First Lady was back.

Until the other shoe dropped.

Chapter 7

⟨⟨⟩⟩

"Fake It Till You Make It"

Hillary's entry into the 1996 campaign year was carefully staged. It was timed to coincide with the launch of her long-awaited book, *It Takes a Village: And Other Lessons Children Teach Us*. *It Takes a Village* was a homey meditation on childrearing and national values. It argued, in sum, that parental efforts to educate and nurture children could only go so far: extended family members, good friends, teachers, clergymen, and community leaders needed to play a role too. In communities where these people were lacking, and when parental resources were insufficient, the government could and should step in to fill the gap.

It was almost a political position paper: a carefully reasoned application of the Clintonite mix of big-government leftism and pull-yourself-up-by-your-bootstraps traditionalism. Hillary wrote:

> How well we care for our own and other people's children isn't only a question of morality; our self-interest is at stake too. No family is immune to the influences of the larger society. No matter what my husband and I do to protect and prepare Chelsea,

her future will be affected by how other children are being raised. I don't want her to grow up in an America sharply divided by income, race or religion. I'd like to minimize the odds of her suffering at the hands of someone who didn't have enough love or discipline, opportunity or responsibility, as a child. I want her to believe, as her father and I did, that the American Dream is within reach of anyone willing to work hard and take responsibility. I want her to live in an America that is still strong and promising to its own citizens and lives up to its image throughout the world as a land of hope and opportunity.

Despite its speechifying tone, *It Takes a Village* was more than a campaign tract. It seemed to be, for Hillary Rodham Clinton, a stab at autobiography: the closest thing to self-revelation that this highly private and deeply wounded woman was willing to deliver to the American public.

It was both a cagey and utterly self-revealing way of avoiding self-revelation. Hillary's meditations on her life were entirely mediated by her thoughts about social policy. The two were inextricably melded. On first reading, this might seem like little more than a way for Hillary to hide her true face. That is to say: the face of a woman who, over the years, has done everything in her power to make her politics and her personal life one and the same. Her marriage has been a vehicle for her political beliefs. Her sense of her self, and the value she gives her life, have been based upon putting those beliefs into action. Trying to scratch the surface of Hillary to get deeper—to a purely personal "true" core of feeling—is probably an exercise in futility. Hillary Rodham Clinton the woman *is* Hillary Rodham Clinton the First Lady. What you see is what you get.

And so, in her book, Hillary called for dress codes in schools, family dinners, mandatory work for welfare recipients, and sexual abstinence until age twenty-one. And so, in her book, she discussed her marriage: "My strong feelings about divorce and its effects on children have caused me to bite my tongue more than a few times during my own marriage and to think instead about what I could do to be a better wife and partner." She made passing references to her husband's personal problems: "Bill had grown up in circumstances that were less than ideal." She illustrated her terror of divorce with the example of her own mother, the one child of divorce she'd ever known growing up, who at age eight was sent alone by train from Chicago to Los Angeles with her three-year-old sister to live with her grandparents. She wrapped up with a statement from a think tank: "The Carnegie Corporation's president describes the ideal landscape in which to plant a child: an 'intact, cohesive, nuclear family dependable under stress.' " And she topped it off with a policy prescription: divorce laws should be tightened for married couples with children.

This was far less revealing than the kind of statements Hillary Clinton had issued in 1992 when asked about whether she had ever thought of divorcing Bill Clinton. "Bill and I have always loved each other," she told *Glamour* then. "No marriage is perfect, but just because it isn't perfect doesn't mean the only solution is to walk off and leave it. A marriage is always growing and changing. We couldn't say, 'Well, this isn't ideal,' and get a divorce."

Hillary's words weren't contradictory either. The shut-down language of *It Takes a Village*, the willful circumspection, simply signaled that from 1992 to 1996 Hillary Rodham Clinton's communication style had profoundly changed. She was no longer interested in being personally known and understood by the public. Her trust—what little there ever was—had been too profoundly betrayed.

Because she lightly teases her husband and is gracefully self-deprecating in the book (she chastises Americans for overeating and underexercising and then casts a rueful eye at her own hips and thighs), and because she acknowledges that, for all her preaching, her own practice of family life hasn't been perfect, Hillary emerges from *It Takes a Village* immensely likable. And that was the whole point. *It Takes a Village*, her allies said as the book launch began, would finally allow Hillary to introduce herself to the country in her own words—to break through the stereotypes binding her to images of career witch and harridan and show instead who she really was: a devoted wife and mother whose first priority was caring for the nation's children. "I am a wife and mother and daughter," she said on the eve of the book's publication. "I am a friend. I am a Christian." The country would forget Hillary the schemer, the power monger, the co-president. They would discover Hillary the "soccer mom"—a social conservative committed to family values.

That, at least, was the way things were supposed

to happen. Fate would deal Hillary a very different hand.

One day in January 1996, as Hillary was polishing the talking points for her newly articulated vision of clean living and family values, White House aide Carolyn Huber decided to clean out her office. Huber was an old family friend of the Clintons'. She'd been the office manager at the Rose Law Firm. Chelsea was said to regard her as a third grandmother.

Under a table Huber came upon a box of "knick-knacks"—odd books and gifts that she'd quickly thrown together and carted out of a storage area on the third floor of the White House residence. She stopped short when she reached a pile of computer printouts. At first sight she recognized them as Rose Law Firm billing records. And not just that—billing records that detailed Hillary Rodham Clinton's legal work for the Madison Guaranty savings and loan.

"I was surprised," Huber later told Senate investigators when they called her before them to testify about her strange find. "I just sat down for a few minutes and thought."

The computer printouts were covered in Vince Foster's handwriting. Foster, everyone knew, had been working on Whitewater issues for the Clintons just before he died. (A box of records marked *Whitewater* had reportedly been moved from his office just after his death.) Investigators had been issuing subpoenas for precisely these billing records for two years. How—and when—had they ended up in a room off Hillary's residential office accessible only to the Clinton family, their guests, Huber herself, a few other personal assistants, and the housekeeping staff?

"Maybe the butler did it!" shouted Senator Lauch Faircloth of North Carolina, breaking up the Senate Whitewater hearings.

Huber didn't want to ponder the mystery for too long. She immediately called her lawyer. Then she called Hillary's.

In the less than two years that had passed since Hillary Rodham Clinton was forced to declare defeat in the health care reform effort, Whitewater had taken on a life of its own. The Republican landslide victory in the 1994 midterm elections had given Clinton opponents in Congress a green light to pursue ever more pointed and costly investigations. Both the House and Senate had mounted special Whitewater investigating committees, and amid speculation that the Whitewater mess was one of the affairs that had driven Vince Foster to suicide, two independent counsels had been appointed by Congress to seek the truth, ostensibly without partisan bias.

Whatever scandal lay buried in the Ozarks mud was now generally believed to be much more sinister and far-reaching than the story originally reported by the *New York Times'* Jeff Gerth in 1992. Then the issue was whether or not Bill Clinton, as governor of Arkansas, had pressured state regulators not to shut down the ailing savings and loan Madison Guaranty because it was run by his hapless Whitewater business partner James McDougal. Now the story was of mind-numbing complexity. And it was much more centered on Hillary.

After all, it was Hillary, as the legal representative for Madison at the Rose Law Firm who had gone before a state regulator, Beverly Bassett (who happened to have been appointed by Clinton). What exactly had been the extent of Hillary's involvement with Madison Guaranty? How much money had she earned? Was it true that, despite the obvious conflicts of interest, she and Bill had begged McDougal to employ the Rose firm because Hillary was being blamed there for spending too much time out campaigning for her husband and not enough drumming up business for the firm?

How much had she worked on Castle Grande—another sham real estate deal involving McDougal and Seth Ward, father-in-law of Webster Hubbell (formerly Hillary's law partner, subsequently Hillary's White House collaborator, later to serve jail time for having double-billed clients while at Rose)? Castle Grande had earned Madison executives millions in fees and had cost taxpayers millions more when the savings and loan went belly-up. Had Hillary profited too?

And what was the significance of Vince Foster's notations? Had he been killed because he knew too much? Had Hillary been blocking investigators from digging into his death ever since?

Hillary had clearly known for a long time that her work for Madison Guaranty could spell trouble. In 1988 she had ordered the destruction of most of her legal files dealing with the savings and loan. When reporters during the 1992 campaign had asked to see her Madison billing records, they'd been told that those records had disappeared. Huber's miraculous sighting now came at a suspiciously fortuitous time. Just days earlier the statute of limitations had expired for a number of civil lawsuits that could be brought against professionals who had fraudulently advised corrupt savings and loans. At the same time the Resolution Trust Corporation, which had supervised the bailout of the savings and loan industry, had closed up shop. In its dying hours the RTC had issued a report saying it would not bring suit against either Clinton for the losses Madison had incurred in partially financing Whitewater.

The confluence of circumstances was just too perfect. And the story of how Huber had come to find the billing records was just too weird. The White House is one of the most closely guarded buildings on earth. Every paperweight, every calendar that Bill and Hillary Clinton received was duly checked and catalogued. How could someone have "accidentally" stuck a set of subpoenaed billing records in with the junk?

Even Hillary's closest allies were hard pressed to make the White House's version of events seem plausible. Their stories did Hillary Rodham Clinton no good whatsoever. The irony was, the billing records more or less exonerated her. They supported the story that she'd told all along: that her work for Madison Guaranty had been minimal. She had worked about sixty hours over a period of months, billing about $7,000 for the law firm. The records didn't clear her in the matter of Castle Grande, however. Instead they showed that she'd spoken to Seth Ward fourteen times while the land deal was being put together. This made Hillary's 1995 testimony under oath claiming that she couldn't recall anything about the deal highly suspect.

For independent counsel Kenneth Starr, who had

been boring the American public senseless with the minutiae of the Whitewater investigation for two years, the Rose billing records seemed to pose a golden opportunity. He had long been laboring to prove that the White House was engaged in widespread obstruction of justice and was hiding Hillary's billing records to thwart investigators. Now he believed he had his smoking gun. At the very least, the billing records were concrete, something the public could visualize and understand. He issued a new subpoena. Hillary Rodham Clinton became the first First Lady in American history to be required to testify under oath before a grand jury.

On January 26, just before two o'clock, she pulled up to a federal courthouse in a gray Cadillac Fleetwood limousine. She emerged from the car smiling and waving to the press. She nodded thanks to the protesters who had turned out to support her and ignored those who'd turned out to berate her. Her aides called it the "Head Held High" strategy. It helped Hillary make it through the day. But it didn't do her any lasting good with the public. Hillary came out of her grand jury appearance the most unpopular First Lady in history. Fifty-one percent of Americans now had an unfavorable opinion of her. The launch of It Takes a Village was utterly sabotaged. On the Midwestern leg of her book tour Hillary couldn't even fill all the seats at a speaking engagement in Chicago.

Trouble never seemed to stop coming. The very same week that Hillary appeared before the grand jury, there was another surprising "find" at the White House. This time it was a memo from former head of White House Management David Watkins that seemed to put the travel office fiasco squarely at the feet of Hillary Rodham Clinton. "There would be hell to pay," its author had written, "if we failed to take swift and decisive action in conformity with the First Lady's wishes." Watkins, who had eventually been fired from his job after he'd used a presidential helicopter for golf course "reconnaissance," denied his note's seeming implications. At the time of its writing, he said, he'd merely believed, through hearsay, that Hillary was ordering the firings. He'd later learned that he was wrong.

It hardly mattered. The image of Hillary as White House "enforcer"—a terrifying witch representing the dark side of the presidency—stuck. It reinforced the stories of a White House staff cowed into impotent silence by a tyrannical First Lady. It made Bill Clinton look all but irrelevant to the goings-on in his own presidential mansion.

The charges couldn't have come at a worse time. Hillary's rival for the job of first lady in 1996 was Elizabeth Dole, a woman so charming and sweet-talking that her nickname was "Sugar Lips." In pitching his wife to the American public, the President's challenger, Republican Senator Bob Dole, stressed, above all, that she *wasn't* Hillary. He said: "When I'm elected, she will not be in charge of health care. Don't worry about it. Or in charge of anything else."

It was a measure of the saint-like Elizabeth's steadfastness that she didn't take umbrage to such belittlement. But then, she was strong enough to withstand it. In fact, as far as power was concerned—both personal and political—"Liddy" could out-Hillary Hillary. After all, the First Lady, who'd given up a Washington career to stand by her man down in the boonies, was a poor excuse for an ambition-crazed careerist. Liddy Dole, an older woman who'd married late and never had children, was the real thing. She was known to be her husband's closest adviser, with influence over policy and staff and his "chief surrogate" out on the campaign trail. She was the only woman ever to have served in two cabinets— as secretary of labor and secretary of transportation, and for two different presidents. And she'd been mentioned in the past as a possible vice-presidential candidate. But she had one skill that Hillary, with all her prestigious education, had never mastered. She knew how to act like a "real" First Lady.

She smiled all the time. She had impeccable manners. She downplayed her strengths. She never seemed to think too highly of herself—above all, never more highly of herself than of her husband. She could mime a form of traditional femininity that she completely eschewed in real life. It was a skill she'd learned while coming of age as a debutante in the South. It was also a survival technique that she'd learned early on, building a career in the pre-feminist era. She didn't try to be part of the "boys' club" of Washington; she thrived outside it. She didn't try to revolutionize the system; she charmed it into doing her bidding. As First Lady, Hillary had worked her political will like a kamikaze pilot. Liddy in the White House would be a Stealth bomber. Everything about her made Hillary seem overmuch. Even her born-again Christianity made Hillary's activist Methodism seem like godless humanism.

The Republicans made mincemeat of Hillary and her big-government prescriptions in *It Takes a Village* at their party convention that summer. The Democrats limited her speechmaking presence to "Family Night" at their convention, and tried to pass her off as wife and mother to a nation. In November a strong economy, plus the fact that the country simply never got around to liking Liddy's husband, won Bill Clinton a second term. The "new and improved" Hillary was given a second chance too.

"Fake it till you make it," she joked to her friends, borrowing a phrase someone had once repeated to her from an Alcoholics Anonymous meeting. And bizarrely, unbelievably, the public fell in love with her once again. *It Takes a Village* became a number one best-seller. The nation gave Hillary's "micro-agenda" of serving as President Clinton's "eyes and ears" on social issues such as welfare reform and child care its blessing. This time around, Hillary made clear that her role would be to work as an "advocate" for change—not a policy maker. Within a year her popularity ratings went through the roof. Fifty-nine percent of respondents to a *U.S. News and World Report* poll said they viewed her favorably—her highest approval rating since 1993. Her job-approval rating—67 percent—topped her husband's highest rating up to that date. Internal White House polling showed that the percentage of people who disliked her "viscerally" had fallen from 35 to about 25 percent.

Hillary received a hero's welcome in Chicago as

she headed homeward to celebrate her fiftieth birthday. As she mused about the challenges of middle age, baby boomers around the country nodded appreciatively. They were already feeling her pain over the departure of Chelsea, a month earlier, to faraway Stanford University. Hillary had shown up for cheery orientation day dressed in black, making no secret of the fact that she viewed Chelsea's departure as an occasion for mourning. She would have preferred for Chelsea to have chosen a college on the East Coast— California seemed so far away, she wailed to friends. But she had also taken care not to let her own strong feelings influence Chelsea's choice. "She didn't want to override Chelsea's point of view or individuality," says Dr. David Hamburg, a frequent collaborator on White House special events and President Emeritus of the Carnegie Corporation, with whom Hillary shared her thoughts. But once Chelsea did decide upon Stanford, even Hillary had to agree that it was a good choice. Friends told her that the campus' laidback atmosphere, and fair-sized celebrity contingent would protect Chelsea from excessive star-gazing. She came away from parent's weekend impressed with the college and its administration. So she kept a stiff upper lip.

She and the president helped Chelsea move her suitcases and boxes. She saw the dorm room, met the roommate, checked out the bulletproof glass in the windowpanes, and approved the food at a parents' lunch.

Hiding behind a big, wide-brimmed hat, she displayed little emotion. But in her syndicated column she gave free reign to her anguish. She worried about

Chelsea's safety and privacy—freedom from the prying eyes of the media and the dangers of public exposure. She recalled her own "caffeine-fueled all-nighters during finals" and "long walks through city streets or across campus that ended in a tender moment with a handsome new boyfriend" and worried that Chelsea, pursued by reporters, would never know the same.

Parents of grown children around the nation held her hand through the trial of "empty nest syndrome." They chuckled as she wrote, "Most of the time, I'm wondering why I ever agreed to let her skip third grade." They enjoyed tales of her trying to learn how to keep in touch with her daughter by e-mail. She was apparently gearing up for computer literacy on a Gameboy. That was endearing. And her new, baby-steps approach to reform programs was hitting the mark too. The pundits cheered that after a first term filled with false starts, Hillary had finally hit her stride as First Lady.

But there had been a huge price to pay. The Hillary Rodham Clinton who traveled the world addressing adoring crowds abroad, and who was trying to learn to communicate by e-mail with her daughter in California, simply wasn't the same woman who had swept into the White House four years earlier. Coming into the White House, she said that she communed spiritually with her predecessor Eleanor Roosevelt. Now she was finding common ground in the political sufferings of figures like Nelson Mandela and Aung San Suu Kyi of Burma, the democracy fighter and Nobel prize winner who had spent years of her life under house arrest. To a degree, her travels around the world had become a kind of personal pilgrimage, a way to see people who suffered *even more* than she did. "These people gave her a sense that she wasn't alone," says a friend. "They told her: never let hatred of your enemies corrode your soul." She tried to ward off hate and self-pity, but she radiated unhappiness. Her "smile doesn't match her eyes anymore," her mother told friends.

Hillary was sad, exhausted, stressed to the breaking point. She'd turned off, tuned out. A number of her key associates had left the White House—they just couldn't take it anymore. Not the legal bills, not the subpoenas ("They were coming in at the rate of three or four a day," recalls one former staffer), not the stress. "I was fried," says one of Hillary's former aides. "You just hit a wall." Friends said that the constant attacks on her personality and professional integrity had left her utterly depressed. "How could a woman who all her life was universally respected suddenly find herself under such a cloud?" one confidante mused. Her entire sense of personal competence had been shaken to the core. "The more I see of the world, the more impressed I am that the vast majority of people [get up in the morning] every day," she told an associate, as reported by journalist Bob Woodward. "You know, it's amazing to me that people actually stop at stop signs, that they do feed their children."

No matter how many successes she raked in abroad, at home it sometimes seemed that forces were conspiring against the entire edifice of selfhood that Hillary Rodham Clinton had painstakingly worked all her life to construct. Her activist approach to social welfare was ridiculed as totally out of step with the times. Her efforts to reform the health care system were credited with nearly costing Bill Clinton a second term. And what saved him, eventually, was a political initiative that flew in the face of every principle, every goal Hillary had ever held dear in her adult life.

Clinton had made the move in August 1996, just one day after he'd handed Hillary a crumb of satisfaction on health care by signing a bill allowing workers to maintain their health insurance coverage if they changed or lost their jobs, and barring insurance companies from denying coverage to people with "preexisting" medical conditions. Then, as if he'd put his conscience at ease, he'd signed a bill putting an end to America's six decades–old welfare system. With a stroke of a pen Clinton eliminated one of the few surviving remnants of Franklin D. Roosevelt's New Deal. He signed a new law imposing a five-year lifetime limit on welfare benefits, and requiring most adults to find a job within two years of first receiving aid. The law also abolished Aid to Families with Dependent Children, the staple of the welfare program, which provided monthly cash benefits to 12.8 million people. "Today we are taking a historic chance to make welfare what it was meant to be: a second chance, not a way of life," Clinton said in a signing ceremony in the White House Rose Garden.

By the administration's own estimates, the bill would force a million children into poverty. It would force unskilled mothers of small children into full-time jobs that paid less than the minimum wage. And it would not guarantee decent, affordable day care for those children.

Some members of Clinton's own cabinet expressed revulsion for the new welfare law. Hillary's old friend Marian Wright Edelman, president of the Children's Defense Fund, attacked it as a "moment of shame" for the country and led a protest march in Washington against the signing of the bill. Hillary remained largely silent. When she tried to defend the new welfare law, she seemed unconvincing.

"I don't think it's fair to subsidize some people and say they shouldn't have to leave their children when millions of women do it every day," she told *Time* magazine. But, she added feebly, "I think they ought to have child-care support, and they ought to have some benefits to take care of their children medically." In the years following the new welfare bill's passage into law, Hillary's efforts on behalf of child care and more accessible medical care for children can almost be seen as a form of damage control. Once again, as she had in the past, and would again in the not so distant future, she was left cleaning up the mess of one of Bill Clinton's betrayals.

The sad truth was, Hillary could no longer trust her heart to tell her what road to take in public life. Overconfident with good intentions, she'd grossly underestimated the country's potential mistrust of an unelected official making public policy. Now she knew better—but if she made the tiniest move beyond the incremental changes promised by her new "micro-agenda," she was blown out of the water all over again. Her early hopes of playing a "formal role" in implementing welfare reform were quickly quashed under the weight of public reaction. "We've finally got the chance to move people off welfare, and we really don't need the tender loving care of Hillary Clinton to mess it up," said Governor Tommy Thompson of Wisconsin, a pioneer of one of the nation's most draconian state welfare reform programs. Even friends on the left said that overt help from Hillary would amount to "the kiss of death" for the administration's new welfare policy.

Her response to Whitewater had been a disaster. She'd resisted releasing information from the very beginning. The public didn't need to know, she first said. It wouldn't understand. It didn't really *want* to know—it just wanted scandal. The more papers were released, she argued, the more questions would be raised. "Hillary reacts with her defense lawyer training: you hold things tight, you manage it closely, you reveal only what you have to," an aide told Elizabeth Drew.

Hillary's reticence only fanned the flames of scandal. Her famous "pink press conference" of April 1994, so named because the First Lady showed up in a shocking pink jacket—was so intentionally unenlightening that reporters who previously had shunned the dreary details of Whitewater got the message loud and clear that behind the obfuscation, there was something worth finding. When Hillary's loyal staffers suddenly started suffering memory losses every time they were called before Congressional investigators, it just thickened the stew.

The Senate Whitewater Committee was considering asking for perjury charges to be brought against Susan Thomases and Maggie Williams. A scabrous book by a recently retired FBI agent, Gary Aldrich, accused Hillary of having masterminded "File-gate"—the early Clinton administration's improper acquisition of hundreds of confidential FBI files. Aldrich also, in *Unlimited Access: An FBI Agent Inside the Clinton White House*, alleged that the Clintons had signed a deal during the 1992 campaign granting Hillary all eventual authority over domestic policy if she agreed not to leave Bill Clinton. And he said that Clinton, hiding in the backseat of an unmarked car, used to dodge his security detail and slip out of the White House late at night to meet women in a Washington hotel.

Aldrich's allegations were backed up by testimony from a high-paid call girl, Sherry Rowlands, who had (temporarily) sunk the career and wrecked the marriage of Clinton campaign guru Dick Morris when the political consultant was photographed on a Washington hotel balcony with her in a bathrobe. Aldrich and Rowlands were easy to discredit. Her information was based on pillow talk (which, Morris said, she hadn't understood), and his stories were uncorroborated. But Hillary's enemies believed them, her friends were forced to answer them, and the press had a field day. "Look, there are people around here who think Hillary Clinton is responsible for the weather outside," former White House press secretary Michael McCurry erupted in exasperation during one of his darker moods.

Many people both in and out of the Clinton camp now agree that if Hillary had allowed a full disclosure of all documents and records related to her business dealings with Madison Guaranty at the time they were first requested, the Whitewater scandal never would have come into being at all. After all, in March 1996—*after* the lost billing records were found—an independent review prepared for the Federal Deposit Insurance Corporation, the agency which insures most American consumer bank accounts, backed up Hillary's claims of innocence. It found no evidence that she'd played any role in financial schemes to defraud Madison Guaranty. As far as Castle Grande was concerned, the FDIC report said that Hillary had drafted one document related to the shady deal but was unaware of any wrongdoing connected with it. The agency noted too that the document had been poorly drafted and had to be redone—either because Hillary had hurried through it or lacked the expertise needed to do it right. But Hillary, it appears, simply couldn't stand the thought of losing face. And she hated the image of herself— as financially hungry, politically naive, shortsighted, even negligent—that the Madison and Whitewater papers revealed. As one close friend explained it to the *Washington Post:* "She said, 'It's embarrassing. It's nothing wrong or illegal. It makes us look unsavory. It makes me look incompetent.' "

Every one of her political instincts had turned out to be wrong. Her belief in the rightness of her convictions and desire to control every detail of her work had made her reject the kinds of input into the health care reform effort that could have saved the project from total failure. Parts of her personality which in her past had been prized—her deep protectiveness of her friends and family—now passed for arrogance, duplicity, and paranoia. She had been deeply distrustful of the permanent White House staff from the very outset. Once stories of the Clintons' private life started leaking out to the press, this fear of spying eyes turned into a near obsession. She apparently saw potential betrayal lurking everywhere—in ushers, telephone operators, kitchen workers, Secret Service and FBI agents and, of course, the travel office staff. She wanted these White House insiders checked for loyalty; according to Elizabeth Drew, she had Bernard Nussbaum require that even the lowest-level White House staffers fill out the personal questionnaire he'd drafted to vet political appointees.

Her mistakes had helped turn the tragedy of Vince Foster's suicide into a scandal. After Foster's death Hillary had been understandably concerned with protecting both the deceased man and his family's right to privacy. But there were so many questions left unanswered after Foster's life came to an end. There were many strange incidents in the hours and days after his death. And so many of the dangling threads seemed to lead right back to Hillary. For example; Foster's office hadn't been sealed off until ten-fifteen in the morning on the day after his death. The previous evening Bernard Nussbaum and her chief of staff, Maggie Williams, had gone to Foster's office, allegedly to look for a suicide note. They stayed there for two hours. By the time outside investigators moved in for a look, some papers regarding the Clintons' personal affairs had been sent to their Washington attorney. This seemed particularly troubling once the billing records reappeared with Foster's handwriting on them.

Another mystery centered around Foster's despairing note—the twenty-seven torn pieces from a yellow legal pad, said to have been found in the bottom of Foster's briefcase, with one piece missing, a week after his death. The White House said at the time that it had delayed its release in order to give Foster's widow, Lisa, and the president time to study it. But a memo discovered in August 1996 tied the secrecy once again to Hillary. What in other circumstances might have been seen as a very human reaction was now called obstruction of justice.

Nothing she did escaped scrutiny. Hillary had made headlines during the 1996 campaign for bringing in record sums of money for the Democratic party, especially from women. Now she and her aides were embroiled in one of the Democrats' many campaign-finance scandals because of a check her chief of staff had carelessly accepted from a Chinese American businessman. Even her reputation as a lawyer had come under attack. Her *National Law Journal* ranking as one of the top hundred lawyers in America, a point of pride for the Clinton campaign in 1992, was now called into question. "Some doubt she was one of the top hundred lawyers in Little Rock," *Newsweek* scoffed. And just to cap things off, her personal finances were in ruins. The Clintons' legal bills now outweighed their assets.

Things were becoming more and more surreal. Hillary tried to hold on to the memory of her life as she'd once known it. Her staff struggled to schedule her some time just for herself. And sometimes, all too rarely, she treated herself to slivers of normality. She'd make a lunch date with Tipper Gore, and they'd stroll together through the Corcoran Gallery. People sometimes came up to her shyly.

"Do you know," they'd ask, "you look just like Hillary Clinton?"

"I've been told that," she'd reply.

She craved solitude, anonymity. She began taking long walks through Washington incognito in a baseball cap and dark glasses, her Secret Service contingent stripped down to the absolute minimum and keeping a discreet distance. She was like a woman lost in a city she'd once known and understood well, but which had now changed in ways she could barely fathom. Washington was a giant fishbowl; she was on display, and there was nothing more lonely than living life in the public eye. When she'd worked for the House Judiciary Committee, preparing a case against President Nixon, she'd been young and inexperienced, and she'd felt like an insider. Now she was First Lady, and she felt utterly alienated from the political culture surrounding her. She'd never seen fit to cultivate the grandes dames of Georgetown, and they'd made her pay for it. She hadn't struck strategic alliances with other powerful Washington insiders. She'd tried to go it alone, with her own people, her own friends, and many of them hadn't made it through with her.

Hillary began grasping at straws, for solace, for spiritual and intellectual guidance. She began consulting with Dr. Jean Houston, a writer and self-described "sacred psychologist" who specialized in "mind-expansion studies." Houston encouraged Hillary to seek answers from Eleanor Roosevelt and Mohandas Gandhi by engaging in imaginary conversations with their spirits. She did. (Hillary refused, however, to talk to Jesus in Houston's presence.) The sessions with Houston, first reported in Bob Woodward's book *The Choice* set the tabloids screaming. Hillary was engaging in "seances," her critics raged. "This was an interesting intellectual exercise to help spark my own thoughts . . . not a spiritual event," the First Lady protested. Houston herself explained she'd done no more than help Hillary brainstorm for her book. But "pushing the membrane of the possible"—as Houston described her work—wasn't really what most people wanted to see going on at the White House. It was ultimately preferable for Houston simply to withdraw from the scene. And for Hillary, once again, to "brainstorm" alone.

"In our country we expect so much from the woman who is married to the President—but we don't really know what it is we expect," Hillary reflected on a trip to Australia early in her husband's second term. The only way to "escape the politics of one's time," she told an audience, is "to totally withdraw and perhaps put a bag over your head, or somehow make it clear that you have no opinions and no ideas about anything—and never express them, publicly or privately." She added: "There is something about the position itself which raises in Americans' minds concerns about hidden power, about influence behind the scenes, about accountability. Yet if you try to be public about your concerns and your interests, then that is equally criticized. I think the answer is to just be who you are and do what you can do and get through it—and wait for a First Man to hold the position."

The crowd, largely women, went wild. Crowds of women in China, South Africa, Ireland, and Latin America did too. Hillary would spend as much time as she could traveling overseas. It was as though, having lived too long in the borrowed confines of the White House, she had begun to feel homeless in America.

Chapter 8

"Bimbo Eruptions"

One of the worst thoughts lurking in Hillary Clinton's mind in the campaign year had been that one day soon her husband might be dragged before prosecutors and made to pull down his pants to show whether he had "distinguishing marks" on his genitals. The leader of the free world doing a one-man "Full Monty" show. And all because of a former Arkansas state employee with short skirts and big hair named Paula Jones.

On May 8, 1991, Paula Jones was handing out name tags at a "Governor's Quality Management Conference" at the Excelsior Hotel in downtown Little Rock. She allegedly caught Governor Clinton's eye. A little while later, she says, one of the state troopers guarding Clinton approached her and said that the governor wanted to make her acquaintance. He sent her upstairs to a guest room. Paula has since said she believed Clinton wanted to offer her a job.

So the twenty-four-year-old, $6.35-an-hour secretary with the Arkansas Industrial Development Commission went upstairs. She and the governor briefly made conversation. Then, she claims, he pawed her. He opened his fly and exposed himself and said, "Kiss it."

"I'm not that kind of girl," Paula allegedly said.

"Well," said the future president, "I don't want to make you do anything you don't want to do." And the encounter ended. "Let's keep this between us," Clinton said.

Jones wanted nothing better. But in December 1993 the *American Spectator* magazine published David Brock's "Troopergate" article. In it Brock mentioned a certain "Paula," who'd been summoned for a brief hotel room rendezvous with Clinton and had emerged saying she was available to be Clinton's "girlfriend."

Jones was mortified. She'd told the story of Clinton's come-on to friends and family. Everyone in Little Rock knew everyone. The last name of the slutty-seeming "Paula" wouldn't remain a mystery for long. She had a husband now (a Mr. Corbin). She had a reputation to preserve. There was, she figured, only one thing to do. She sued President Clinton for sexual harassment, "embarrassment, humiliation, fear, emotional distress, horror, grief, shame, marital discord, and loss of reputation." She claimed that after she'd turned down Clinton's advances, her supervisors at the Arkansas Industrial Development Commission, a state agency headed by a Clinton appointee, had discriminated against her. She'd never gotten a raise. And, her complaint stated, on April 22, 1992, Secretary's Day, she'd been the only clerical worker in her office not to receive flowers.

Paula Jones went public with her charges at a press conference in February 1994. She told reporters that Clinton had tried to kiss her and grope her and had asked her to perform a "type of sex." She wouldn't provide more details because, she implied, such indelicacy offended her sense of propriety. The correspondents laughed.

The case languished for the better part of two years as Clinton's lawyers argued that a president could not be tried for sexual harassment while in office. They said he had "never been alone in a hotel" with Jones. Then, in January 1996, a judge ruled that Jones's case could go forward. Bill Clinton, ever mindful of his place in history, became the first sitting president to testify in his own defense in a court case.

Paula Jones claimed to have noticed distinguishing characteristics of the then-governor's genitalia which, if confirmed, would prove the veracity of her account. Her lawyers submitted a request for names of doctors "who performed surgery or other procedures on the President's genitalia." They dug for dirt throughout Arkansas, tracking down every whiff of scandal they could out of Clinton's past. Clinton was deposed and questioned about Jones and about a long list of other women. He reportedly admitted to having had an affair with Gennifer Flowers. But he denied any recollection of the encounter with Jones.

Jones's case was easy to discredit. The only airtight piece of evidence she had was confirmation from co-workers that she hadn't in fact received flowers that Secretary's Day. As far as pay raises were concerned, she'd received two after the alleged incident with the governor. She'd received a promotion too. As the case wore on, even some of Jones's family members turned against her. A brother-in-law said she was a manipulative tease. An ex-boyfriend tried to sell nearly nude photos of her to *Penthouse* magazine. The women's rights community treated her harassment claims with distaste. Eventually, in April 1998, an Arkansas judge dismissed Paula Jones's lawsuit, ruling that "the governor's alleged conduct does not constitute sexual assault." The former governor, it seemed, was cleared.

But the President was in serious trouble.

In trying to establish a pattern of behavior by Clinton, Paula Jones's lawyers had interviewed a twenty-four-year-old former White House intern named Monica Lewinsky. Under oath Lewinsky had denied ever having had an affair with Clinton. Under oath Clinton had done the same. Now secret tapes emerged that argued otherwise. They also suggested that Clinton was guilty of perjury, suborning perjury, obstruction of justice, and witness tampering for trying to deny and cover up the affair. That was very bad news.

Kenneth Starr was having a field day.

After four years and nearly $40 million, his Whitewater investigation had essentially run dry. He was starting to shut down his Little Rock operation. His Arkansas grand jury hadn't indicted anyone in almost two years. It had never brought charges against either of the Clintons. "Travelgate" had gone nowhere very interesting. "Filegate" turned out to have been an administrative error. Vince Foster's death once again had been ruled a suicide.

Watching his investigations dissipate, Starr had tried to jump ship once, accepting a job as dean of Pepperdine University Law School in California. But he'd ruffled so many feathers—and cost so much taxpayer money—that the country had refused to accept his resignation. Chastened by public outcry, he'd toiled on. He discovered that Clinton associates had gathered more than $700,000 for Webster Hubbell after he left his Justice Department job and served time in jail. He dug to see if it had been "hush money" to buy Hubbell's silence on Whitewater. He sent scouts to question the now infamous Arkansas state troopers. Clinton's alleged women friends, he explained, might have gleaned information about the Whitewater land deal from pillow talk.

Starr had over the years scored some partial triumphs. He'd convicted James McDougal, his ex-wife Susan, and then Arkansas governor Jim Guy Tucker on fraud charges linked, for the most part, to Madison Guaranty. Susan McDougal, who had refused to cooperate in Starr's efforts to accuse Bill Clinton, had been jailed for contempt of court. Little Rock businessman David Hale had pleaded guilty to fraud as well. Now Starr's most cooperative witness, Hale had provided the independent counsel with what he hoped would prove to be his "smoking gun": testimony that Hale and McDougal had met with then governor Clinton to discuss Hale's providing a fraudulent government-backed $300,000 loan to Susan McDougal. That loan had partially been funneled into Whitewater. It had never been repaid.

The problem with Hale, however, was that he was now a convicted felon—not the most credible of star witnesses. When James McDougal died in prison and the state troopers were discredited—Betsey Wright stated that they hadn't abused their state employee positions to procure women for the governor; they'd used their uniformed power to procure women for *themselves,*—the troopers denied this allegation—Starr was pretty much left empty-handed.

Fortunately for Starr, richer pastures soon bloomed closer to home. In January 1998, exactly four years after the first Whitewater independent counsel, Robert Fiske, had been named to look into Vince Foster's death and the troublesome $300,000 loan, Starr was contacted by a Pentagon aide named Linda Tripp. Tripp told Starr that her co-worker Monica Lewinsky was having an affair with the President and that they both were conspiring to cover it up.

Tripp had befriended the much younger Lewinsky after both women were transferred from positions in the White House to the Pentagon. She'd quickly become the young woman's confidante. When Lewinsky had confided in her that she was having an affair with the President, she'd started secretly recording their phone conversations. When she contacted Starr on January 12, she had twenty-two hours of tapes to offer, recordings in which Monica, sometimes tearfully, called Clinton "schmucko" and "the creep" and painted a sordid picture of sex, lies, and the President. The tapes suggested a stream of damaging allegations: sexual activity in the White House. Phone sex. Presidential fluids preserved on a stained blue dress. (Put it in a Ziploc bag, Tripp told Lewinsky.) And there was a written document in Tripp's possession, a memo called "Points to make in an affidavit," suggesting ways that Tripp, if subpoenaed, could lie about Clinton's purported extramarital activities.

If the tapes were real, and their assertions of a sexual affair were accurate, then the President had committed perjury in the Jones case. He had lied in a civil suit, a felony under federal law. If Clinton had encouraged Lewinsky to lie, it meant he had suborned perjury. His friend Vernon Jordan, a powerful Washington insider, had tried to secure a job for Monica in New York. If, at the President's instructions, he had been trying to buy the former intern's silence, then it was obstruction of justice. And if Clinton had played a part in writing the memo, it was witness tampering.

Why was Linda Tripp taping Monica Lewinsky? And why did she sell her out to Starr?

Rewind to November 1993. Linda Tripp, who'd initially been hired to work for Republican president George Bush, was sick of Bill Clinton's White House. She hated the kids and the anything-goes atmosphere. There was something about Clinton himself that she found *unpresidential.* On November 29, she was walking through the West Wing when she came upon a former White House volunteer named Kathleen Willey. Willey, the wife of a successful Virginia real estate lawyer and major Democratic party donor, was looking "disheveled." As Tripp said, in a now famous (and highly disputed) assertion to *Newsweek*: her "face was red, and her lipstick was off. She was flustered, happy, and joyful."

Willey had little reason to look happy that day. She'd just learned that her husband, Edward, had been accused of embezzling hundreds of thousands of dollars and that she herself was implicated in some of the debts. She was in Washington trying to find a job. She'd come to see Bill Clinton in the hope that he could help her out with a position at the White House.

According to Willey's friends and her own statements, Clinton offered the pretty former flight attendant some coffee. Close to tears, Willey confided in him about her personal problems and said she needed a job. Clinton hugged her and kissed her. "I've always wanted to do that," he allegedly said. He allegedly groped her and tried to get her to fondle him. His face, Willey later told friends, was beet red.

The encounter was interrupted by the voice of a presidential aide. Willey hurriedly left Clinton and ran into Tripp, whom she told about the encounter. When she got home, she learned that her husband had killed himself.

Subsequently, Clinton secured a temporary job for Willey as a secretary in the White House counsel's office—where she sat next to Tripp. He later arranged other favors for her and her son.

An anonymous caller brought Willey to the attention of Paula Jones's lawyers. Willey was issued a subpoena to testify about Bill Clinton's standards of conduct. So was Tripp. By now her regard for Bill Clinton had reached rock bottom. When she told her story to the press and was belittled by Clinton's lawyer Robert S. Bennett as "not to be believed," her hatred of the Clinton White House redoubled.

The Rutherford Institute, a conservative legal firm contributing funds to Paula Jones's lawsuit, began receiving answering machine-messages from an anonymous woman caller in October 1997—just about the time when Linda Tripp began recording Monica Lewinsky. The caller suggested that Paula Jones's lawyers might like to interview Lewinsky about an affair she was having with the President. A subpoena to Lewinsky soon followed. The story then veered further into the scary and absurd.

On January 12 Tripp contacted Kenneth Starr. She'd been subpoenaed to testify in the Paula Jones case, and now she was frightened. She'd learned that it was illegal in her home state of Maryland to tape someone without his or her permission. When she was called upon to tell what she knew about Lewinsky under oath, she'd implicate herself. Kenneth Starr, she thought, could offer her immunity—if she sought protection as a federal witness in his investigation.

On January 13 Tripp, wearing a wire, met with Lewinsky for lunch at a Ritz-Carlton hotel in suburban Virginia. Over a cheeseburger they discussed Bill Clinton. On January 16 the Justice Department expanded Starr's inquiry to include the Lewinsky case. Starr arranged another Ritz-Carlton Hotel lunch for Tripp and Lewinsky.

Monica arrived first. As she waited in the hotel's food court, she saw Tripp coming toward her down an escalator. As she stepped forward to greet her, two FBI agents moved in, flashed their badges, and told her she was under investigation. She said she wouldn't talk without her lawyer present. The agents, she later testified, told her a lawyer wouldn't do her any good. They took her up to a hotel room. Some of Kenneth Starr's deputies were there. They told Monica that she was going to go to jail—possibly for twenty-seven years. They told her that they were going to send her mother to jail—for allegedly advising her daughter on ways to keep Tripp from testifying. When Monica asked to place a phone call to her mother, a deputy told her, "You're twenty-four, you're smart, you're old enough, you don't need to call your mommy." They let her out of the room just to eat and, bizarrely, to go window-shopping.

Monica Lewinsky could not have picked a worse confidante than Linda Tripp. But then, that was one of her shortcomings—she confided too much, to too many people. At the Pentagon, where she had been transferred after a senior White House aide had noticed her loitering excessively around the Oval Office, she talked too much and too easily about her personal life. She talked about her father, Bernard Lewinsky, a Beverly Hills oncologist, and her mother, Marcia Lewis, a gossip writer, who once, to promote a biography she'd written on the sex lives of Luciano Pavarotti, Jose Carreras, and Placido Domingo, had written a jacket blurb suggesting she'd been "more than friends" with Domingo. Lewinsky talked about their divorce (the mother claimed the father verbally abused the children, and the father claimed the mother abused his credit cards) and about her very expensive rounds of psychotherapy. Her openness and her obvious vulnerability were to many people what made her appealing as a friend. "She has a naive quality that was endearing and made me want to shelter her," one former colleague told the *New York Times*. For Bill Clinton, an alcoholic's stepson, always eager to "save" and to please, such openness and vulnerability were downright irresistible.

When the scandal broke, they gave him a built-in cover story. Monica, he could say, was an unstable and sweet young woman who had latched onto him as a friend and mentor. She had come to him in need, and he had helped her. He had, in a well-chosen word, "ministered" to her—as he had to hundreds of young people, in Arkansas and Washington, over the course of his years in power. That, at least, was what he told Hillary.

He awakened her in the dark morning hours of Wednesday, January 21, the day the story broke in the press. According to Hillary's own account, Clinton nudged her as she slept and said: "You're not going to believe this, but . . ."

"What is this?" she asked.

"I want to tell you what's in the newspapers."

The story had been whispered about in Washington for some time. It was the kind of thing that made reporters drool and made editors very nervous. When it broke on the Internet, the mainstream media had to react. To Hillary it seemed axiomatic. There'd been nothing but good news for a while. There had to be a backlash.

Just a week earlier she had launched her first major political initiative since the health care fiasco four years earlier: an ambitious campaign to improve child care in America. This time she'd taken care to cast her role as simply that of an advocate for children and an information gatherer for the president, and the public was on her side. Clinton himself, for that matter, had never been more popular. The Clinton couple had never seemed more perfectly in synch. They'd recently been seen dancing together alone on a beach in the Virgin Islands.

Bill told Hillary that he'd probably been imprudent in befriending Monica Lewinsky. He said that he'd grown emotionally close to her—"too close," he said—but the relationship had never become sexual. He said that he and the woman three decades younger had become friends by sharing stories about their emotionally deprived childhoods. He said that on the tapes she'd either been fantasizing or exaggeratedly boasting about physical contact.

That story raised eyebrows when it leaked out of the White House. Clinton's former chief of staff, Leon E. Panetta, went on record voicing his doubts about Clinton's future. If the allegations turned out to be true, he said, it would be better for the Democrats if "[Vice President Al] Gore became president and you had a new message and new individual up there." George Stephanopoulos, spin doctor of the 1992 campaign, broached the possibility of impeachment. Inside the White House there was embarrassed silence. No one wanted to touch this story. No one could quite stomach it.

No one, of course, but Hillary.

She was always at her best when Bill was at his worst. Now, as she had so many times before when "bimbo eruptions" (as Clinton's former chief of staff Betsey Wright had so memorably named them) threatened to wreck the entire edifice of their shared lives, she went into battle mode. While Clinton went around looking pale and defeated, she busily set about the business of helping him govern. "We've been through worse than this," she told an aide in the hall. "We'll be okay." She had spent the weekend of her husband's deposition in the Paula Jones case cleaning out her closets. "You have to box it off," she had said when asked how she dealt with the press of scandal into her daily life. "There's no way that you can let people with their own agendas, whatever they may be, interfere with your life, your private life or your duties."

She hit the airwaves. "I have seen how these charges and accusations evaporate and disappear if they're ever given the light of day," she told the Associated Press. She went to Maryland to give a speech about race relations. "From the time my husband announced he was going to run for president, for reasons I don't fully understand, he was considered a threat to certain ideological and political positions that are held by certain people, deeply, in our country," she said as she boarded the train. "And there has been a concerted effort to undermine his legitimacy as president, to undermine much of what he has been able to accomplish, to attack him personally when he could not be defeated politically."

Exactly six years to the week since Gennifer Flowers had gone public with the story of her alleged twelve-year affair with Clinton, the Bill and Hillary show was back in action. Bill Clinton called in his former political rival, the black politician and Protestant minister Jesse Jackson. As they had in the 1992 campaign year, the two men watched the Super Bowl on TV. Then they bowed their heads and prayed. "As the storm rages, choose prayer over panic," Jackson said. "Remain focused and faithful. God will prevail."

Hillary got on the phone. She called in old advisers to help control spin. In meetings she discussed the Lewinsky allegations as though they concerned a legal client—and not her husband of more than

twenty years. Even as Clinton's own staff admitted
that they questioned his honesty, she defended his
honor. She had to. There was no way that the country
would believe in Bill Clinton's innocence if his own
wife didn't.

No one knew if she believed him or had just decided to believe him. It didn't really matter. She pro-
jected belief. She committed herself to the act of
believing. The rest was easy. It was familiar ground:
political idealism and faith. Hillary could meditate
upon all the good things her husband had done for
the country during his time in the White House. She
didn't have to think about the bad things he might
have done just steps away from the Oval Office. She
wouldn't ask, and he wouldn't have to tell.

And so, ironically, the scandal brought the Clintons together—during work hours at least. With the
constant threat of subpoenas hanging over the White
House, Clinton couldn't talk to even his closest aides
about his relationship with Monica Lewinsky. Hillary
became his closest adviser, the only one besides his
personal lawyer, who by law could not be made to
testify against him. She encouraged Clinton to issue
categorical denials of the affair with Lewinsky. She
emerged as his strongest defender. Soon she was
seen as his best weapon for launching a counter-of-
fensive against Kenneth Starr.

As Clinton's defense slowly began to take form,
the White House released stories of how Lewinsky
had been so infatuated with the President that she
would arrive at events hours early to find a place in
the rope line to see him. Clinton's lawyers were
blessed with a phone call that led them to a former

high school teacher of Lewinsky's who said he'd had an affair with her and called her a home wrecker. Soon other long-lost acquaintances were recalling Lewinsky as a liar, gradually drowning out the early voices from friends and former classmates who'd agreed, above all, that she was "nice." *Penthouse* magazine offered her $2 million to pose and tell her story. The negative spin was taking on a life of its own.

Meanwhile, Hillary had her own spinning to do. On the day that Clinton was to deliver his State of the Union message, she went on national television to blame the Lewinsky accusations on "the unfortunate, mean-spirited give-and-take of American politics right now." She then threw the media a bone that would keep it busy for weeks to come: "The great story here, for anybody willing to find it and write about it and explain it, is this vast right-wing conspiracy that has been conspiring against my husband."

Her rhetoric may have been slightly overheated. But in pointing to the conservative forces allied against her husband, forces that had spent years and millions of dollars scratching the Arkansas dirt, Hillary Clinton had a point.

From the time he ran his first race against Representative John Paul Hammerschmidt in 1974, Bill Clinton had inspired gut hatred. Not just dislike or political disagreement, but real, visceral detestation. There had long been a solid core of Clinton haters in Arkansas waiting to bring him down. They claimed it was his moral failings that enraged them: his womanizing, his lying, all the "Slick Willie" wiliness that never seemed to wash clean.

There was Larry Case, a Little Rock private investigator who in 1992 had served as a virtual encyclopedia for Clinton philandering stories, spending his life on the phone with reporters and political opponents (and taping the calls).

There was Cliff Jackson, a native of Hot Springs, Arkansas, whose hatred of Clinton dated back to the late 1960s, when they'd both studied at Oxford on prestigious scholarships. When Clinton ran for president, Jackson formed a political action committee to oppose him. Afterward, he brought the Arkansas state troopers' stories of soliciting women for Clinton to the public eye.

There was Larry Nichols, the self-avowed "smut central" for Clinton opponents, who was fired from his Arkansas state job in 1988 for allegedly making personal calls to the Nicaraguan contras. He had nourished a grudge against Bill Clinton ever since. He'd set up Gennifer Flowers with the tabloid press. Then he helped produce a right-wing documentary, *The Clinton Chronicles*, which accused Clinton of crimes including drug running and treason. Videos of the film sold in the tens of thousands, thanks to the help of the right-wing television evangelist Jerry Falwell, who hawked them on his *Old Time Gospel Hour*. The video fed a mini-industry of Clinton conspiracy theories which charged, among other things, that the president had terrorized Arkansas with "death squads," and that Vince Foster had been shot on the White House grounds and then moved to Fort Marcy Park.

Then there was James McDougal, Clinton's partner in the Whitewater land deal, who claimed to have turned against Clinton when the then governor bilked him on a promised job. When McDougal, burning papers in his yard, had come upon his old Whitewater documents one day in 1992, he'd taken them to Sheffield Nelson, another long-term Clinton foe. Nelson had put him in touch with the *New York Times*. Burning trash begetting Whitewater begetting Kenneth Starr begetting Monica Lewinsky.

Nefarious though the Arkansans turned out to be, they were small change compared to the power brokers who turned their guns on Clinton once he came to Washington. Among the most powerful: Richard Mellon Scaife, a Pittsburgh millionaire and supporter of various right-wing causes. Scaife provided the main financial support behind the Arkansas Project— a $1.8 million special effort by the *American Spectator* magazine to dig up scandal on Clinton. He allegedly funneled money to Starr witness David Hale. (Both Scaife and Hale have vigorously denied this.) According to now repentant "Troopergate" journalist David Brock, another big money source in the Clinton scandals was Peter W. Smith, a Chicago financier who gave thousands of dollars to the Arkansas troopers and to lawyers and public relations consultants who peddled their story. Brock admitted on CNN: "There is a right-wing [apparatus] and I know what it is. . . . I've been there. I was part of it and, yes, they were trying to bring down Bill Clinton by damaging him personally . . . by any means necessary."

The Paula Jones case, whatever validity it may or

may not have had (and the truth now never will come out—in November 1998, after endless threats of appeals, Clinton and Jones settled their case for $850,000—a sum to be largely furnished by Hillary Clinton's own savings), was clearly one such means. Brock has said that a Jones lawyer told him once that he didn't necessarily believe in her sexual-harassment story. Jones herself has made no secret of her link to right-wing lawyers and financiers. Her case was bankrolled by the conservative Rutherford Foundation, and her suit was announced at the 1994 Conservative Political Action Conference in Washington.

As for Linda Tripp, she'd first gotten her job in the Bush White House through a prominent tobacco lobbyist, employed by an industry deeply hostile to Clinton's politics. She was a friend of Gary Aldrich, the former FBI agent and author of *Unlimited Access*. She had approached Aldrich's publisher, the conservative Alfred Regnery, with a book proposal dealing with Vince Foster's death. She was also friends with Lucianne Goldberg, a New York book agent and avid Clinton hater who had previously represented the ubiquitous Arkansas troopers. Goldberg was a fan of covert operations. Earlier in her career she'd worked briefly as a Republican spy in the 1972 presidential campaign of George McGovern. She encouraged Tripp to tape Lewinsky. And, according to *Newsweek*, she—via Alfred Regnery, via Peter Smith—put Jones's lawyers onto Tripp and her tapes.

This leads to Kenneth Starr. He is the son of a Church of Christ minister. He was raised to consider smoking and drinking moral lapses, and his hobby in junior high school was polishing shoes. He went on to top Justice Department posts for Republican presidents Ronald Reagan and George Bush. He publicly denounced Clinton in the Paula Jones case and argued against Clinton's claims of immunity while in the White House. In the $1-million-per-year private practice he maintained while investigating the Clintons, he represented a major tobacco company. He was allied with a number of conservative groups openly opposed to Clinton. The post at Pepperdine University that he was eventually forced to turn down was subsidized in part by Richard Mellon Scaife.

So why was he named "independent" counsel?

The first independent counsel, Robert B. Fiske Jr., had been selected in January 1994 by Clinton's attorney general, Janet Reno. These were exceptional circumstances; the law enabling a panel of federal judges to pick an independent counsel had expired. Later that year the law was renewed, and the panel's powers were restored. One of the judges went to lunch with two conservative senators from the tobacco-rich state of North Carolina, Jesse Helms and Lauch Faircloth. Faircloth said that Fiske wasn't investigating Whitewater aggressively enough. Kenneth Starr, he said, would do a better job. Soon after, the panel judged that Fiske's investigation was tainted by a conflict of interest—the independent counsel had, after all, been appointed by a Clinton cabinet member. Fiske was out; Starr was in.

Americans love conspiracy theories. In this case, Hillary's theory appeared to hold water. At the very least, it bought the Clintons some time. It deflected attention from the fact that, where his own defense was concerned, Bill Clinton was floundering badly.

He was just too slippery. On January 22 he issued a written statement denying having had an "improper relationship" with Monica Lewinsky. When that was criticized as too vague, he elaborated. "There is not a sexual relationship." Only when quizzed on the "is" did he correct himself: "The relationship was not sexual."

That didn't inspire confidence. It was too much like the time that Clinton explained away his one experience of marijuana smoking by saying, "I didn't inhale." Finally, after a few coaching lessons in miming firmness from his friend the Hollywood producer Harry Thomason, and with Hillary standing by his side, he went on the offensive. "I want you to listen to me," he said, glaring at the cameras on the day before his State of the Union address. "I'm going to say this again, I did not have sexual relations with that woman . . . Miss Lewinsky." He spat out the name as though it were distasteful. "I never told anybody to lie, not a single time—never. These allegations are false. And I need to go back to work for the American people."

The problem was, no matter how much Americans wanted to believe their president, and how far they were willing to go in believing that right-wing forces were gunning to bring him down, the fact was that Bill Clinton had dug his own grave with Monica Lewinsky. He'd gotten her into something that was way beyond her league—and she was scared senseless. She didn't want to go to jail. She didn't want to send her mother to jail. So she lawyered up. She got the blue dress out of safekeeping. And at the end of July, she handed it over to Ken Starr, cutting an immunity deal in exchange for truthful testimony about Clinton.

The independent counsel immediately asked for a sample of Clinton's DNA. A date was set for the President to make a grand jury appearance. As August heated up, Clinton felt the White House walls closing in on him. Two bombs went off at American embassy compounds in Tanzania and Kenya. On August 13 Clinton attended a memorial service for the ten Americans who had died. He cried. Then he and Hillary came home to the White House. In the privacy of their very public home, he told her the truth about Monica. The relationship had gone on for eighteen months. It had been physically intimate. He was sorry.

The next morning the *New York Times* reported that Clinton was considering admitting to a sexual relationship with Lewinsky. That was it—there was no "zone of privacy" at all left for Hillary. She was the victim of a double betrayal. It appears that she had trusted her husband. She'd certainly wanted to badly enough. When he'd promised her six years earlier that he'd put all his wandering behind him, he'd really seemed to have meant it. And perhaps he did: according to a confidant, Clinton said he'd worked hard to "turn off" his body once he'd come to the White House. She'd bought into the business about "ministering" to Monica Lewinsky. "The president had come from a broken home," she'd explained to White House aide Sidney Blumenthal, according to Blumenthal's later grand jury testimony. "It was very hard to prevent him from ministering to these troubled people." (Clinton had actually taken the charade one step further. When Blumenthal warned him to stay away from Monica because "troubled people can get you into incredible messes," Clinton responded, "It's difficult for me to do that given how I am. I want to help people.") As another White House aide put it to the *Washington Post:* "[Hillary] obviously believed him until she couldn't anymore."

There was a second article of faith. Hillary had implicitly trusted Clinton to shelter her from the kind of soul-battering publicity she'd endured in 1992. Her decision to defend him at all costs in the Monica Lewinsky affair rested upon a kind of bargain: she'd protect him politically and he'd protect her personally. There wouldn't be any more bad surprises. No more airing of their dirty laundry in public. "She was misled," her spokeswoman, Marsha Berry, dryly explained, when in the days following Clinton's confession to Hillary, reporters clamored to find out exactly what she had known and when. "She learned the nature of his testimony over the weekend."

The evasive answer raised a question that has never been—and no doubt will never be—answered. Had Bill Clinton in fact sworn to Hillary that he'd never had an affair with Monica Lewinsky? Or had he just promised her that she'd never be forced to see him admitting one to the nation? After all, from the very beginning Hillary's defense of her husband had been worded with lawyerly precision. "[T]he important thing now is to stand as firmly as I can and say that, you know, the President has denied these allegations on all counts, unequivocally," she had proclaimed in January. "You won't be hearing any more from my husband." She also said: "I'm not only here because I love and believe my husband. I'm also here because I love and believe in my country." In the light of later events, it was no longer clear that Hillary's early resolve to defend her husband had really been a defense of his honor. It might well have simply been a defense of her right to privacy—and of the country's right to a higher level of political discourse.

Whatever the original goal was, the plan had run aground. With Clinton set to admit to an "improper relationship," Hillary was destined to look either like a fool, a victim, or a liar—all images she repudiated with equal disgust. It wasn't just a question of embarrassment. It was a question of the most profound kind of self-betrayal.

There was a fifty-second birthday party scheduled for Clinton on the White House South Lawn later that day. Hillary greeted guests through gritted teeth. For once she made no effort to hide her rage and fatigue. Then she shut herself in the White House residence for the weekend. She exercised. She called her mother. She prayed. Clinton called his closest advisers in one by one and debriefed them on the "improper relationship" with Lewinsky. On Sunday morning he took a break to attend church with Hillary. On Sunday evening the Reverend Jesse Jackson came by and led the Clinton family in a reading of David's prayer for mercy after his seduction of Bathsheba. "Wash me thoroughly from mine iniquity, and cleanse me from my sin," they recited.

The following day, so cleansed, Clinton began his

grand jury testimony. It was transmitted from the White House Map Room to the grand jury chamber. The President read a prepared statement, admitting to an improper relationship with Lewinsky. Starr's lawyers badgered him to provide more details. He refused. Afterward he was furious. As he prepared for a nationally televised speech, his aides implored him to put his anger aside, play humble, and beg for forgiveness. But Hillary was tired of playacting. "It's your speech," she told Clinton. "Say what you want."

The speech, a masterwork of Clintonism, is worth reproducing almost in its entirety:

This afternoon in this room, from this chair, I testified before the office of independent counsel and a grand jury. I answered their questions truthfully . . . questions no American citizen would ever want to answer.

Still I must take complete responsibility for all my actions, both public and private. And that is why I am speaking to you tonight.

As you know, in a deposition in January, I was asked questions about my relationship with Monica Lewinsky. While my answers were legally accurate, I did not volunteer information. Indeed I did have a relationship with Miss Lewinsky that was not appropriate. In fact, it was wrong.

It constituted a critical lapse in judgment and a personal failure on my part for which I am solely and completely responsible.

But as I told the grand jury today, and I say to you now, at no time did I ask anyone to lie, to hide or destroy evidence, or to take any other unlawful action.

I know that my public comments and my silence about this matter gave a false impression. I misled people. Including even my wife. I deeply regret that.

I can only tell you I was motivated by many factors. First, by a desire to protect myself from the embarrassment of my own conduct. I was also very concerned about protecting my family. The fact that these questions were being asked in a politically inspired lawsuit which has since been dismissed was a consideration too.

In addition, I had real and serious concerns about an independent counsel investigation that began with private business dealings twenty years ago—dealings, I might add, about which an independent federal agency found no evidence of any wrongdoing by me or my wife over two years ago.

The independent counsel investigation moved on to my staff and friends. Then into my private life. And now the investigation itself is under investigation. This has gone on too long, cost too much, and hurt too many innocent people.

Now this matter is between me, the two people I love most, my wife and our daughter, and our God. I must put it right. And I am prepared to do whatever it takes to do so.

Nothing is more important to me personally, but it is private. And I intend to reclaim my family life for my family. It's nobody's business but ours. Even presidents have private lives. It is time to stop the pursuit of personal destruction and the prying into private lives and get on with our national life.

The religiosity, the Alcoholics Anonymous–derived language of responsibility and recovery—this was the stuff of Clinton's innermost being. The petulant anger, the sense of injustice, it was the Bill Clinton most often described in off-the-record remarks and former aides' memoirs. Not the President as he was normally packaged for prime-time TV. The real thing.

Clinton's aides were mortified. They guessed that, in large measure, the speech had aired Hillary's own grievances: "The family feels that whatever the fault of the father and the husband, the fact that the mother and the daughter have had to endure this excruciating public venting of this issue—Ken Starr's responsible for that," one aide told the *New York Times*. Later in the day Hillary released her own tersely worded statement. "Clearly this is not the best day in Mrs. Clinton's life," her spokeswoman, Marsha Barry, said, "This is a time that she relies on her strong religious faith. She's committed to her marriage and loves her husband and daughter very much and believes in the President, and her love for him is compassionate and steadfast." After that the Clintons went on vacation.

Their walk across the South Lawn to the helicopter waiting to take them to the Massachusetts island of Martha's Vineyard was like a forced march. Hillary looked straight ahead in her sunglasses. Bill Clinton sported an artificial smile. The Clintons walked holding hands with Chelsea between them, separating them as they mimed togetherness. Hillary seemed to cringe away from Clinton's touch as she entered the helicopter. It was going to be a long two weeks at the beach.

Clinton made a run for Washington less than twenty-four hours later. He'd decided to bomb suspected terrorist bases in Afghanistan and Sudan. Then he beat it out of Washington as fast as he could. Monica Lewinsky was back before the grand jury. She was clearing up some discrepancies between her testimony and Clinton's. First, on the question of lying: she insisted that he had, if not in so many words, then by sending a clear signal, told her that she should hide incriminating evidence and encouraged her to lie. Then, on the question of sex: Clinton had made it sound like it had all been oral, performed "on the deponent," as he put it; i.e., by her on him. This was an important legalism; when he'd testified in the Paula Jones suit, Clinton's lawyers had defined sexual relations as occurring "when the person knowingly engages in or causes contact with the genitalia, anus, groin, breast, inner thigh, or buttocks of any person with an intent to arouse or gratify the sexual desire of any person." Sticking by this definition and admitting only to having *received* oral sex allowed Clinton to claim he hadn't perjured himself by denying a "sexual relationship" with Lewinsky in the Jones case. And it allowed him, in his grand jury testimony, to continue to deny having had sex with her.

This was all well and good for the President, but it made Monica Lewinsky very angry. On August 20, under oath, she complained that this "suggests some kind of service contract—that all I did was to perform oral sex on him and that's all this relationship was." It was much more than that, she said. The president had "touched and kissed her bare breasts" nine times, she revealed, in videotaped testimony she'd given privately to female prosecutors. He had "stimulated" her genitals four times and brought her to orgasm three times (once multiply). There had been fifteen episodes of phone sex (Lewinsky didn't like it; the President fell asleep) and one unfortunate episode involving a cigar.

Hillary and Chelsea didn't bother showing up at the airport when Clinton flew back to Martha's Vineyard. They didn't accompany him when he took his dog Buddy out for long walks on the beach. In the past, the Vineyard vacations had been a rare chance to semi-casually socialize. Hillary would lunch and play tennis with local A-crowd women like William Styron's wife, Rose, Vernon Jordan's wife, Ann, and the *Washington Post*'s Kay Graham. Bill Clinton showed off his literary knowledge to the likes of Gabriel García Márquez and Carlos Fuentes. Before a dinner party at the home of a mutual friend, the cartoonist Jules Pfeiffer had once driven the Secret Service nearly mad by parking his rental car in the spot reserved for the President and then locking his keys inside. (The Secret Service agents finally bashed in the window with a rock.) This time around there was no such fun. The Clintons kept largely to themselves. The "repair work" which a White House spokesman had promised would take place in the beach house seemed to be going rather slowly. "The healing process," announced spokesman Michael McCurry, "is underway, but it's not done yet."

The project of "family recovery," launched by Jesse Jackson and now monitored daily by the press corps, was becoming a grotesque spectacle. Hillary's anger,

Clinton's contrition, Chelsea's peace-brokering efforts—it was like the staging of a Greek tragedy, punctuated by doomsaying commentary from a veritable chorus of Hillary's friends and colleagues. The President and First Lady, it was whispered to the press, were more estranged than ever before. Hillary's whole life project had been betrayed. They had never seen her so angry. They'd never seen her so self-critical. " 'What do I owe him? What couldn't I feel? What couldn't I do? What couldn't I give him?' " one friend chanted, rephrasing Hillary, to *U.S. News & World Report*. Sometimes there was a dissenting voice to break up the lament of Hillary's martyrdom: "He probably has to do everything she wants," one pal said. "He is pretty much owned by her now."

The seemingly endless flow of "insider" commentary turned the stomachs of Hillary's true intimates. "No one really knew anything of what was going on between them. They were really private about it, and their true friends, if they knew anything, weren't about to go around saying so," notes a close friend and former colleague of the Clintons. "There were a lot of people who just wanted to look like they were in the loop." But the pack of journalists paid to cover the Clintons didn't care who they were quoting. They had to generate copy. And in the long run, the build-up of verbal garbage worked to the Clintons' advantage. A disgusted public began to tune out the pundits, the experts, and the "friends."

Things started to get better. Clinton's popularity ratings, which had held steady throughout the scandal, were on the rise. Kenneth Starr released videotapes of the grueling and humiliating grand jury interrogation of the President, and the American public was horrified. The people were turning against Starr. Clinton left his prison by the beach. On a day of commemoration for the thirty-fifth anniversary of the great civil rights marches on Washington, he addressed a church in Oak Bluffs, a resort town on Martha's Vineyard. "It is important that we are able to forgive those we believe have wronged us, even as we ask for forgiveness from people we have wronged," he told the crowd of four hundred mostly black supporters. "The anger, the resentment, the bitterness, the desire for recrimination against people you believe have wronged you—they harden the heart and deaden the spirit and lead to self-inflicted wounds. . . . I'm having to become quite an expert in this business of asking for forgiveness," he said. "It gets a little easier the more you do it."

Clinton and his supporters joined together to sing the hymn "We Shall Overcome." Speaking for the congregation, Charles Ogletree Jr., a professor at Harvard Law School, told the President: "I want you to know that the people here understand and feel your pain, believe in redemption."

Clinton was saved.

Or was he? There was just one monkey wrench in the machinery of national recovery. Hillary wasn't playing along. When reports were leaked from the West Wing that she was about to give a speech absolving her husband, she had her spokespeople deny it. More and more information was coming out about Monica Lewinsky's grand jury testimony. It was get-

ting harder and harder for Hillary to forgive. Certain
details of Clinton's dalliance were just too awful.

Most of his encounters with Monica had taken
place while Hillary was away traveling. But sometimes, it appeared, he'd met with Monica just before
or after he'd been with Hillary. He'd had Monica
perform oral sex on him while he spoke on the phone
to members of Congress. He'd told Monica that he'd
had "hundreds of affairs" before turning forty. He
said he thought he "might be alone in three years."
And once, according to the testimony, after oral sex
he'd told Monica that he "hadn't had that in a long
time."

It was positively stomach turning. But eventually
the sheer number and volume of Clinton's apologies
wore Hillary down. That is to say, apparently, she
just could not bear the sound of his asking for forgiveness one more time.

On September 10, when Hillary finally issued a
statement stressing "her support, her love and forgiveness of her husband," Clinton had been out of
control for two days, apologizing left, right, and center after Starr released an early version of his damning report on the Lewinsky matter to Congress.
"Pray for me," he'd asked a group of Democratic
senators. "I was not contrite enough," he then told
a group of clergymen at a White House prayer breakfast. "I have sinned . . . I have repented."

After her time in deep freeze, Hillary had clearly
come to some kind of inner resolution. She held her
head high at a state dinner for Czech Republic president Vaclav Havel and danced with her husband.
She turned her anger outward, toward the press. On

the day before Starr's report was released, she scanned the unusually large crowd of reporters who'd turned out for a White House event promoting more frequent screenings for colorectal cancer and declared herself "thrilled by the concern the press is showing for colon cancer." She then invited members of the press into the Green Room to undergo a rectal exam.

As the Starr report hit the Internet, she bantered with guests at a reception for key players in the Irish peace effort. As the crowd quieted for speeches, she sat down at the podium and put her hand on the President's leg. She smiled magnanimously and whispered in his ear.

"She's moving on," a friend observed. "It's vintage Hillary."

Chapter 9

~~~~~

Understanding Hillary:
Faith, Love, and Politics

It is hard to believe now that there was once a time when Hillary Rodham Clinton was considered a dangerous radical. To conservatives, like the commentator and sometime presidential candidate Patrick J. Buchanan, she was the enemy within, a godless feminist, hell-bent on wrecking the American family. She was the incarnation of evil in post-Cold War America. She was nothing less than a Lady Macbeth-like monster, defined, as the *American Spectator* magazine put it, by her "consuming ambition, inflexibility of purpose, domination of a pliable husband, and unsettling lack of tender human feeling."

Never mind that Hillary was far from a radical feminist. She'd given up her name to stand by her man. She'd deferred the dreams of her youth to help him realize his. And as far as ambition was concerned—she probably could have gone further as a full political player without him. Staying with Bill Clinton caused Hillary to trade in on her personal ambitions, not fulfill them. With her husband earning only $35,000 a year as governor of Arkansas and spending much more than that biannually on his re-election campaigns, she had to practice corporate law to keep her family financially afloat. His utter disregard for financial affairs made the full weight of the Whitewater mess fall squarely in her lap. To fulfill her role as Bill Clinton's wife, Hillary made so many compromises with her independence and integrity that, as her former law partner Webb Hubbell later put it, "her real self was forced to live so far inside her that she sometimes didn't know who she was."

But what was that real self? The answer, in the past, was said to lie in the paper trail Hillary left behind her as a children's rights lawyer and activist. There were, for example, the legal articles Hillary had written as part of her advocacy work on behalf of children's rights in the 1970s. Her most often quoted comment came from an article she'd written for the *Harvard Educational Review* in 1973. It was entitled "Children Under the Law." In it Hillary Rodham wrote: "The basic rationale for depriving people of rights in a dependency relationship is that certain individuals are incapable or undeserving of the right to take care of themselves and consequently need social institutions specifically designed to safeguard their position. . . . It is presumed that under the circumstances society is doing what is best for the individuals. Along with the family, past and present examples of such arrangements included marriage, slavery and the Indian reservation system."

Although this statement was interpreted by conservatives to have, as Daniel Wattenberg of the *American Spectator* put it, "likened the American family to slavery," it clearly did no such thing. It described how the law had historically treated certain classes of people as dependents on others, without the legal right to speak for themselves. In doing so, it simply reiterated certain well-known facts. Until modern times married women had few legal rights and were considered legally dependent upon their husbands. Considered one body under the law with their husbands in the nineteenth century, married women in some states were forbidden to own property in their own names or to file lawsuits.

The fact that there were indeed clear parallels between slavery and marriage in the past in terms of the distribution and administration of power was not a radical concept. Neither was Hillary's consideration of what the role of the state should be in intervening in family life when parents were shown to be incapable of adequately caring for their children. It focused particularly on the issue of the need for children to have their own views expressed through court-appointed representation.

Children had virtually no legal rights when Hillary, as a lawyer for the Children's Defense Fund, wrote her 1973 article. Whereas delinquent children were provided counsel in court, the "dependency relationship" that children necessarily had with their parents assumed that non-delinquents did not have a separate right to independent legal counsel. This, Hillary Rodham argued, was a gross oversight, and deprived children of a fair chance to have their special needs and interests recognized by the law. She suggested abolishing the legal status of minority, along with the presumption that children are legally incompetent, and said that all procedural rights guaranteed to adults under the Constitution should be granted to children whenever the state or a third party moved against them. In later writings as well, she made the point that the legal reasoning that characterizes as "minor" everyone under eighteen or twenty-one was artificial and simplistic, and did not take into account the dramatic differences in competency among children of different ages. Hillary argued in favor of creating a scale of graduated maturity, through which the increasing competence of children would be taken into account.

Another frequently quoted statement of Hillary Rodham's comes from a chapter in a 1979 book called *Children's Rights: Contemporary Perspectives*. "Decisions about motherhood and abortion, schooling, cosmetic surgery, treatment of venereal disease, or employment and others where the decision or lack of one will significantly affect the child's future should not be made unilaterally by parents." This was taken by conservatives to mean that Hillary favored teenagers suing their parents to have nose jobs or liposuction. But in fact she never even addressed the question of child-parent lawsuits. The citation at issue was actually part of a longer paragraph that sought to limit the kinds of "extreme cases" in which courts might intrude in resolving conflicts between children's rights and their parents.

Conservatives have seized upon Hillary Clinton's writings to say that the First Lady is a proponent of more government interference in the home. In fact, time and again in her writings over the years she has argued that less is best. Although it is true that her idea of granting children competency would make it easier for the state to remove them from parental control in abuse situations, Hillary Rodham was actu-

ally one of the first legal scholars to warn against
excessive government interference in family life
through social service agencies. And she did so long
before lawsuits against state child-welfare systems
for violating the rights of both parents and children
became commonplace.

"It is important to recognize the limited ability of
the legal system to prescribe and enforce the quality
of social arrangements," Hillary wrote in 1973. Most
families, she argued, are much better equipped to
take care of children than the government, she wrote,
expressing a fear of "arbitrary and harmful state intervention." The state "has the responsibility to inter-
vene in cases of severe emotional deprivation or
psychological damage if it is likely that a child's development will be substantially harmed by his continued presence in the family." But, she said, "the
state does not provide an adequate substitute parent
in many of the cases where intrusion is resultant in
the removal of a child from his home." The thrust of
the argument is that state efforts should focus on
preventing abuse, not removing children from their
homes once it has occurred.

Hillary Rodham's legal writing embodies an early
version of the much more conservative, responsibil-
ity-minded social welfare views that both Clintons
would later espouse. This is particularly evident in
Hillary's assertion that granting children rights also
means demanding of them responsibilities, and thus
establishing a relationship of dual responsibility between parent and child. This idea was incorporated
into state law in Arkansas when the state passed a
requirement that pupils stay in school in order to

receive and retain driver's licenses. It turned into a rationalization for forcing welfare mothers to work when Bill Clinton did away with Aid to Families with Dependent Children in 1996. It is the most mainstream form of American political thinking possible.

But critics still point to Hillary Clinton's radicalism. Look, they say, at her tenure, from 1978 to 1981, on the Legal Services Corporation board, which she chaired for two years. The LSC funds legal-aid clinics for the poor. Its affiliates filed some controversial suits during Hillary Rodham's tenure. One suit, filed in Connecticut, asked the government to pay for a sex-change operation. Another sought giving over two-thirds of the state of Maine to Indian tribes.

Then there is Hillary's work for the Children's Defense Fund, a nonpartisan lobby which she chaired from 1986 to 1992. In 1991 the CDF advocated increasing taxes on inherited wealth and doubling taxes on tobacco and alcohol—radical stuff. It also sent Hillary Clinton to the "socialist" country of France to study child care. With a team of child-care professionals, Hillary spent two weeks in France in 1991 visiting schools and speaking with ministry officials, educators, and health professionals. She was impressed by the fact French women enjoy government-mandated, paid maternity leave, which was nonexistent in the United States at that time. She also liked the inclusion of preventive health services in French child-care programs, and noted that preschool teachers were paid better, trained better, supervised better, and given more job security than in the U.S.

"What we saw was a coordinated, comprehensive

system, supported across the political spectrum, that links day care, early education and health care—and is accessible to virtually every child," she wrote in an op-ed piece published in the *New York Times* that year. "Much more significant, though, are the pervasive beliefs in France that children are a precious national resource for which society has collective responsibility, and that one goal of a child-care system is to help children develop and thrive."

Her conclusions put her directly at odds with mainstream American orthodoxy. "Throughout the 1980s, debate over child care in the U.S. always seemed to focus on 'family values,' " Hillary wrote. "This assumes that parents alone can always determine and then provide . . . what's best for their children and, hence, society. . . . But this view has allowed our government and, to a much larger extent, business to ignore the needs of America's children and their parents." She called upon the American government to learn a lesson from France.

But there would be no form of government-mandated maternity leave granted American women until Bill Clinton became president (and then women were granted only six weeks of paid leave). Despite Hillary's consciousness-raising efforts, there is still no wide-reaching, quality-controlled, affordable government-backed child care. "If you want to open the floodgates of guilt and dissention anywhere in America, start talking about child care," Hillary acknowledged ruefully in *It Takes a Village*. "It is an issue that brings out all of our conflicted feelings about what parenthood should be." The year 1998 was supposed to be when Hillary would launch headfirst into that conflict. Unfortunately, it was Monica Lewinsky instead who would open the floodgates of guilt and dissension.

Interestingly, Hillary's work for the Children's Defense Fund put her at odds with Bill Clinton. Clinton, as head of the National Governors' Association, consistently opposed the CDF's demands that the federal government impose national standards on child-care centers and verify the credentials of child-care workers. He also fought against Hillary's demand that more state money be allocated to subsidize better health care for poor pregnant women and children. He complained that this money would drain funds from education and other vital services. In other words, as he would later as president, he expressed the resentment of middle-class taxpayers who felt they were receiving less and less from the government while the poor received more and more. "Bill's position, which is a responsible position for a governor to take, is more of a budgetary position," Hillary explained carefully to the *Arkansas Democrat.* "Our position is a policy position. In the long run, this country is going to have to resolve the differences between the two."

In the long run, Bill Clinton's positions would win out. He would become president. A political culture of nickel-and-diming expediency would win out over idealism. And Hillary, as First Lady, would stand silently by.

How much did it hurt? It's hard to say. For the truth is, Hillary Rodham Clinton has always been a pragmatist at heart. She steered clear of radicalism even in her most outspoken years as a student activ-

ist. Though her principled stands didn't change over
the years, she tolerated her husband's penchant for
tailoring his stances on issues to public opinion polls.
Friends who know both Clintons well point out that
even if Hillary leans a bit more to the left than does
Bill, the practical ramifications of that difference are
all but nil. It was she, after all, who called in the
political consultant Dick Morris to engineer the woo-
ing of center-right voters that cemented Bill Clinton's
1996 presidential victory. It was she who pushed
the President to balance the federal budget. She
was willing to take a chance, to mince her words,
on welfare reform. "They're both very pragmatic,"
says Hillary's friend Carolyn Ellis. "And pragmatism has no labels."

Hillary's pragmatism, developed against the backdrop of politics in the conservative Southern state of
Arkansas, has led her to take positions that don't
conform to anything like conventional American leftism. She was an outspoken critic of the American
"culture of poverty" long before her husband made
that criticism law by ending the welfare system. She
has long advocated putting welfare recipients to
work for their money. She has also advocated other
"personal responsibility" measures like requiring
welfare recipients to prove they have immunized
their children in order to continue receiving benefits.
As First Lady she had been an outspoken advocate
of teenage chastity. Just as Nancy Reagan once ex-
horted the nation's youth to "Say No to Drugs," Hillary has urged teenagers to say no to sex. It is
morally wrong, she explains, "for children to engage
in sexual activity. It violates every traditional moral

code, and it unleashes emotions and feelings and experiences that children are not equipped to deal with." In Arkansas she fought teen pregnancy by promoting not contraception but abstinence. "It's not birth control but self-control," she said.

The key to Hillary's seeming contradictions, and the source of her political pragmatism, may well be her religion. Hillary belongs to the United Methodist church, which was founded in the eighteenth century be John Wesley, a British social reformer who spent his later life evangelizing among the poor. She has taught adult Sunday school classes, and at one point lectured around Arkansas about "what it means to be a Methodist." She has also made an effort to continue studying the teachings of John Wesley and other theologians throughout her adult life.

"Do all the good you can, in all the ways you can, in all the places you can, at all the times you can, to all the people you can, as long as ever you can," was John Wesley's credo. His church still preaches his gospel of social justice and personal and social responsibility.

Reinhold Niebuhr, a theologian who greatly influenced Hillary's early mentor, Don Jones, wrote that humankind's capacity for justice makes democracy possible, whereas our inclination to evil makes democracy necessary. That dialectic, Jones says, directly influenced Hillary's world vision. "She's more pragmatic than she is liberal ideological," says Jones. "And I think that her pragmatism has something to do with her faith. She is a deeply spiritual person. And I also think that her social concerns, her sense of social responsibility, rests on a spiritual foundation. Even her feminism. I think it's her faith that keeps her from becoming overly ideological about anything. If you're a secular feminist, it's pretty easy for feminism to become the religion, to become the lens through which you view everything. I don't think that could ever happen to Hillary. That doesn't mean that she is less concerned with feminist issues. The extremely important thing about her personality is that she will affirm something, like being pro-choice, but she's able to stand back and entertain some criticism of that position. When Bill was once making a decision about whether to commute a sentence with a capital punishment for a serial killer and rapist, Hillary agonized over this, asking me what I thought. And I said, 'Well, I believe there is such a thing as punitive justice; that's part of the whole concept of justice. And I think some people have forfeited their right to life because of the heinous deed that they've committed.' And she said, 'Well, I think I agree with you.' But she was struggling with the question of could she conscientiously as a Christian say that. There was a tad of uncertainty about that. And I attribute that to her faith," Jones says. "It almost makes her dialectical."

Hillary's Methodism requires more than "doing good by doing well." It requires her to do well by doing good. She tried at one point to apply this moral imperative to the life of the nation. This was in 1993, at the high point of her White House prominence, before the health care reform effort failed and she retreated into the shadows of the East Wing. She unveiled her thinking publicly in a speech in Texas. America, she told her audience, was plagued by "alienation and despair and hopelessness," suffering from a "crisis of meaning" that amounted to a "sleeping sickness of the soul." Borrowing a phrase from the liberal Jewish thinker Michael Lerner, she spoke out in favor of a "politics of meaning." Lerner had defined that vision of politics as one that would seek "to build a society based on love and connection, a society in which the bottom line would not be profit and power but ethical and spiritual sensitivity and a sense of community, mutual caring, and responsibility." Hillary called it an effort to "remold society by redefining what it means to be a human being in the twentieth century." The *New York Times*, in a quietly damning article called "Saint Hillary," likened her quest to "something on the order of a Reformation: the remaking of the American way of politics, government, indeed life."

The "politics of meaning" didn't serve Hillary Rodham Clinton very well. For one thing, it had no constituency. The social conservatives who might have sympathized with Hillary's calls to reestablish acceptable moral standards of behavior and stop "defining deviancy down," wanted nothing to do with the First Lady herself. The social liberals who normally sang Hillary's praises were made uncomfortable by her attacks on moral relativism and on the "right" to lifetime welfare. There was another problem too: in the long term, Hillary's moral crusading made her look like a hypocrite. Her 1993 *New York Times* interview was a setup for disaster. When asked how the White House could put a "politics of meaning" into action, she said it was just a question of applying the Golden Rule:

How do we just break this whole enterprise down in small enough pieces? Well, somebody says to themselves: "You know, I'm not going to tell that racist, sexist joke. I don't want to objectify another human being. Why do I want to do that? What do I get out of that kind of action? Maybe I should try to restrain myself."

If Bill Clinton could have managed to restrain himself, the "politics of meaning" might have had a fighting chance. But, unfortunately, that wasn't to be.

Clinton is a believer too. But he was raised a Southern Baptist, and the religion that shaped him is quite different than Hillary's. "Methodism stresses the balance between the attention to personal, spiritual faith and social expression of that faith," Don Jones says. "The concern is for the underprivileged and the children, for the reformation of the world. That's not characteristic of the Southern Baptist church. That is, they're very preoccupied with personal salvation, conversion, and that sort of thing. And while the Methodists don't eschew that, they tend to emphasize the social-responsibility side." One might note that salvation is predicated upon sin; in other words, that Clinton's religion cut him a bit more slack, behavior-wise, than did Hillary's. It must have seemed like that sometimes to Hillary Rodham Clinton.

In Little Rock, Bill and Hillary worshiped separately, Bill Clinton at the socially conservative Immanuel Baptist Church and Hillary at the more progressive First Methodist. An incident that occurred during the Gulf War illustrated the difference between their churches. After church, on the Sunday that churches across the nation consecrated as a day of reflection on the war, the Clintons met up with an old friend for brunch.

"What did the pastor say at your church this morning?" Hillary asked the friend.

"He prayed that all men and women everywhere would be safe and no life lost," the friend, who had attended a Baptist church service, said.

"Mine too," said Hillary, a teasing smile playing around her lips. "And yours, Bill?"

His had been a rather hawkish call for a swift and valiant American victory. He smiled and didn't say anything.

There came a point, when Chelsea was about ten, that for the sake of family unity, Hillary gave being a Baptist a try. She attended Bill's church and sent Chelsea to the Baptist Sunday school. But the experiment was short-lived. Though it was important to her that Chelsea freely choose her own church affiliation, and that the choice be as meaningful as Hillary's own confirmation into Methodism had been, she was nonetheless relieved when Chelsea chose Methodism. Dorothy Rodham was glad too. She had been accused of blasphemy by Chelsea, who was then attending a Southern Baptist Sunday school, for saying, "Oh, my God!" when she had accidentally knocked a glass off her kitchen counter. Some of the lay Sunday school teachers at Bill's church were extremely conservative. Dorothy Rodham didn't relish the idea of a fundamentalist Southern Baptist grandchild.

Methodism was strongly ingrained in the Rodham

family. Hillary's great-grandparents had been part of the Wesleyan evangelical sweep through England. She had grown into her own faith as a teenager in Don Jones's Youth Ministry, and then continued in college by reading theology by Karl Barth and C. S. Lewis and studying the Old and New Testaments in an academic framework. She didn't, however, become an active churchgoer until the early 1980s. As she recalls, her return to actively practicing her faith came about after she had a picnic in the backyard of the Little Rock governor's mansion with Vic Nixon, the minister who had married her and Bill. Nixon gave her a copy of the United Methodist Church's new Book of Discipline, a statement of the church's basic principles and beliefs, and they discussed it. Afterward, she has said, "I was ready to focus on spiritual matters again."

Was it accidental that this meeting took place just after the Clintons had passed through a stretch of marital discord? Perhaps not—Hillary has repeatedly stressed that her religious beliefs, as much as anything else, have borne her through her marriage. It's been widely reported that in the late 1980s the Clintons briefly considered divorce. Infidelity seems to have been the prime issue. Bill Clinton's inability to run for president in 1988 because of his personal problems was just too infuriating, Hillary told her friends. What was she supposed to do with the rest of her life? Serve tea in the Arkansas governor's mansion? Clinton apparently broached the subject of divorce in the intimate setting of the National Governors' Association. Political considerations clearly were never far from his mind. But in the end faith—

some kind of faith—in the marriage prevailed. Hillary told Betsey Wright that she was too invested in her marriage to let it go so easily. "They both wanted their marriage," Wright says. "They went through the hard work it takes to move on." Hillary herself once told a friend: "I really believe you can change the way you feel and think if you discipline yourself." In other words, grace can come through hard work and faith.

Is religion really the key behind Hillary Rodham Clinton's decision to stay with Bill Clinton? In an abstract sense, yes. Hillary's faith demands that she sublimate personal feeling to a greater, abstract ideal. "Life can have some transcendent meaning," she said once in a graduation speech at Hendrix College, a Methodist school in Conway, Arkansas. "Work toward the achievement of a universal human dignity, not just your own personal security."

Hillary appears, when times have been tough, to have made a conscious effort to focus on the transcendent aspects of her marriage. By all accounts, she has always believed in Bill Clinton's larger mandate—passionately believed in the good he could do for the country. She also knew that to accomplish that mandate, he needed her beside him: both as a wifely presence and as a political adviser. She also, by all accounts, has always loved him. "That love was something so much a part of us that it was impossible to think of ending it or cutting it off or moving beyond it," she told David Frost in 1992. These days that love often sounds like something more akin to Christian charity. "[H]er love for him is compas-

sionate and steadfast," Hillary's spokeswoman read
after Bill Clinton's grand jury testimony this summer.

That sounds like *agape*—the highest form of love
of all, some might say. Others might venture that,
with a married couple, it is a degraded emotion. At
any rate, the spectacle of a First Lady called upon to
justify her love in a press release is mind-boggling.
But then, it's been a long time since the Clintons
could carry on their married life in private. And
maybe the heavy Christian overtones of Hillary's par-
don of Bill Clinton weren't accidental. They would,
after all, have been perfectly in keeping with the sin-
and-pardon spin cycle that the White House had or-
chestrated around the Monica Lewinsky affair. Unless, of course, it all goes deeper. It is always possible
that the dance of sinning and pardoning is part of
the glue that keeps the Clinton couple together. As
a CNN commentator said after the House voted to
impeach Clinton, nothing anymore can be said to
be surprising.

There is clearly some kind of charge that keeps the
Clintons together. In larger measure, friends say, it's
intellectual. They read books together and discuss
them, debate policy and fight for hours over their
ideas. Hillary likes to "get into it," she once told
family friend Carolyn Staley, according to a conversation recorded in David Maraniss's biography of Bill
Clinton *First in His Class.*

But there's clearly a more personal form of conflict
as well. And conflict can be binding—much more so
than complacency. "I have a lot of friends whose
marriages are solid but routine," says Betsey Wright.
"And it's not routine to Bill and Hillary." The tension

between complicity and rage has been the defining characteristic of their bond for as long as anyone can remember. "I see two people who despite their differences really love each other," says an old friend. "I can't imagine them apart." Some friends even consider the difficulties in their marriage to be the flip side of its strength: the unique coming together of two very strong, very smart, and very complicated people. "Their relationship is extraordinarily difficult and extraordinarily rewarding," says another friend who has known the Clintons for more than two decades. "That's been true from day one, and they always knew it at some level." But, she adds, her voice dropping an octave, "we didn't realize that he was as sick as he obviously is. I think to live with it, Hillary has to see it in a similar light. She has to see it as a sickness—otherwise, how do you deal with it?"

The study of Bill Clinton's "sickness" has practically become a new discipline in the practice of popular psychology. "Sex addiction," a disorder which became popular in the past decade, has now been redubbed the "Clinton Syndrome." Last year the *New York Times* diagnosed Clinton as having a "documentably dysfunctional personality." The *New York Post* and *Time*, borrowing a term from the recovery movement, diagnosed the American public as a nation of Clinton "enablers." One of the president's advisers likened Clinton's slow process of contrition to the stages people pass through in coming to terms with death: denial, anger, acceptance, and a desire to move on. Next will undoubtedly come "closure."

With the build-up of such commentary the Clintons' complex personal history has been reduced to the terms of talk-show TV. Their marriage, once discussed as a model of modern political partnership, is now considered a case study in "co-dependency." The story of the co-dependent Clinton marriage goes like this: Bill Clinton, as the (step)child of an alcoholic father, exhibits the classic personality pattern of a child of alcoholics. That is to say, as one commentator encyclopedically put it, "a strong desire to smooth things over and to please; volatile temper, low self-esteem, addictive behavior in the form of compulsive politicking and sexual activity. Trying to please everyone through manipulation and lying." He has had almost no choice but to reenact with Hillary his legacy of family dysfunction. His insatiable need for affirmation and approval, for "unconditional love," drives him toward other women— particularly at times of personal failure, when his own self-flagellation, coupled with Hillary's disappointment, becomes too overwhelming.

Hillary by this reckoning has become Bill Clinton's "enabler"—the recovery movement's term for the person who keeps an addicted person from hitting rock bottom and getting help. Standing by her man, she has made it possible of him to cheat without taking responsibility (an important stage in recovery). By playing the role of "enforcer," trying to keep him focused, surrounded by the right kinds of people, home in the evenings for family dinners with Chelsea, she contained his "sex addiction." She dispatched watchdogs like Betsey Wright and Evelyn Lieberman, a former assistant to the First Lady who went on to become Clinton's deputy chief of staff, to keep an eye on the "bimbos." (Lieberman was responsible for transferring Monica Lewinsky to the Pentagon.)

Going one step further in this story, Hillary the "enabler" has become "enmeshed" with Bill Clinton as she has devoted her life to managing his personality problems. She has thrived upon saving him from self-inflicted defeat. She has been strong when he has been weak. She couldn't possibly leave him. She is too "co-dependent."

Does this story have anything, in fact, to do with the Clintons? Maybe, and maybe not. Hillary Clinton has always dismissed such psychologizing with distaste. Friends call it "psychobabble"—the ramblings of journalists who have no access and no insights, selling ideas that go over easily with the public, like intellectual candy. In the end, the psychological portraits of the presidential couple that proliferated so wildly in the months following the Monica Lewinsky controversy probably say more about the journalists who write them (and the readers who devour them) than they do about the Clintons themselves. They're works of projection generated by a society obsessed with making excuses for its own moral failings, political contradictions, and psychological weaknesses.

"Psychobabble" currently is the lingo through which Americans construct and understand their world. It's aging-baby boomer-ese, the self-indulgent stuff of a universe where God and his moral strictures and the sharp black-and-white distinctions of political ideology have faded before the all-encompassing Ego. It is *not* the language by which Hillary Rodham Clinton understands her life. "She doesn't adhere to the psychological point of view," says a friend. "She's always been much more interested in people's ideas than in their emotions—particularly her own," says Diane Blair, a political science professor at the University of Arkansas and one of Hillary's closest friends. "She would never go on a talk show and talk about her emotions." "She has almost no capacity for self-pity," says another friend. "She takes great comfort in the Bible and feels that, compared to Job, she has it easy."

In the wake of the Monica Lewinsky affair, commentators frequently intoned that the major Clinton project of the post–White House years would be therapy—couples therapy, at least. Maybe Bill Clinton will go for it. Hillary is much more likely just to stay wedded to her faith.

Chapter 10

⟡

"The Habits of the Heart"

On the morning of Saturday, December 19, 1998, Hillary Rodham Clinton went to Capitol Hill to make a speech. She received a half dozen standing ovations. When she was finished speaking, the members of Congress crowded around to hug her. "She's so terrific," gushed Representative Dennis Kucinich of Ohio. "It's lucky for America we have a woman with the strength to lead the nation."

Later in the day the Congress voted to impeach President Bill Clinton.

It was a dynamic that Clinton watchers had seen countless times before. "Billary," the powerful Clinton & Clinton machine that kicks into action whenever the male member of the team falters, was back.

In the past, Hillary had often seemed to be up when Bill Clinton was down. But never was Clinton so very low. And never before had Hillary soared to such heights.

She was credited with giving new life to the Democratic party. The steadiness of her speeches, the seriousness of her ideas, the connectedness she could create with voters—the very "groundedness" that friends had for decades said was the core of her being—had made people sit up and take notice. Hillary was credited with giving people back their faith; giving them the feeling that their leaders in Washington cared about the concerns of their day-to-day lives, and not just about internecine power struggles, character assassination, and more and more sordid affairs.

Amazingly, out of the ashes of the worst presidential embarrassment in history had come a Clinton ready to do battle and more. Hillary seemed strangely charged by the scandal. She was committed to rising above, to looking ever outward from the mess of her personal life to remember the voices and needs, ideas and dreams of the people she'd met during her five and a half years as First Lady. She kept a photograph of Eleanor Roosevelt in her office, an Eleanor perched on the edge of her chair, listening intently, optimistic and ready for action. She seemed obsessed with the work of being First Lady, which, says a staffer, she saw as the business of "improving individual lives, but in the process of improving lives helping to transform society."

For what was all the scandal mongering really but a sign of the failure of American civil society? What was the impeachment proceeding really but a sign that American politicians had gotten far away from their electorate? What was the fact that children were learning the term *oral sex* from the evening news but a sign of the country's overall moral decay? It was a sign, Hillary reasoned, of a rot that had set into people's hearts.

And so, in the months that followed Bill Clinton's televised interrogation, she pursued her agenda with ever greater purpose, Just weeks after her husband was forced to confess to his illicit affair, she called together a meeting of two dozen experts in the field of international affairs and held a half-day White House conference to explore the issue of how to make Americans understand the country's need to engage in world affairs. "I spent three days in and around the White House, and I came away really depressed," says Dr. David Hamburg, president emeritus of the Carnegie Corporation in New York, who organized the conference at Hillary Clinton's request. "Everything had gotten so poisoned. But I marveled at the way she withstood it. She had a very strong feeling that the scandal should not deflect her from her agenda. If anything, it reaffirmed her dedication to the issues she believes in."

Hillary delivered speeches in Northern Ireland and in Uruguay. And when she spoke to the nation on her campaign stops, it was to do more than get out the vote for the Democrats. It was to get people talking—about the "serious and important" things in their lives, to strengthen that inchoate thing that Hillary Clinton calls "civil society"—"the third part of the triangle of democracy . . . what the citizens do on their own to make conditions better." Talking, she believed, was good for them, and for the life of the nation. "[I]n a democracy," she has said, "people's personal concerns can become political if they use their voices—and their votes—to define them." As far as she was concerned, she was rebuilding civil society.

It was—and remains—a grandiose project. But then, Hillary Rodham Clinton has always had grand dreams. And once she hit her stride as First Lady, she came to realize that, though she couldn't have a private life, couldn't go to a movie or take a walk alone, she could have an amazing effect on other people's lives. It was a do-gooder's dream: she could hear people out, note their problems, and then, as if with a swipe of a magic wand, she could make things better. She could meet a young couple on a rope line in Chicago and hear what it was like to have an epileptic daughter and not have enough money to provide her with adequate care. She could go back to Washington and see that federal funding for helping people with epilepsy was increased. She could attend a health care event and hear a woman talk about having health insurance that didn't cover the cost of having a suspicious breast lump removed, and what it was like to live with her doctor's words, "Well, we'll just have to watch it," hanging over her head like a death sentence. She cherished the memory of the Senegalese village ("my village," she called it) that, after a wide-reaching educational campaign, banished female genital mutilation. She brought a very sick little boy to the White House. She made him happy—at least temporarily.

And then she lobbied for greater awareness of children's health needs. She prided herself on legislation passed in Congress that expanded health care coverage for five million children whose families didn't qualify for Medicaid and couldn't afford private health insurance. She saw child immunization rates sharply increase. She saw legislation passed that allowed Americans to carry their insurance with them after they lost or left their jobs. Federal funding for women's health, and particularly for breast cancer research, skyrocketed. Medicare coverage was expanded for older women to reimburse one mammogram per year. She drew national attention to the daily agonies of working mothers who couldn't afford the top-quality day care they desired. Afterward, she saw Congress pass an additional $200 million for afterschool programs and nearly as much for state efforts to improve child care quality. She shrugged off comments from people who tried, sympathetically, to suggest she'd be glad when her term as First Lady was finally over. "They don't see what I see," she'd tell her staff. "They don't know that I see every day how very blessed I've been and what I've been privileged to do."

The personal anecdotes she collected became woven into a political theory. It was a theory that eschewed abstraction. It avoided policy formulations derived from ideology rather than informed compassion. It rejected dogmatic theoretical feminism in favor of concrete measures that could visibly improve women's lives: micro credit, increased access to health care and family planning, and above all education. It was a politics of daily life, Hillary Clinton explained, in a speech to women's groups in Australia in 1996. And it was, she believed, the wave of the future. "For the first time in America," she said of the recently passed presidential elections, "a new set of concerns took on political importance—concerns about enhancing the quality of our lives, about raising children, about meeting the demands of work and family. . . . They are real issues on people's minds—kitchen table issues." She concluded: "What women are saying today—loudly and clearly—is that national politics is not just about *realpolitik*. It's also about *real life politik*, how we live together." In other words, the future of politics would now reside in making the personal political.

There was a certain irony to that. After all, the Monica Lewinsky scandal had, arguably, been created by the thinking that "the personal is political." The media had armed themselves with that right-thinking excuse to justify digging into the most private aspects of Hillary Clinton's marriage. Certain feminists had called both her and her husband to task because their private lives now appeared so jarringly at odds with their professed feminist beliefs. And the religious right—well, they had a field day. Thanks to the belief that the personal was political, private life was seen as a mirror of the soul, and the soul—for public figures—was subject to the same rules of "full disclosure" as tax forms and financial records.

Hillary Rodham was part of the generation that had brought this state of affairs into being. But back in 1969, when "the personal is political" came into being as a feminist slogan, it had a very different meaning. Back then it hadn't been about "outing" adulterous men. Indeed, it wasn't about men at all. It was about encouraging women to see how the unequal power relations of a male-dominated society played themselves out in their private lives. It was deeply liberating for women in the "consciousness-raising" groups of the late 1960s to learn that their personal problems as housewives—boredom, frustration, resentment, anxiety—weren't personal problems at all; they were the political problem of a class of people denied the full exercise of their human potential. Housework didn't bore and depress them because they were neurotic; it bored and depressed them because it was boring and depressing.

By giving a political reading to some of the darker aspects of private life, feminism helped bring the family out of the dark ages. Domestic violence was no longer a side effect of women's natural "masochism." Incest was no longer an unfortunate slip-up by men who loved their daughters too much. Politicizing personal life took a whole class of women's problems beyond the hands of psychotherapists and into the realm of the courtroom. And this was a very good thing for women's empowerment.

Hillary *Rodham* always thought so. And Hillary *Clinton* did too. Her positions in support of children's rights, her early attempts to raise awareness of rape and domestic violence, her later efforts to change the health care system, ease adoption laws, provide better day care, increase awareness of women's health issues, all were based on this original understanding of the personal as political. The feminist movement's original stress on speaking out—on bearing witness as a means to bonding together to achieve social change—was central to her thinking too. So was a certain utopianism. Feminism anticipated that if egalitarian ideals were put into practice in society at large, feminist men and women would follow. That is to say: women would exhibit independence of mind and spirit, and then would show their commitment to egalitarianism in every private encounter. Men would not, for example, demand oral sex from interns. This, of course, turned out to be an utter fallacy, but the idea behind it, that people are transparent, that their private selves are mirrored in their public acts and—on a larger scale—their private beliefs are mirrored in their public institutions, lives on. It particularly lives on in the thought of Hillary Rodham Clinton.

She likes to cite Alexis de Tocqueville. She likes to note that he identified democracy, self-reliance, and egalitarianism as the "habits of the heart" of the American people in the early nineteenth century. The American "habits of the heart," Hillary has said, are "what it is that we felt inside ourselves about the role of the individual, about the respect for people who were not like ourselves," as she put it in a speech in Siberia in 1997. On an African tour in 1997, she elaborated further: "Democracy's success . . . will not depend solely upon free elections, open markets, or government policies. It will depend ultimately on the internalization of democratic values in people's hearts, minds, and everyday lives."

What Hillary Clinton is out to change in America—indeed, in the world—are the "habits of the heart." This is little less than an evangelical mission. "Her aim is to transform people's vision," says Diane Blair. "She believes that you have to picture a new and better world and bring people to that vision." This is not a mere matter of the "feminization of politics," a shift in emphasis from "big" issues like defense, diplomacy, and trade to "women's issues" like child care and education. It's the "humanization of politics": a "politics of meaning" at last ready to be carried forward into action.

She's likely to be in for some disappointment. People's hearts and people's actions often tend to work in contradiction. Making the "habits of the heart" the province of public officials might turn out to be a very bad idea.

But Hillary Rodham Clinton's real-life politics do offer a great opportunity. Even if Hillary isn't able to overhaul the country's habits of the heart, she could lead the country to a new consensus on the need to separate and protect private life from political manipulation. She may help usher in an era where "real life" politics take precedence over the cynicism of *realpolitik:* Maybe a real life politics of caring compassion will inspire greater measures of the same in the hearts of America's citizens. Perhaps Hillary Rodham Clinton, having survived a decade of the politics of personal devastation, will be able to find a dignified and positive way to make the personal political. And in so doing humanize politics in America in the twenty-first century.

Penguin Putnam Inc.
Online

Your Internet gateway to a virtual environment with
hundreds of entertaining and enlightening books from
Penguin Putnam Inc.

*While you're there, get the latest buzz on
the best authors and books around—*

Tom Clancy, Patricia Cornwell, W.E.B. Griffin,
Nora Roberts, William Gibson, Robin Cook,
Brian Jacques, Catherine Coulter, Stephen King,
Jacquelyn Mitchard, and many more!

**Penguin Putnam Online is located at
http://www.penguinputnam.com**

PENGUIN PUTNAM NEWS

Every month you'll get an inside look at our upcoming
books and new features on our site. This is an ongoing
effort to provide you with the most up-to-date
information about our books and authors.

**Subscribe to Penguin Putnam News at
http://www.penguinputnam.com/ClubPPI**